Woman Suffrage & Citizenship
in the Midwest, 1870–1920

IOWA AND THE MIDWEST EXPERIENCE

Series editor, William B. Friedricks,
Iowa History Center at Simpson College

Woman Suffrage & Citizenship

in the Midwest, 1870–1920

SARA EGGE

University of Iowa Press, Iowa City

University of Iowa Press, Iowa City 52242
Copyright © 2018 by the University of Iowa Press
www.uipress.uiowa.edu
Printed in the United States of America

Text design by Judy Gilats, Peregrine Graphics Services

The University of Iowa Press is a member of Green Press Initiative and is committed to preserving natural resources.

Printed on acid-free paper

Cataloging-in Publication data is on file at the Library of Congress.

ISBN 978-1-60938-557-6 (pbk)
ISBN 978-1-60938-558-3 (ebk)

To Mark

Contents

Acknowledgments

DURING THE YEARS I have worked on this project, I have accrued many debts. My interest in woman suffrage in the Midwest began as an undergraduate at North Dakota State University and was fostered by a pair of scholars unmatched in their dedication to students. I thank David Danbom and Claire Strom for cheering me on all those years ago. David also read the manuscript in its entirety, and I thank him for his valuable suggestions. While a graduate student at Iowa State University, I received excellent advice from my mentor, Pamela Riney-Kehrberg. She supported me even when my plans were sketchy at best, and I am grateful for all that she has done for me. My thanks to her for reading the manuscript and offering well-timed feedback. I also appreciate the contributions of the members of my graduate committee, as well as the camaraderie and collegiality of my graduate school cohort at Iowa State. Jenny Barker-Devine has remained a steadfast supporter and friend, and I thank her for her prescient comments on the manuscript. Dorothy Schwieder and Deborah Fink listened carefully as I explained my vision for the project during its early stages, and their advice was unparalleled. My colleagues at Centre College have sustained my intellectual development, and I am a better teacher and scholar because of them.

In addition to the community of scholars who have supported this work, archivists across the country contributed their expertise to this project. At the New York Public Library and the Library of Congress, archivists uncovered important documents and correspondence. At the State Historical Society of Iowa, South Dakota State Historical Society, and Minnesota Historical Society, I benefited greatly from the dedicated staff members who work tirelessly to preserve state history. I especially thank Susan Jellinger and Mary Bennett in Iowa, Ken

Stewart in South Dakota, and Debbie Miller in Minnesota. I am also grateful to the staff at the Iowa Women's Archives for their assistance. Jan Louwagie, the archivist at the Southwest Minnesota History Center in Marshall, provided kind and patient help and pointed out collections that I had overlooked. Staff members at the University of South Dakota were also incredibly supportive.

Local history is vital to this project, and I am grateful to the countless people in Clay County, Lyon County, and Yankton County who dedicate themselves to preserving the history of their communities. At the Clay County Heritage Center in Spencer, Cindy McGranahan and Holly Kellogg went above and beyond the call of duty. In one case, they contacted the Clay County Extension Office on my behalf so that I could track down a lead. In Lyon County, volunteers at the Lyon County Historical Society, as well as workers at the Minneota Public Library and Lyon County Public Library, dug up valuable documents I did not know existed. At the Dakota Territorial Museum in Yankton County, Crystal Nelson and her volunteer staff were exceptional resources. I also appreciated the impressive number of microfilm newspapers at the Yankton Public Library.

This book exists because of generous financial support. The U.S. Department of Education awarded me a Jacob K. Javits Fellowship that funded four years of graduate education. I thank Jennifer Rivera for her tireless efforts at managing the paperwork that the award required. I also received a research grant from the State Historical Society of Iowa, a professional development grant from Phi Alpha Theta, a travel grant from an anonymous donor to Iowa State University's History Department, and an Enduring Questions grant from the National Endowment for the Humanities to investigate citizenship. Centre College has provided annual faculty development funds to support the revisions to this project, and five students have served as summer research assistants: Sarah Welch, Ashton Spangler, Hadley Judson, Nicolaus Stengl, and Peter Shirley. I have tremendously enjoyed working with each one.

Family and friends have made the seemingly endless work on this project bearable. Research trips to South Dakota and Minnesota meant fun visits with Dana Suing, Ashli Maddox, and Jen and Tyler Everson. In New York, Laurie and Jose Vazquez offered me a warm bed and plenty of conversation, while Ben, Kelly, and Jayne McGovern were lovely hosts in Washington, DC. J. D. and Vercie Webb sustained me during long research days in Clay County with plenty of scrambled eggs and toast. I got to know them through my dear friends, Sam and Kimberly Isburg, with whom I spent many restful and relaxing weekends away. I thank my in-laws, Dorothea, Richard, and Paul, for their support, and I am sorry that Richard did not live to see the book. My parents, Alan and Sharon, and my siblings, Alison and Jon, taught me to appreciate my roots, and I owe them more than I can ever repay. I wrote drafts while thinking often of my grandmothers, Harriet Namminga and Dorothy Egge, who embody the strength of the midwestern women I study. Finally, I thank Mark for seeing me through this project. I look forward to many more years with him and our children.

Woman Suffrage & Citizenship
in the Midwest, 1870–1920

Introduction

CITIZENSHIP, COMMUNITY, AND CIVIC RESPONSIBILITY IN THE MIDWEST

IN 1914 THE RESIDENTS of Yankton County, South Dakota, experienced their fifth campaign to enact a woman suffrage amendment to the state's constitution. In the spring suffragists had formed the Yankton Universal Franchise League to promote the cause, and they relied on Edith Fitch, the district press chairman, to produce editorials for the campaign. By the fall, local newspapers were printing her articles, and she laid out a compelling claim to the ballot. Fitch argued that women deserved the right to vote because of their civic contributions to their communities. Midwestern women were at the forefront of community engagement, gaining public acclaim by raising the money needed to build churches, libraries, schools, parks, post offices, and other civic institutions. Fitch explained that the "welfare of any community depends upon the amount of civic responsibility which its members assume." In the Midwest, Fitch claimed, women had fulfilled this civic responsibility with determination and grace. But even though women had proven their worth as citizens, they still could not vote. Instead, they foundered as "half citizens" with birthright citizenship but without political rights. Denying women the ballot was a major flaw in the promises of American citizenship. "Our American republic rests on the broad principle that the people can be trusted," Fitch wrote, "and that the fullest participation of its citizens in the government is the best safeguard of liberty." Women's civic contributions not only uplifted communities but also upheld foundational democratic principles. Unfortunately for the members of the Yankton Universal Franchise League, locals voted against the woman suffrage amendment, defeating it by almost a two-to-one margin.[1]

Edith Fitch's editorials revealed the profound ways that suffrage advocates asserted their claims to the ballot in the Midwest. By basing her message on citizenship, gender, and community, Fitch spoke to cherished principles that middle-class, white midwesterners had prized since settling the region in the mid-nineteenth century. These values centered on the intersection of belonging and civic activism, a site where women found great success and public recognition. Examining woman suffrage in terms of community and citizenship adds depth to previous scholarship on woman suffrage because it illuminates the complex political identities women built. These midwestern suffrage advocates, who were mostly Yankees with kinship ties to the Northeast, claimed the right to vote by combining their domestic roles with their position in the community as civic leaders. The woman suffrage movement flourished at the grassroots level in the Midwest, as women demanded the ballot out of well-established civic identities. While national leaders orchestrated sudden bursts of activity during campaigns to achieve woman suffrage, their presence was irregular and did not sustain the cause over time. Instead, local advocates did more to advance woman suffrage by claiming the ballot as loyal citizens who held highly respectable records of civic activism.

Investigating woman suffrage in the Midwest reveals how gender shaped the region's political culture between 1870 and 1920. In the small towns and villages that made up counties, residents established bonds of community despite tensions stemming from blurred boundaries of inclusion and exclusion. These tensions, along with diverse ethnic, religious, and political characteristics, shaped the outcomes of campaigns and advocacy on behalf of the suffragist cause, requiring a comparative approach that investigates the differences among three states in the upper Midwest—Iowa, Minnesota, and South Dakota. This analytical strategy illuminates how people living in the same vicinity had vastly different experiences with woman suffrage. Even though the same set of national leaders used similar directives and strategies, many tested for the first time in the Midwest, campaigns in these three states were distinct and diverged in marked ways.

Further investigation at the county level confirms the complexity of woman suffrage in the Midwest. It also reveals that woman suffrage was not a single issue, despite attempts by national suffrage leaders to make it one. As much as national suffragists wanted voters to separate the suffragist cause from other political concerns, like temperance or taxes, these issues shaped debates about woman suffrage. A large ethnic population that was against the prohibition of alcoholic beverages could kill a woman suffrage measure, while a powerful Yankee element could push forward a suffrage initiative with ease. Local communities either inspired or rejected woman suffrage activism, and it is critical to account for contextual differences. Moreover, studying the fight for woman suffrage in three counties, one in each state, uncovers the unexpected and remarkable ways that ordinary men and women understood female enfranchisement. Midwesterners were neither ignorant nor backward about the cause, despite what national leaders sometimes assumed. The counties studied in this book are Clay County in northwest Iowa, Lyon County in southwest Minnesota, and Yankton County in southeast South Dakota, which were chosen for their similar geographical characteristics, settlement histories, and economic outlooks. (See figures 1, 2, and 3.)

Examining woman suffrage in these local contexts was an intentional choice made for its methodological value. If decades of local civic engagement had politicized Yankee suffragists, then focusing on community and all its intricate elements was key. Leaving local issues out to consider only efforts at the state and national levels creates a

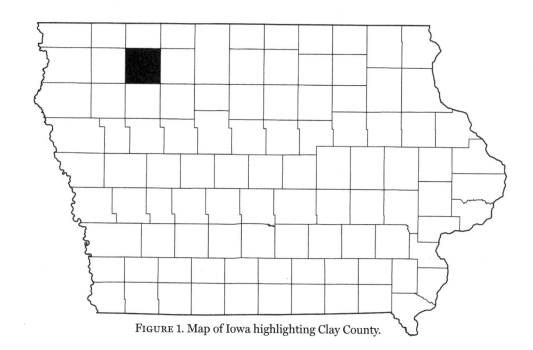

FIGURE 1. Map of Iowa highlighting Clay County.

lopsided and incomplete narrative. Incorporating local advocates required comprehensive archival research, which made Iowa, Minnesota, and South Dakota ideal for study. The respective historical archive in each state contains large collections deposited by state and national suffrage leaders, which served as exceptional resources. Finding local advocates in the three counties under study, however, was challenging, and suffrage activists in small towns left relatively few records of their own. Locating them meant diving into local newspapers, community histories, church documents, and other records collected by dedicated librarians, preservationists, and curators in public libraries, community centers, and museums in each county. Clay County's Heritage Center, Lyon County's public libraries, the Southwest Minnesota History Center, Yankton County's public library, and the Dakota Territorial

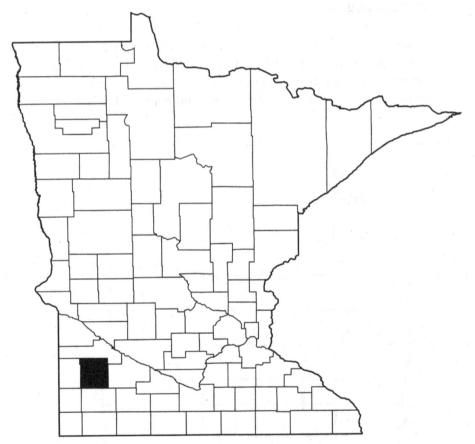

FIGURE 2. Map of Minnesota highlighting Lyon County.

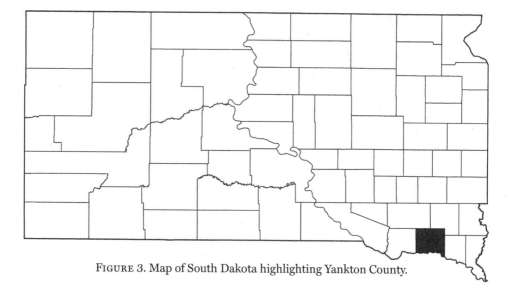

FIGURE 3. Map of South Dakota highlighting Yankton County.

Museum offered reams of microfilmed newspapers, boxes of correspondence, and minute books galore. Newspapers were especially helpful. Each one was unabashedly political but remarkably personal, featuring everything from news "around home" to state, regional, and national bulletins. When woman suffrage campaigns flourished, newspapers covered them closely. In these publications there vividly emerged midwestern political culture and women's place in it.

Studying woman suffrage in comparative, local contexts was also a deliberate decision because the Midwest lacks any consistent regional definition. Missing the kind of "geographical coherence, historical issues, and cultural touchstones" of other regions, the Midwest has baffled historians who have struggled to delineate its boundaries, describe its people, and construct its identity. Diverse groups of people, living hundreds or even thousands of miles apart, from western Pennsylvania to the plains of the Dakotas, have claimed a midwestern identity, creating a vast conglomeration of loosely affiliated individuals. Searching for general patterns amid such dizzying complexity fails to acknowledge the importance of community. Instead, selecting a smaller geographic area illuminates the particularities of place that shaped woman suffrage and honors the emphasis on the local experience. Choosing three states in the upper Midwest was prudent because few historians have examined woman suffrage there. Future scholarship may confirm that the conclusions offered here reach beyond the borders of this study. For now, studying woman suffrage in Iowa, Minnesota, and South Dakota offers compelling suggestions about how midwesterners across the region understood politics, gender, and citizenship.[2]

Middle-class Yankee suffragists did not select the message of civic responsibility in haste. They carefully constructed the idea to reflect the emerging political and cultural contexts that came to define the Midwest before World War I. In particular, they built their case for woman suffrage around liberal and republican theories of citizenship because midwesterners both embraced and contested the meanings of citizenship. Settlers, especially Yankees, who were typically middle-class residents with Anglo-Saxon ancestry from the Northeast, saw the spirit of civic engagement as the hallmark of community life, and they encouraged it among their neighbors and themselves. Communal institutions, as well as market involvement, were cultural touchstones for Yankees, and they sought to build communities, complete with schools, churches, and local governments, out of the "barbarism" they saw on the frontier. In the process they partnered with immigrants, mainly from northern Europe, who arrived during the 1880s and 1890s. These immigrants came from diverse ethnic and religious backgrounds and some, particularly Germans, resisted assimilation to the culture the Yankee settlers had established. What emerged was a contested political terrain that called into question ideas of American citizenship, giving Yankee women an opening in which to claim the ballot. Initially, they struggled, and nineteenth-century campaigns often failed because most midwesterners embraced gender inequalities and strict interpretations of traditional gender roles. Woman suffrage was radical at the time, and most people opposed it fervently. In the early twentieth century, however, Progressivism upended these political assumptions and emphasized cultural uniformity to a single "American" identity. In 1917, America's entry into World War I transformed civic obligations into wartime sacrifice as the mass mobilization of the country's economic and manpower resources occurred. Midwestern Yankee suffragists responded wisely and wholeheartedly to these domestic and international political developments, building their arguments on the civic responsibility and loyalty they displayed during wartime to win the right to vote.[3]

Citizenship

Understanding woman suffrage in the American Midwest begins at the intersection of citizenship, community, and civic activism. White, middle-class, Yankee midwesterners privileged community membership, based on participation in communal institutions, and set standards for belonging on the basis of these civic expectations. Citizenship was complicated, however, and people often disagreed about its meanings, especially in the modern nation-state. Legal decisions and legislation regarding citizenship were inconsistent, and racial, gender, and ethnic inequalities led to contradictions and ambiguities. In general, researchers have examined citizenship in the United States within two major political traditions. The liberal model embraces the individual as the bedrock of civic and political life. In a liberal society, private, individual rights are paramount. By contrast, the republican tradition upholds a communitarian or participatory society through common civic institutions. In a republican model, membership in the community through active contributions is a key tenet of citizenship. Both traditions influenced thinking on American citizenship, producing a constellation of meanings that created confusion, uncertainty, and conflict.[4]

Scholars have attempted to study these two models in a historical context with mixed results. T. H. Marshall argued that citizenship developed in a linear fashion over time. White men achieved civil rights in the eighteenth century, political rights in the nineteenth century, and social rights in the twentieth century. Extending the right to vote to a diverse population was a nineteenth-century struggle, born out of industrialization. While Marshall opened new avenues of scholarship on citizenship, his study was narrow. It focused on white men, mostly workers living in Great Britain, and ignored racial and gender hierarchies. His ideas were also too convenient and did not account for how much citizenship changed in messy ways. Nation building was a fraught process, with no clearly defined patterns. Major disruptions like war, labor unrest, or other geopolitical phenomena could challenge and transform the meanings of citizenship. In some cases, political rights actually came before civil rights or after social rights. Instead of a straightforward model, Marshall's critics advocated a more complex take on citizenship that included these contradictions.[5]

Since the 1990s, scholars have begun to incorporate those people and perspectives that Marshall's work overlooked. Rogers Smith argued that conceptions of citizenship were idealistic rather than realistic in the United States. A historical analysis of citizenship in practice reveals contradictions, inequalities, and the denial of citizenship to most adults for much of American history. Race, gender, ethnicity, religion, and other markers of identity prevented large numbers of people from sharing in the political opportunities that citizenship allegedly afforded. As Smith argued, "inegalitarian ascriptive" traditions used characteristics like race, gender, or age to constrict the full meanings of citizenship, creating a system of "second-class citizenship." In other words, the ambiguity of citizenship disguised the limited rights that accompanied it for many segments of the population. Other scholars found similar patterns in the Midwest. According to Andrew Cayton, it was "white men [who] created a political nation . . . [and] to be a citizen was to be male and white and to share a general commitment to liberty, equality, and (implicitly) fraternity." Most midwesterners believed passionately that the United States "was by rights a white nation, a Protestant nation, a nation in which true Americans were native-born men with Anglo-Saxon ancestors." They derived their ideas about citizenship from eighteenth-century Enlightenment philosophers who championed principles like liberty, equality, and self-government but inhabited a worldview that privileged the rule of wealthy white men.[6]

The abundant discourse about freedom, independence, and liberty masked the uncertainty in these concepts. As Carroll Smith-Rosenberg argues, fear, racism, and distrust made instability the hallmark of American national identity. Even at the founding of the nation, there was "no common history, no governmental infrastructure, no shared culture" to bind people together. Instead, diversity—religious, gender, ethnic, cultural, and racial—defined the people who gave birth to the United States. To foment a sense of unity, the founders had to create myths for Americans to embrace. Essential to this project were outsiders, who were perceived as "dangerous, disdained as polluting, demanding expulsion." Exclusion, not belonging, was the hallmark of citizenship in the United States for most of its early history, and social outcasts, including African Americans, Native Americans, and other poor or marginalized groups, remained outsiders. Accounting for difference, then, is paramount. Citizenship was neither universal nor equal, and people approached citizenship from identities marked by gender, race, ethnicity, and culture.[7]

Prior to the twentieth century, white, free men gained citizenship in the United States through a simple, albeit haphazardly enforced, process. In theory, men became citizens by birth or naturalization. The first piece of legislation that established criteria for citizenship was the Naturalization Act of 1790. It restricted citizenship to "free white" people who had lived in the United States for two years. Five years later Congress passed the Naturalization Act of 1795, which extended the residency requirement to five years. In both cases, the law stated that men became citizens when they vowed their loyalty to the United States in court. Women were not permitted to testify in court, so their citizenship status was unclear. Not until the passage of the Fourteenth Amendment in 1868 did the federal government explicitly confirm that all people, including women, gained citizenship by either birth or naturalization. Because naturalization took place in state and local courts, record keeping was chaotic, and many clerks did not preserve petitions or affidavits. Officials routinely destroyed or lost files, misspelled or changed names, or used initials. Scholars estimate that 25 percent of all foreigners listed on the censuses from 1890 to 1930 did not become naturalized. When they did, they followed a two-step process. After two years of residency, a foreign-born male took out a Declaration of Intention, also known as first papers. Three years after filing first papers, the immigrant then submitted a Petition for Naturalization, or second papers. After the court granted the petition, the man received a Certificate of Citizenship. He had to provide sufficient knowledge of the Constitution and prove that he was a moral and upright individual with allegiance only to the United States. It was not until 1906 that Congress passed a Naturalization Act that created the Division of Naturalization, part of the Bureau of Immigration and Naturalization. For the first time, naturalization became a federal matter, although it took years for officials to sort out the mess left by local and state courts.[8]

Ambiguity over citizenship led people to attempt to define its parameters, but in the process legislators, judges, and other authorities often made matters worse. Much of the contradiction came from competing ideas about ethnicity and gender that created exceptions to the naturalization process. In almost two-dozen states, economic boosters who wanted to attract immigrants won legislation that allowed foreign-born men to vote after receiving their first papers. This loophole created "alien suffrage," which let noncitizens cast ballots in elections. Poor enforcement added to the problem, making it possible for some immigrants to never become citizens but remain enfranchised for decades. Naturalization also broke down in terms of gender. In 1855 Congress confirmed "derivative citizenship," which allowed a foreign-born woman who married a citizen of the United States to receive citizenship. Marriage, not the naturalization process itself, became the naturalizing act for a woman born outside the country. Fifty years later, Congress stripped native-born women of their citizenship using similar logic. According to the Expatriation Act of 1907, any American-born woman who married a foreign-born individual lost her citizenship. This decision not only rendered women who married noncitizens politically neutral, but it also subjected them to deportation and deprived them of the protection of the state and the right to hold or inherit property. While the Fourteenth Amendment had confirmed birthright citizenship and upheld naturalization, the laws passed in 1855 and 1907 defied it. These two measures revealed that citizenship status could change over a person's lifetime to match an ascribed characteristic or marital status.[9]

Legislation, court cases, and political traditions reveal how inconsistent citizenship was until the early twentieth century in the United States, but they also provide only a partial view, considered as a product of the modern nation-state. Long before nationalism reshaped political ideologies, philosophers had offered simple metrics for citizenship, advocating that a citizen was anyone involved in local affairs. According to Aristotle, citizens held each other responsible to participate in local governance. Contributing to the community was a civic duty that was both a selfless act and an obligation imposed by others. Communal expectations encouraged autonomous citizens to sacrifice for the common good. Citizenship was relational, therefore, constructed through social bonds with and among other citizens. Many of the earliest American thinkers, from Benjamin Franklin to Thomas Jefferson, embraced Aristotle's vision of citizenship by identifying civic virtue as a hallmark of American political life. They underscored its importance to the survival of the republic, and they celebrated the American citizen as independent and virtuous, free and responsible. They argued that a citizen had to give up a certain amount of personal liberty to make government possible, which created a vital link between private virtue and public life. During the nineteenth century, civic virtue became a powerful idea among Americans, especially people living in the Midwest. Community relationships encouraged people to establish mutual interests and shared experiences, inspiring civic engagement and shifting the focus of citizenship away from who a citizen was to what a citizen did. As citizens acted on behalf of the community, they constructed, deconstructed, and reshaped their own civic identities. Voting in the nineteenth century was not a solitary act but a "performance of community directed to the locale." Understanding the importance of community in the United States changes the emphasis of citizenship from law to action and illuminates the ways that people worked around the legal restrictions that limited citizenship.[10]

Historians who study the history of community in the United States focus on its common elements and shared meanings. Communities can contain almost infinite complexity, which makes defining them in terms of size, geography, or character nearly impossible. In a community a multiplicity of entities, both real and imagined, converge to encompass the fabric of life, from public institutions like schools, local governments, and libraries to intimate matters like families and the home. At its heart, a community is simply a "network of social relations marked by mutuality and emotional bonds." People living in a community share "a common interest in a particular locality," which sets them apart from other communities. While the physical boundaries of place define communities, cultural or social bonds can also transcend these boundaries. These two elements—the physical place and the shared experience— are foundational aspects of community that intertwine and intersect in unexpected and tangled ways.[11]

Understanding the link between community and citizenship is critical to the study of woman suffrage in the Midwest. The suffrage movement began to arise at the same time that Yankees and immigrants from northern Europe arrived in the region. As the population increased during the 1870s and 1880s, proximity helped to establish communities out of scattered settlements and neighbors grew close, relying on mutuality to survive a harsh climate in a land that was seemingly a wilderness. Together, Yankees and European immigrants created physical boundaries and infrastructure by establishing small towns and villages. In these places, people formed relationships based on social exchanges, economic transactions, and shared cultural values. Immigrants practiced chain migration, preferring to settle in separate enclaves and marrying within their particular ethnic groups. In this way, place became a significant component of midwestern community identity. It developed out of the shared experiences of late-nineteenth-century settlement as well as an array of different ethnic ties, cultural traits, and religious beliefs. The process of community development was profoundly gendered, and women played an instrumental role in what they saw as domesticating the wilderness and bringing civilization to the desolate prairies. In the absence of local government, women stepped into public service, creating a direct connection to civic activism. By making significant contributions to emerging communities, they saw citizenship as an obligation to their small towns and villages, making civic duty a key component of their identities as midwestern women.

Nineteenth-Century Gender Norms and Women's Rights

The importance of civic virtue to American political life exposed the inequalities of citizenship in the Midwest, especially for women. Community membership raised expectations for civic involvement, but gender distinctions stymied women's participation in public affairs. Since the founding of the United States, gender had imposed limited and unequal citizenship on women. Gendered notions of the domestic ideal, propagated during the late eighteenth and nineteenth centuries, helped to create a system of second-class citizenship for women. Most Americans embraced the idea of separate spheres that placed men in public life and women in private life. Men were heads of household who represented their families in politics and business. Women were dependents who served the interests of the home and the family. Nineteenth-century prescriptive literature venerated women's virtue, purity, and piety as a response to increased industrialization, corruption, and competition in public life. Women were to preserve morality against threats of vice and dishonesty. They did so through their domestic responsibilities, including cooking, cleaning, and child care. Coverture, which traditionally defined women's legal status under English common law once they had married, reinforced the domestic ideal and sought to protect women from public life. In reality, it restricted women's political rights. Under coverture, in most states women could not own property, enter contracts, or testify in court. Some of the earliest American political observers confirmed that women were not civic equals to men. Alexis de Tocqueville believed that American women were of "equal worth" to men, but he saw gender as a limitation that denied them certain political rights, including the right to vote. Women were passive citizens, present in the nation-state but incapable of active participation in it.[12]

By the middle of the nineteenth century, women's rights activists had cut to the heart of gendered inequalities of citizenship. Advocates clamored for legal recognition in the form of rights to inheritance, contracts, and divorce. They also argued for the right to vote. In the 1840s, women like Lucretia Mott, Elizabeth Cady Stanton, and Susan B. Anthony began to demand full political and legal equality. In resolutions like the "Declaration of Sentiments," published in 1848, they claimed that women ought to enjoy the inalienable right to consent to the laws that governed them. They spoke to liberal political ideas that venerated the individual and prized justice for all. After the Civil War, Stanton, Anthony, and other leaders sought to organize nationally, but differences in strategy, especially about working for the rights of African American men, led to disagreements. In 1869 two competing associations, the American Woman Suffrage Association (AWSA) and the National Woman Suffrage Association (NWSA), formed, and for two decades they advocated for women's rights simultaneously but separately. The AWSA, led by Lucy Stone and Henry Blackwell, supported rights for African Americans as well as women while the NWSA, headed by Stanton and Anthony, focused on attaining individual liberties, especially the vote, for women only. In particular, the NWSA argued that birthright citizenship, established with the Fourteenth Amendment, gave women the same constitutional rights as men. During the late nineteenth century, many Yankee suffragists in the Midwest followed the NWSA's lead and called for equality within a liberal tradition. While this argument gained some converts, it did not secure women's right to vote. Most Americans, including a majority of midwesterners, still viewed female autonomy as radical, and they opposed woman suffrage as a threat to the home. Coverture, and the patriarchal representation it produced, meant that men voted on behalf of their family members, including their wives.[13]

By the late nineteenth century, suffragists, including many Yankees in the Midwest, began to reconsider their approach to achieving the vote.

In 1890 the AWSA and NWSA merged, creating the National American Woman Suffrage Association (NAWSA). While Stanton became its first president, her election was largely symbolic. Anthony quietly ran the organization for two years until Stanton retired in 1892, becoming the second president that year. Under her leadership, NAWSA shifted tactics. According to Sara Graham, suffragists were "ideologically diverse," holding a variety of positions. Some, like Anthony, began to celebrate domesticity when agitating for the ballot as a matter of expediency, recognizing that demanding individual liberty was a dead-end strategy as long as gender norms reinforced women's differences from men. Others embraced the feminized ideal out of a genuine desire to defend the home and family, advocating for a "home protection" ballot. Among the groups to champion this rhetoric was the Women's Christian Temperance Union (WCTU), led by Frances Willard. For midwestern Yankee suffragists, many of whom came to woman suffrage from temperance work, "home protection" was a common late-nineteenth-century refrain that reflected their commitment to their families and communities and highlighted women's "higher, selfless nature." While the "home protection" argument softened opposition to woman suffrage, it also upheld rigid gender roles. To those for whom domesticity was suffocating, "home protection" offered only limited options.[14]

As "home protection" reshaped woman suffrage rhetoric, women across the United States also developed political identities through voluntary associations and clubs. Nineteenth-century club work in benevolent societies and federated women's clubs taught women important political lessons in partisanship and electoral politics and gave them their first taste of leadership. Female voluntary associations were extremely popular among Yankees in the Midwest, and almost every small town had some sort of women's club. Their activities were mostly local and largely steeped in moral and social reform efforts. They also usually focused on single issues meant to improve their communities, bringing the hallmarks of domesticity into public life. In 1890 the General Federation of Women's Clubs (GFWC) created a coalition of organized women dedicated to community uplift. They built libraries and schools, advocated for better nutrition for infants, and initiated sanitary measures like garbage disposal services. Their efforts challenged the boundary between public and private, and women soon began to understand politics in sophisticated ways. By the early twentieth century, it had become difficult for clubwomen to separate the home from politics, and they began to embrace public affairs. Clubwomen in the Midwest recognized that building a park or opening a library only scratched the surface of the major cultural and social problems that plagued their communities. It became imperative to seek direct government action to solve complex civic issues. Clubwomen increasingly turned their attention to the government as individuals with civic virtue, advocating for legislation that targeted the root of social problems.[15]

By the early twentieth century, suffragists across the United States had reshaped their messages to respond to major political changes. By this time, many Americans were embracing Progressivism, which increased expectations for state intervention in society and the economy. Moving away from laissez-faire liberalism, Progressives rejected limited government and demanded reform through state intervention, especially at the federal level. Political involvement shifted away from partisan loyalty, and people began to advocate for direct democracy. Reforms such as the primary, initiative, referendum, and recall moved people closer to the government as individuals, which eroded patriarchal representation. While Progressives upheld ideals of popular democracy, they also embraced organizing interest groups and advocating for certain policies, like woman suffrage, through associations acting as pressure groups. In the process, they championed shared social responsibility and redrew the alleged line between the public and private realms. At the same time, the state assumed many of the functions of the home, taking up social policies like sanitation, public health, child labor, and infant nutrition that granted protections from impersonal economic forces. People began to perceive the government as nurturing.[16]

The spirit of Progressivism encouraged suffragists like Carrie Chapman Catt to expand upon "home protection" and add a utilitarian approach to their strategy. It was part of a grand redesign taking place in NAWSA. As national leaders revised their approach, they embraced direct power politics by training national organizers, organizing at district and precinct levels, and staging popular demonstrations to exert pressure on politicians. Their goal was to convert public sentiment to favor woman suffrage. To do so, they claimed that women sought the ballot to contribute to the government as women with special skills and interests rooted in the home. Voting was not only a right but also the duty of "municipal housekeepers" who knew how to clean up filth and protect the innocent. In this way, woman suffrage made women better wives, mothers, and citizens and politics less corrupt and more effective. By the second decade of the twentieth century, NAWSA had moved away from the WCTU's "home protection" ballot, preferring the "municipal housekeeping" argument for its ability to link motherhood, public service, and the home.[17]

"Municipal housekeeping" corresponded to twentieth-century ideological changes occurring among suffragists across the country. It privileged an elitist vision of governing and social reform in which white, Anglo-Saxon, and upper-class women directed efforts. While conservative forces like these were not the majority in NAWSA, they held strong sway. Many Southern suffragists linked the cause to maintaining white supremacy. Other national figures, like Stanton, Anthony, and Catt, had made imperialist arguments as the United States expanded into new, overseas territories in the 1890s. At issue were meanings of citizenship and national belonging, and imperialism turned the vote into a matter of civilized behavior, not natural rights. While these discussions were meant for international contexts, they resonated in domestic ones like the Midwest, where inhabitants increasingly linked community membership to a broad sense of national belonging. Midwestern suffragists became some of the first to question "alien suffrage." They claimed that the ballot in the hands of native-born women would counter the sinister influence of inferior, but enfranchised, immigrant men. In this line of thinking, woman suffrage became a conservative measure, elevating the special qualities of elite, educated, and native-born citizens of Anglo-Saxon heritage who would "clean up" society and maintain control of popular democracy. They also echoed Catt, who explicitly argued that Germans, as outsiders wedded to their liquor interests and hostile to democracy, had ominous plans to defeat woman suffrage at every opportunity. It was no wonder that when World War I broke out, the primary effort among Yankee suffragists was the "Americanization" of foreigners, especially the ethnic Germans living in their midst.[18]

Twentieth-century midwestern Yankee suffragists both embraced and expanded upon "municipal housekeeping" when they advocated for civic responsibility. Like national leaders, middle-class Yankees linked the home and the vote in powerful ways, arguing that with the ballot, they could protect their families. Where they differed was in their emphasis on community obligation and loyalty. Voting was not just an individual right; it was the act of members whose duty was to the community, and with the outbreak of World War I, to the nation. They understood how Progressivism redefined citizenship, emphasizing "good" and "active" citizenship to improve the community by enhancing social bonds and uplifting mutual interests. While civic responsibility embraced the ideals of midwestern political culture, it also subverted patriarchal authority by giving Yankee women power through their social relations with other community members. In addition, by linking woman suffrage to civic virtue, the activists pledged to serve the common good like any other white, Anglo-Saxon citizens. They promised to uphold the founding principles that distinguished the United States as a beacon of liberty and justice. As Edith Fitch explained, the fate of the American republic rested on the "amount of civic responsibility which its members assume." Liberty was safe only when white, virtuous citizens participated fully in community affairs. Midwestern Yankee suffragists struck gold when they chose civic responsibility as their message. It not only combined Progressive visions of community-based citizenship with midwestern values of civic duty, but it also envisioned women as individuals who were capable, virtuous, and patriotic.[19]

Before World War I, Yankee suffragists crafted civic responsibility out of midwestern political values about community and gender, amplified by Progressivism. While this helped advocates dull the radical edges of the suffrage cause, it did not secure the vote for midwestern women alone. It was World War I that created an extraordinary political and military situation that placed women in a position to participate in the war effort. In fact, contributing to wartime activities was not just accepted, it was expected of midwestern women. More than "municipal housekeeping" ever did, civic responsibility created a direct bridge between decades of civic activism and patriotic war service. Whereas "municipal housekeeping" retained the language of the home and family, civic responsibility deliberately shed the confines of domesticity. It cast midwestern women as virtuous native-born citizens and the vote as one of the many obligations they fulfilled out of loyalty to community and country.

As midwestern suffragists advocated for women's right to vote, they were careful to avoid feminism. They understood that demanding gender equality was unpopular in the region, and they often couched their claims in the rhetoric of home and domesticity to protect their reputations. Avoiding feminism often curtailed the visibility and significance of their activism, leading some scholars to believe that midwestern women disdained politics entirely. Others disagreed, however, and noted the power of mutuality to give women the ability to engage in community affairs. The bonds between home, family, and community created social and political networks that propelled midwestern women to positions of influence. Community membership compelled civic activism, which led middle-class midwestern activists to demand equal political rights. While civic responsibility was an effective argument, it contained an implicit feminist rhetoric by implying that midwestern women sought the ballot to be civic equals to men. Midwestern activists understood the danger of this feminist overemphasis, so they framed their arguments with precision. As Andrew Cayton and Susan Gray have suggested, midwestern women outwardly rejected feminism and embraced public activism as "upholders of private virtue." They participated in politics to promote a "republican good life" for their communities, not for individual gain or gender equality.[20]

Defining Midwestern Political Culture

During the early twentieth century, white middle-class suffragists in the Midwest found success in arguments that championed their civic responsibility to their homes and communities because most residents highly valued civic virtue. Midwestern political culture came to venerate volunteerism, civic duty, and community pride because of a strong Yankee influence. Yankees were among the first arrivals in the region, claiming a majority in the decades after the Civil War. They typically hailed from the Northeast and set high expectations for civic engagement and encouraged others to participate in public affairs. Many became farmers or started businesses to serve farmers, which instilled agrarianism as a central component of midwestern identity. Agrarianism was a way of thinking that valued farming and the way of life it inspired. American political figures, especially Thomas Jefferson, venerated farmers as independent producers who gained powerful wisdom and political insight from property ownership and self-sufficiency. As Jon Lauck has argued, midwesterners embraced agrarianism, proclaiming a powerful affinity with the "American tradition of Lockean liberalism" that embraced "property rights, economic freedoms, and civil liberties." Personal attributes were vital to the survival of the republic, and Jefferson mythologized farmers as the backbone of democracy, arguing that they embodied the hallmarks of civic virtue. In this way, independent and self-sufficient farmers were best suited to champion republican values. Only they understood the importance of personal virtue in maintaining communities and preserving the republic. Lauck noted that most midwesterners placed a high value on "social capital," or the degree to which people participated in civic life.[21]

While civic engagement and agrarianism influenced midwestern identity in powerful ways, they were only ideals. Many people living in the region contested their meanings and created identities that diverged from these standards. As much as Yankees attempted to shape midwestern political culture, others, most notably immigrants from northern Europe, also influenced the region in dramatic ways. Although some came before the Civil War, it was during the 1880s that many foreigners arrived from countries like Germany, Norway, and Sweden. They were responding to regional boosters, many of whom were Yankees, who enticed European immigrants to come to the Midwest. The region desperately needed laborers, especially farmers, for economic development. Migrants, both native and foreign, poured into the region during the 1880s. Iowa gained half a million new inhabitants between 1870 and 1880, and by 1890 it claimed a population of almost 2,000,000. Minnesota also grew by leaps and bounds. In 1870 its population was just under 440,000. Ten years later, over three-quarters of a million people lived there. By 1890 the figure was 1,300,000, meaning that the state population had tripled in just two decades. The percentage of foreign-born residents differed markedly between Iowa and Minnesota. In 1870 and 1880 about 17 percent of all people living in Iowa were foreign born, compared to about 35 percent of the population of Minnesota. South Dakota remained a territory until 1889, with a population of only about 389,000 at that time.[22]

By the 1890s, the presence of foreigners had made Yankees both grateful and wary. Although the majority of residents were native-born in the three states, it was the perception of foreigners as outsiders that mattered most. Immigrants to the Midwest often settled in enclaves outside small towns and were able to hold steadfastly to their ethnic identities for years. Varied settlement patterns, difficult topography, sparse populations, and religious fragmentation encouraged isolation, reinforced ethnic distinctions, and created a region of vibrant diversity. People spoke a slew of languages, practiced an assortment of religious beliefs, and expressed their heritages with traditional food, drink, and dress. Like Yankees, many embraced community development, but they did so on their own terms, while preserving their ethnic identities and resisting pressure to assimilate. Among immigrants, Germans were the most insular, protecting their ethnic heritage with separate religious, educational, and cultural institutions. What resulted was a region full of "complicated landscapes and networks of social relations" and characterized by "many voices together continually contesting, negotiating, and redefining the Midwest."[23]

Chapter 1

HARDSHIP AND BOUNTY:
BUILDING MIDWESTERN COMMUNITIES

IN NOVEMBER 1894 Andrew A. Meek, a farmer from Lyon County, Minnesota, challenged readers of the *Lyon County Reporter* to see life there as more than just "loneliness and hardships." He explained that recent population growth had fostered a deep sense of community on the prairie, and he pointed to specific examples to make his case. Friendships had blossomed among neighbors, who always were "ready to accord a hearty welcome to new settlers." Residents of nearby small towns had erected a number of notable public institutions, including courthouses, public schools, churches, and banks. Educational and religious activities added social events to schedules already filled with near-constant "social intercourse." Fertile land had enticed a diverse group of farmers from outside the United States, particularly from Germany, Norway, and Sweden, to borrow money, buy land, and plant crops, and they reaped bountiful harvests every year. Railroads like the Great Northern Railway provided ready access to national markets. Economic success produced wealth, and Meek noted the construction of many "luxurious" houses that were "exceedingly neat and well adapted to the climate." He even praised Minnesota's seasons, with its "delightful" summers and "superb" winters that beckoned people outdoors even in "extreme cold." He boldly proclaimed that the "skies of Minnesota more nearly resemble those of Italy than any other." Meek undoubtedly left many readers dizzy as they read his embellishments while shaking their heads in disbelief.[1]

Meek produced his utopic vision by glossing over the conflicts and problems that characterized community building in the American Midwest. When he chose to highlight neighborly cooperation and prosperity, he consciously downplayed the many difficulties to which residents had grown accustomed. Despite his best efforts, Meek could not avoid the "loneliness and hardships" that gripped his community. Minnesotans faced political turmoil with the rise of a powerful third-party option, the Populists, only a few years earlier. Partisan bickering grew markedly, and the political climate became polarized and hostile. While Meek took no stance on political matters, his piece appeared in the *Lyon County Reporter*, a Republican newspaper. The paper's editor often took great delight in criticizing Democrats and Populists without mincing words or sparing feelings. In addition, the Panic of 1893 created financial difficulties that made people vulnerable to market vacillations. Rock-bottom crop prices and insurmountable debt forced farmers into insolvency, which drained banks and stalled the local economy. When Meek pointed out that there were plenty of "fine farms" available for "reasonable figures," he admitted that land was abundant because farmers were "simply overburdened with debt." Finally, the sociability that Meek celebrated was somewhat limited. Along with his neighbors, Meek was Scottish, and he lived in an isolated colony of Scottish farmers. He was one of many thousands of immigrants who had arrived in Minnesota in the late nineteenth century and had skewed the ethnic and religious composition of the state. Ethnic differences fomented suspicions of outsiders, and native-born people resented foreign-born groups, especially Germans. Meek admitted that native-born residents assumed that Scots were clannish and aloof, but he assured Americans that there was "no cause for such a state of matters." His words failed to assuage the public's fears, and his article reveals the contradictions embedded in the immigration process. As immigrants helped to settle regions and establish communities, their presence left many native-born people feeling unsettled.[2]

The *Lyon County Reporter* published Meek's article at a transformative moment in the history of the American Midwest. Less than half a century earlier, only a few white people had lived scattered across the prairies. After the Civil War the federal government aggressively removed powerful Native American tribes like the Dakota (also called Sioux), which opened land to Americans and European immigrants. Communities grew during the late nineteenth century, and small towns and villages slowly began to connect farmers living in the countryside. Railroads linked these places to national markets, orienting midwestern communities to distant urban centers. Despite national influences, the rural landscape was harsh, promoting isolation and encouraging people to construct identities rooted in locality. The settlement process was uneven, and populations remained scattered over vast distances. In other words, while people with shared interests attempted to forge relationships and cultivate social connections, the endless stretches of terrain sometimes limited their ability to do so. Community grew out of geographic and social conditions; it was both a place and an experience.[3]

Midwesterners defined themselves primarily as members of local communities, of small towns and villages. In doing so, they established belonging as an essential midwestern value. While community was a powerful idea in other regions, the timing of settlement in the Midwest made it a primary way of organizing life. People, especially middle-class Yankees, embraced community engagement and encouraged a strong spirit of civic responsibility. Arriving in vast, unbroken prairies, Yankees planted communities while simultaneously giving them meaning. These residents typically hailed from the Northeast and expected active participation in public affairs so as to boost the prospects of their small towns and improve the overall quality of life. In turn, building communities promoted republican notions of citizenship, and Yankees typically supported shared civic institutions and celebrated communitarianism. They believed that individuals, including women, had a duty to their community, and they conceived of citizenship in terms of contribution and involvement. Public acts were key for community acceptance. When Meek praised nearby small towns for constructing public buildings, he tapped directly into those sentiments. The link between citizenship and community also fostered an emphasis on status, and reputation and loyalty became significant measures of belonging. By fulfilling their obligations to their communities, individuals proved themselves worthy citizens who could enjoy the privileges of membership. Inclusion was Meek's aim when he exaggerated the community life of Lyon County. He desperately wanted to belong, and his article was an attempt to establish an honorable reputation. Meek was like most midwesterners at the time who constructed their identities at the intersection of community development and active citizenship.[4]

While middle-class Yankees understood civic engagement as a major component of midwestern values, they never agreed on what citizenship meant or how it should appear. They had vague notions as to the character of public service, but they failed to establish any definitive standards until World War I forced the issue. Contradictory goals of "mobility and stability and volunteerism and collective discipline" created tensions among community leaders. As Andrew Cayton and Peter Onuf note, perhaps the "most striking fact" about the Midwest in the late nineteenth century was "the constant struggle among all its peoples over the ways in which they should live their lives." A kaleidoscope of immigrants, mostly from northern Europe, brought an array of ethnic, religious, political, and economic ideas that challenged any attempts to impose a uniform vision of active citizenship. In an ironic twist, one of the most vital features of midwestern identity became one of its most contested ones as vibrant ethnic diversity challenged a single Yankee standard. While belonging was significant in other regions, ambiguity about it made it all the more important in the Midwest. At the core of these debates were the meanings of citizenship itself. Most midwesterners thought the premise of citizenship straightforward, but it did not take long for individuals to see that contradictions abounded. Birthright citizenship was silent on civic expectations, and until the early twentieth century, the state did little to enforce citizenship laws. Some people avoided involvement in public affairs without consequence. Others contributed as non-naturalized residents. Conversely, gender, ethnicity, race, and class could limit civic engagement for those who wanted to participate, imposing hierarchies based on difference. American citizenship was ambiguous at best and, more often than not, failed to accommodate diversity and distinction. The political culture of the Midwest exposed these fundamental flaws in citizenship and revealed a startling paradox. In a region where people prized civic engagement, inequalities of citizenship restricted the ability of all its residents to do so.[5]

Gender also informed community development in the Midwest by blurring the alleged line between the public and private spheres. The home and family were central to community life, and it was impossible to separate political concerns from domestic ones. Friendship and familiarity characterized both the political and social lives of midwesterners, despite their ethnicity, and locality ensured that people tackled issues more often through face-to-face encounters. Local politics were personal, tied directly to the networks of kinship and sociability that thrived in midwestern communities. Politics and sociability emerged as the two main arenas in which native-born and foreign-born residents, both individually and collectively, made community. People often conflated the two, discussing politics at family or social gatherings or turning political events into parties. In doing so, they confirmed that the boundary between public and private life was elusive at best. At no place was the overlap more pronounced than in the church. Religious activities were at the heart of community life, and midwesterners understood that pulpits could contain both pastors and politicians. Belonging to a church also reinforced ethnicity because both Americans and immigrants sought refuge within familiar religious traditions. For most women, the church became the path through which they first engaged in public affairs, gaining praise for both spiritual and community devotion. In their churches, Yankee suffragists often hosted woman suffrage lectures. Blending public and private created a loophole through which midwestern women of all ethnicities could challenge inequalities of citizenship, and it opened civic issues to people normally excluded from participation.[6]

Bridging politics and sociability did not mean that the Midwest was a bastion of equality. Immigrants often arrived with little economic or political power and smaller populations, giving native-born Americans more prestige and control over civic institutions. While this imbalance did not necessarily sit·well with foreign-born residents, they mostly complied with it because they were still able to retain their distinct ethnic traditions. For nearly five decades, most immigrants managed to celebrate their customs despite covert pressure to assimilate. Ethnic diversity was a hallmark of the Midwest, and it remained so until the outbreak of World War I, when nativism erased ethnic plurality without hesitation or mercy. Just as ethnicity marked community, so too did gender. Even though most midwesterners welcomed women into civic life, they did so while espousing rigid gender roles. When women engaged in community affairs, which they did as soon as they arrived, they explained their involvement in gendered terms. They were wives, mothers, and daughters who were concerned about the prospects for their families. Couching their activism in gender masked their significance in community life. Women helped build the places where politics erupted, and they often controlled public spaces, albeit with restrictions. Their community engagement garnered them reputations as citizens with unquestionable loyalty to their communities. It also set the stage for them to demand the right to vote.

Local communities profoundly shaped the identity of the Midwest and the people who lived there during the late nineteenth and early twentieth centuries. Settlement encouraged midwesterners to foster inclusivity within their political culture, but ethnic, religious, and gendered factors promoted exclusion. Residents had to negotiate this tension between inclusion and exclusion while simultaneously establishing complex social relationships. While people approached civic life in myriad ways, they favored inclusion until World War I forced them to reconsider who belonged and who did not. For Yankee suffragists, midwestern political culture afforded a distinct opportunity. Initially, they struggled to gain support. During the late nineteenth century, settling the land consumed their energy, and cultivating respected civic reputations took time. Working on the front lines of public affairs gave them reputations as loyal community members, however, and by the early twentieth century, middle-class activists had capitalized on decades of community involvement to argue their fitness as responsible citizens who deserved the ballot. As Progressivism called for increasingly universal citizenship standards, midwestern Yankee suffragists carefully structured their claims in those terms.

Settling the Land

In the three counties in this study—Clay County in Iowa, Yankton County in South Dakota, and Lyon County in Minnesota—the land offered vibrant farming prospects to incoming white settlers. Each county benefited from rich, dark, loamy soil that beckoned people onto its grassy prairie landscape. The first settlers arrived to farm the well-watered land, and small towns sprang up as agriculture developed, populations grew, and transportation networks improved. Clay County, located in northwest Iowa, was the first county to gain legal recognition. In 1858 locals cut it out of a neighboring county. With twenty-four square miles of verdant farmland, spliced through by streams, lakes, and the Little Sioux River running north to south, the county was a beacon to farmers. That same year white settlers arrived in Yankton County, located in southeastern South Dakota. Unlike Clay County, the residents of Yankton County capitalized on its location near the Missouri River, which was a major waterway. The Missouri River brought more than just farmers to the area; it promoted trade and commerce upstream. A small town, called Yankton, developed along the river's banks and served as a steamboat landing and trade hub. Yankton County gained official status with the Organic Act of 1861. The act created the Dakota Territory and named Yankton as the territorial capital. Soon stagecoach lines complemented the river traffic, running from the frontier capital to military outposts like Fort Randall, Fort Pierre, and Bismarck. Farmers prospered and new settlers, among whom were many families, arrived to take advantage of the rich, well-watered soil near the James River, a tributary of the Missouri River that cut diagonally across the county from northwest to southeast. As one early observer reported, "Yankton is surrounded by an excellent agricultural country" that complemented Yankton's booming river port.[7]

White settlement appeared at the expense of the indigenous groups living in the area. Through a series of treaties, many later broken, the federal government secured the homelands of Native Americans and forced them further westward. The Dakota (Sioux) had begun to cede their lands to the federal government in 1851, allowing the settlement of white people on the prairies. Even though the terms of the treaties stipulated that the Dakota leave their lands, small bands later returned, ready to fight for survival. From 1857 to 1862, white settlers wrote frequently about the threat of violence from the Indians living in the area. In the spring of 1857, clashes between Indians and settlers in northwestern Iowa left at least thirty-two dead and a sense of terror among white settlers. Relations between the Dakota and white arrivals continued to deteriorate, and violence erupted during the Dakota War of 1862. Angry at the treaties broken by the federal government, the Dakota rebelled, attacking white settlements in southern Minnesota near what became Lyon County. Only with a swift and effective military response from the federal government did the violence abate. The stigma of Indian violence, as well as the Civil War, slowed migration to the area, however, and white settlement stagnated until 1870.[8]

The Dakota uprising prevented much white settlement in Lyon County, located in southwest Minnesota, until 1870, but it blossomed with the arrival of the railroad. By this year, all three counties were experiencing the railroads as a major developmental influence. The railroads did more than just open up new economic possibilities for the Midwest. They carved the landscape, building communities and plotting the town sites along railroad lines at intervals determined by the company. Railroads controlled the fate of small towns, promising vibrant trade potential to communities along the track while sounding a death knell to those the railroad line missed. Yankton County, which included a bustling river port and territorial capital by the late 1860s, benefited handsomely from the construction of railroad lines. Between 1868 and 1890, the Chicago, Milwaukee & St. Paul Railroad, the Chicago & Northwestern Railroad, and the Great Northern Railroad all built lines through the county, connecting the area to eastern cities. In Clay County, railroad construction from 1878 to 1901 cut down shipping costs substantially for farmers and transformed Spencer, a small village, into an important rail hub and the county seat. Rail transport also decreased travel times, which was a boon to livestock owners who developed a strong dairy industry with a national reputation. In Lyon County, market activity blossomed in 1873 with the arrival of the railroads. Competition between the Chicago & Northwestern Railroad and the Great Northern Railroad transformed the landscape substantially, as each company built lines that intersected at the county seat of Marshall. The Great Northern Railroad also built town sites at Cottonwood, Green Valley, Lynd, Russell, and Florence. The era of the railroads in the Midwest dramatically transformed the region, connecting it to national markets and promoting immigration and population growth.[9]

The end of the Civil War, the military removal of the Dakota, the advent of rail lines, and the promise of prosperity hastened settlement in the Midwest. Between 1870 and 1900, the region received a tremendous surge of both native-born and foreign-born immigrants, and mobility came to define the region. In the Dakota Territory, the government distributed more federal land between 1870 and 1890 than in any other place. Immigrants came for cheap land, economic promise, and an agrarian livelihood. An astounding rate of growth transformed the land from vast prairies into fields, farms, and small towns. While state populations ballooned during this period, local populations swelled as well. For example, between 1870 and 1875 the population of Clay County more than doubled from about 1,500 residents to more than 3,500. Every five years between 1885 and 1905, the county gained between two and three thousand people so that by 1905, the population stood at just over 12,700. The foreign-born population was low at less than 20 percent; in 1890, for instance, Germans numbered less than 500. In Yankton County, the population nearly quadrupled over the ten-year period from 1870 to 1880, vaulting from almost 2,300 to 8,400 inhabitants. By

1890 the county's population had reached 10,000 people. Of that number, about 4,000 were foreign-born individuals. Almost one quarter of all immigrants were Germans. The pattern of rapid population growth in Lyon County mimicked that of Yankton and Clay counties. Between 1880 and 1890 Lyon County gained just over 3,000 residents, for a total of about 9,500. Of that number, almost one third, or just over 3,000 residents, were foreign-born individuals. Half of the immigrants came from German, Irish, or Belgian backgrounds. As one county history put it, immigration to Lyon County was a "tidal wave."[10]

Community institutions blossomed with population growth, and Yankee women stood at the helm of creating communal order. Land surveyors platted town sites, making space for businesses, residences, and streets. To establish civilization out of the "barbarism" of the frontier, Yankee women demanded that the first buildings erected be churches, followed by schools, local government buildings, general stores, banks, and homes. Development was rapid. By 1870 Yankton boasted 180 structures within town limits, most of which were homes. Two years later the county was home to four newspapers, including the Republican *Press and Dakotan* and the Democratic *Dakota Herald.* Curiously, the weekly newspaper with the largest circulation in the Dakota Territory, the German-language *Freie Press,* had its headquarters in Yankton. The "Dakota Boom" was favorable to Yankton, and by 1890 Yankton enjoyed a status as the "Mother City" of the Dakota Territory. The county also had prospered, with four small towns, Utica, Lesterville, Volin, and Gayville, and ten post offices dotting the countryside. Only Deadwood had a population larger than Yankton's during this period of prosperity.[11]

Population growth and agricultural development also spurred community building in Lyon County. Wheat production in the 1870s and 1880s was a boon to the county, and settlers constructed four flour mills to process the grain. In Marshall, the county seat, residents noted that a spirit of "boosterism" had caught hold by the 1890s, and the editor of the *Lyon County Reporter* remarked that community pride was a "commendable and necessary" ingredient in creating an "enterprising town." According to one scholar, the history of Marshall boiled down to this sense of "consistent civic optimism." Yankee newspaper editors promoted a sense of mutual cooperation and civic belonging among all residents, drawing "like-minded, even those without kinship ties, into the orbit of community life." They encouraged them to patronize local businesses, join community organizations, and engage in local politics. Marshall's women responded enthusiastically, distributing petitions about local ordinances like curfews, and populating numerous civic associations. To these middle-class Yankees, membership in the community meant contributing to civic life, and by the close of the nineteenth century, the residents of these midwestern counties had cultivated a vibrant spirit of engagement and civic responsibility.[12]

As midwesterners created communities that celebrated civic participation, they did so amid changing geographies of rurality that emerged during the settlement period and developed afterward. People often moved more than once in their lifetime, making mobility an important element of community development. Civic responsibility was a powerful and widely shared sentiment even when mobility was high, and during the late nineteenth century, frequent migration incentivized residents to induct new members swiftly into civic affairs. It also shortened the time it took to establish loyalty to a community, since individuals only had to prove that they wanted to belong in order to participate. The impulse to include newcomers challenged Yankees directly since some immigrants, especially Germans, avoided swift assimilation. It encouraged Yankees, however, to accept foreign-born residents as they were, with their ethnic traditions intact and relatively unchanged. While mobility fostered inclusivity, exclusion emerged along the boundary between town and countryside. Small towns had higher population densities and greater access to national markets, and soon midwesterners began to distinguish the countryside from the town. By the early twentieth century, the divide between the two had widened. Farmers came to dress, speak, and act in ways different than people in small towns. As Michael Goldberg argues, these two worlds "represented a cultural divide" that privileged proximity and encouraged people residing near each other to band together out of necessity. In some cases, the divide reinforced the identities that neighbors already shared, while in other cases, people connected despite different ethnic, racial, or gender features.[13]

In some cases, the animosity between town and country grew so intense that officials shamed small-town residents into welcoming farmers. On the occasions when farm families went to town to conduct business or visit, they often stood out. Goldberg notes that sometimes townspeople used rude nicknames like "clodhoppers" and "hayseeds" to disparage farmers. In 1915 the *Spencer Herald,* one of the newspapers in Clay County, chided readers to examine their prejudices against farmers. "Is your greeting such that he feels that he is with us, but not of us?" the editor asked. Yankee women were some of the first to show hospitality, opening public rest areas, libraries, and churches to country visitors. Ultimately, most midwesterners realized that bridging the divide between town and country was more beneficial than not. While historians acknowledge the growing animosity between farmers and businesspeople that developed during the Gilded Age in the late nineteenth century, they also recognize the practical efforts people made toward cooperation. Navigating the class divide between town and farm was one part of the process of community formation and identity that shaped rural life in the Midwest.[14]

Ethnicity

Community formation required midwesterners to face distinctions between native-born Americans and foreign-born immigrants, which often divided residents into spheres of belonging. Rural and urban differences also exacerbated the ethnic disparities, since immigrants were more likely to settle on farms in rural areas while native-born Americans more often chose small-town living. Some of the first people to settle in these counties after the Civil War were Yankees from the East, mainly from states in the Northeast and Old Northwest. The earliest county histories, often written by Yankees as a form of self-congratulation, described these native-born transplants as "industrious, economical and naturally religious" and "intelligent and enterprising." These people were mobile after the Civil War and desirous of economic prosperity and independent living. Most also sought to replicate the life they had enjoyed further east by re-creating the communities they had left behind, and they eventually dominated life in each county. It was their commitment to progress, prosperity, and public-mindedness that instilled a spirit of "boosterism" and community engagement. As a settler from Sioux County, Iowa, put it, these were "hardworking . . . northern people" who "wanted to get ahead." Gender profoundly shaped Yankee settlement. Although they paid lip service to the separate spheres dichotomy, Yankee men and women

demonstrated mutuality. Any "like-minded" individuals who participated in community development were worthy of inclusion. Yankees
emphasized communal institutions, not kinship or household ties, to
bind people together, which presented women with a golden opportunity. Community membership was achievable through civic involvement, and contributing to institutions demonstrated selfless civic virtue, a hallmark of American citizenship.[15]

While Yankees made plans for the Midwest, massive waves of immigrants arrived, carrying with them traditions and values from the Old
Country. The immigrants came mainly from northern Europe and most
often were Germans, Norwegians, and Swedes. Other groups arrived in
smaller numbers and usually stood out among their neighbors. In Yankton County, a small Czech population along the western border held
steadfastly to their culture. People in Clay County noted the arrival of
Welsh immigrants, while Lyon County became known for its distinct
populations of Icelanders, Belgians, and French Canadians. As Robert
Swierenga explains, these immigrants to the Midwest, particularly Germans and Scandinavians, sought to acquire and hold onto land in the
country. Immigrants practiced chain migration, in which people with
similar backgrounds and places of origin resided together. These immigrant enclaves, separated by ethnic cultures, created a sort of "patchwork quilt" pattern of settlement in the Midwest. As Swierenga notes,
"clustered settlements were the norm on the midwestern frontier. Families migrated to places where kith and kin had already settled and were
able to help them with finding work and housing." This type of migration
promoted endogamy, or marriage within a specific group, which perpet-
uated ethnic identities down the generations. Further division occurred
based on religious preferences, so that neighborhoods and local communities often sprung up around churches. Finally, gender reinforced
ethnicity, and foreign-born residents more often embraced traditional
values. In particular, Germans and Scandinavians did not practice gender inclusivity to the extent that their Yankee neighbors did.[16]

Despite their differences, native-born Americans and immigrants
depended on each other, revealing the tension at the heart of citizenship
and community. Until 1880 settlement was slow, and residents knew
that immigration was critical to the growth of the region. As historian
Annette Atkins explains, "boosters saw newcomers as the fuel for the
engine of development," and officials produced guidebooks, maps, and

images to entice immigrants with promises of fertile land, bountiful harvests, and fantastic wealth. Yankees were desperate for immigrants to help them build communities, and they welcomed them gladly. Local leaders even joined the bandwagon, like Yankee businessmen in Marshall, who pledged money from their own pockets to construct a Catholic church. They hoped to attract Catholic laborers to the town, admitting that failure to do so jeopardized the survival of their fragile community. Economic boosterism promoted political and cultural toleration, and prosperity encouraged ethnic pluralism. Regional promoters did such a remarkable job that by the early twentieth century, the number of foreign-born residents threatened to eclipse the native-born population. In Yankton County foreigners, led by Germans, made up almost 50 percent of the population in 1910. In Minnesota's Lyon County, only 40 percent of the population reported Yankee ancestry by 1920, as Germans, Norwegians, Irish, Polish, Belgians, and French Canadians became the majority. Only in Clay County did Yankees outnumber immigrants, in this case by a margin of about two to one. It was the turn-of-the-twentieth-century shift in population that first sharpened nativist inclinations among Yankees.[17]

While some immigrants, like Norwegians and Swedes, assimilated quickly, others, such as Germans, refused to abandon their ethnic identities, preferring to remain outsiders. They understood Yankee expectations of civic engagement but cultivated distinct ethnic neighborhoods that contained different religious and gender norms. The unintended consequences of immigration baffled Yankee leaders, and they struggled to come to grips with the meanings of American citizenship. While Yankees watched skeptically as first-generation immigrants retained their ethnic identities, they bristled when their second-generation children also failed to assimilate. As American citizens, these children enjoyed political rights and equal standing under the Constitution, but they seemed to reject them by living in isolated enclaves. Second-generation children exposed a weakness of citizenship. Individuals could skirt assimilation because citizenship lacked any coercive mechanisms. While there was pressure to adopt American customs, immigrants could avoid Yankee prescriptions with enough effort.

Yankees soon distinguished among ethnic groups, preferring those who were willing to assimilate to those who were not. Norwegians and other Scandinavians seemed to learn English and adopt American values more quickly than Germans, particularly ethnic Germans from Russia. Germans had first come to Russia under the protection of Catherine the Great in 1773. These Germans settled in the Crimea and Black Sea regions following war with the Ottoman Empire. Germans continued to settle in Russia, especially in the province of Odessa, after Catherine's grandson, Alexander I, added further incentives to relocate. Although the arrangement worked well for almost a hundred years, it ended when Alexander II, who reigned from 1855 to 1881, revoked German privileges in Russia and sought to "Russianize" the immigrants through mandatory conscription and other measures that aimed to strip them of their culture and customs. Germans in Russia, dissatisfied with these new laws, began to look for a new place to settle. Their desire to migrate coincided with the "Dakota Boom," and many Germans from Russia saw great potential to build up their families in the Dakota Territory. In the end, the late-nineteenth-century process of settling the Midwest relaxed Yankee definitions of community building. Inviting droves of immigrants to the region granted foreign-born residents license to adhere to ethnic and gendered visions of community. While belonging was essential to midwestern identity, its meaning was anything but certain.[18]

European immigrants and native-born Americans lived together but separate. For decades, ethnic, gender, and religious differences produced restrained tensions and distrust. The presence of a strong sense of national identity among immigrants "deeply alarmed Anglo-Saxon Protestants," writes scholar John Radzilowski, and the latter "felt these 'foreigners' were out-breeding them." By the twentieth century, immigrants and their children outnumbered native-born residents. In many places, Germans boasted numerical superiority. Rivalries not only brewed between Americans and immigrants but also among immigrants who fought within their ranks, many times over nationalistic issues dating from Old World conflicts. Religious divisions between Catholics and Protestants created antagonisms, and the boundaries of ethnic enclaves or church membership served as much to delineate those who belonged as those who did not. Curiously, as historians Susan Gray and Andrew Cayton point out, immigrants and Yankees shared the same vision. Both groups "saw in the Midwest a promise of untrammeled material and moral progress" and ultimately desired freedom and independence. The ways they defined those terms shaped the boundaries between them. For foreigners, freedom meant the ability to retain their European cultures and customs, while Yankees assumed that freedom only came through assimilation and American citizenship. Ethnic differences characterized the Midwest until World War I erupted and many Germans living in the region openly defended Germany. Many midwestern Yankees became nativists and espoused "Americanization" efforts that forced most immigrants to suppress or abandon their ethnic customs. The war gave Yankees the impetus to enforce a rigid standard of American citizenship. Citizens not only had to adhere to democratic principles, but also had to behave as patriotic Americans.[19]

Gender and Sociability

Ethnic diversity could promote discord among the residents of these developing midwestern communities. With the arrival of new immigrants from Europe throughout the late nineteenth century, Yankees defined themselves in terms of who or what they were not, placing themselves against the "others" in their midst. Defining the Midwest in terms of conflict, however, does not capture the efforts of people to transcend their distinct identities and cultivate friendships and civility. The harsh conditions of settlement promoted neighborly bonds. "People helped each other," noted one Iowan. People were "involved with each other," practicing a deep sense of neighborliness. They shared chores, equipment, food, and gossip out of mutual obligation, crossing boundaries of gender and, in some cases, ethnicity. Common interests in civic improvement, such as constructing a schoolhouse or fixing a road, also brought people together. While ethnic, political, or religious differences could limit the social bonds created through community interactions, people also forged relationships that ignored these distinctions. An array of opportunities for social interaction emerged, reflecting both the diverse backgrounds of midwesterners and their desire for community membership and belonging.[20]

Gender influenced the creation of these social groups in the Midwest, inspiring cooperative relationships between men and women. Some of the first associations were male fraternal organizations, including the Masons, Independent Order of the Odd Fellows, Modern Woodmen of America, and Grand Army of the Republic (GAR). These fraternities emphasized brotherhood and male solidarity, with secret rituals and private meetings. These societies generally drew their membership from Yankees who had carried these associational connections to their new homes from back east. These were normally well-to-do, native-born men, especially the Masons. The Odd Fellows and Modern Wood-men sometimes bucked the trend by including foreign-born men where those populations were prominent. Women often joined auxiliaries to these organizations, such as the Order of the Eastern Star, the auxiliary to the Masons, and the Women's Relief Corps, the auxiliary of the GAR. While fraternal societies attempted to segregate men and women, the sexes often worked together on the same tasks. For example, the GAR and Women's Relief Corps often collaborated to plan encampments, parades, and other events, confusing the fraternal boundary.[21]

While midwesterners sometimes espoused gender distinctions, they practiced gender inclusivity. In a variety of community clubs residents socialized, played music, staged plays, heard speakers, and enjoyed pic-nics. Men and women interacted together to plan annual events. One of the most ubiquitous gender-inclusive organizations in the Midwest was the debating society. These were incredibly popular, particularly in neighborhoods with young people interested in testing their bud-ding knowledge of the world. For example, in Lyon County, the Flor-ence Debating Society regularly chose topics that reflected prominent national conversations. In March 1893, they debated a resolution that declared that "a woman can fill a man's place." A strenuous debate ensued, and the local newspaper reported that the "discussion was hot and ani-mated and the speakers on both sides made some hitting remarks." The Florence Debating Society met regularly through the 1890s, which was a testament to its popularity and importance to locals.[22]

A shared agrarian lifestyle also created organizations that blurred gender distinctions and promoted sociability. These clubs were prom-inent among rural residents in the Midwest, and they acknowledged the importance of family and community to a farming livelihood. While men and women worked together, they did not necessarily share responsibilities equally. Many times, men held executive positions while women served in supporting roles. For example, gender inclu-sivity helped to promote the formation of the Patrons of Husbandry, or Grange. The early 1870s brought economic upheaval and environ-mental issues, like locust infestations, which threatened agricultural production in the Midwest, and Grangers promoted neighborhood cooperation, mutual aid, and economic reform to meet these challenges. Grangers often obscured the line between the political and domestic spheres, welcoming women to participate in these efforts and celebrating their public responsibility while simultaneously praising their domesticity. Sometimes women even became leaders in the Grange. In Minnesota, Sarah Baird presided over the Minnesota State Grange for seventeen years, while in South Dakota and Iowa, women served prominently as lecturers. While some midwesterners enjoyed the Grange for its social benefits, the organization's local branches in Lyon, Clay, and Yankton counties did not last into the twentieth century. Farmers in Clay County formed a chapter of the Grange in 1875, but it fizzled by 1878. Members reported that it "did not prove either profitable or beneficial generally" and soon became a "thing of the past." People liked the idea of the Grange but struggled to apply its national resources to local problems. In Lyon County, residents reported that the Grange never "accomplished much more than ordinary farmers' clubs."[23]

While the Grange was short-lived in some midwestern communities, other agrarian organizations flourished when they emerged organically from rural residents. County agricultural associations were particularly successful in the late nineteenth and early twentieth centuries. The highlight for these groups was the county fair, an annual gathering that brought together farmers, local business leaders, and neighbors to support agricultural growth. Clay County had one of the first county fairs in the state, organized by the Clay County Agricultural Society. The first county fairs were modest exhibitions of livestock and other farm products. In the 1890s farmers added educational opportunities to their work, meeting annually in a series of Farmers' Institutes. These meetings featured speakers, both from state institutions and local groups, as well as demonstrations on topics of "interest to the tiller of the soil." While Farmers' Institutes welcomed women as well as men, by 1897 women had organized additional proceedings, called the "Woman's Congress." At these meetings, women debated a host of issues related to family life on the farm, including domestic economy, children's education, food preservation, gardening, and sanitation. The Woman's Congress, just like the Grange, demonstrated that agricultural interests both transcended gender boundaries and reinforced gender distinctions.[24]

By the first decades of the twentieth century, the Clay County Agricultural Society had reached its zenith. Members had purchased an old church building to accommodate their burgeoning annual exhibition. The poultry shows were especially popular among women. In 1913 the group changed its name to the Clay County Improvement Association and hired an agent, W. F. Posey, to "further the agricultural interest of the county." The first president of the group was a woman, Mina Johnson, who oversaw renewed enthusiasm in agricultural pursuits and garnered widespread respect for her efforts. The group's quarterly gatherings became legendary for their massive attendance records. At one picnic in September 1913, about 4,000 people, almost a third of the county's population, attended a picnic that featured roast ox, football games, and a lecture by the dean of agriculture from Iowa State Agricultural College. In 1914 smaller township chapters sprang up, and both men and women held offices in these local clubs. These leaders helped to foster robust social networks around agricultural promotion, with schedules filled with short courses, picnics, crop shows, soil fertility demonstrations, and other meetings. That same year, the Smith-Lever Act created the Extension Service, and it eventually streamlined these activities under one centralized authority. By the 1920s, the Clay County Improvement Association had become the local branch of the Farm Bureau, and members continued to encourage agricultural development.[25]

Religion

Ethnicity and gender profoundly influenced religious practices and church formation, and churches were essential to midwestern community life. In many cases, churches were the first institutions on the desolate prairies, providing regular gatherings for food, fellowship, and fraternization. The life of the church was more than just Sundays in the pews; it stretched to social activities like weekly Bible studies, sewing circles, and picnics. As Robert Swierenga puts it, "the church was more than a religious meeting place; it was a cultural nest, integrating families, social classes, and nationality groups. It gave members a cultural identity and status and socialized them into the community." Numerous scholars agree with Swierenga, noting the centrality of religion and the church to the Midwest. Jon

Lauck argues that religion "gave meaning to settlers' lives, acted as a social stabilizer and source of community interaction, and provided moral guidance." Religious activities underscored kinship networks and further cultivated the sense of belonging among people living in the Midwest. Tied tightly to church were gender, ethnicity, and culture. Across denominations, women organized societies to promote local, national, and international missions, raising impressive sums through suppers, bazaars, and other fund-raisers. They earned respect and financial power, which they eventually transformed into political influence. Creating churches also promoted ethnic cultures, since religious activities inspired "identity reinforcement." In church, foreign-born residents could speak their native languages, serve ethnic dishes at potlucks, and celebrate Old World holidays. The church and the religious activities that existed within its walls were critical to rural midwestern identity. As Swierenga states, "Rural life was truly church centered."[26]

The first settlers to the Midwest worked diligently to fill the absence of religious life because it bolstered sociability. For almost two decades, during the 1870s and 1880s, residents focused on establishing organized religion. As one early resident of Iowa noted, one reason for church formation stemmed from "a feeling of lonesomeness at being separated from any place" and a "desire to be as near each other as practicable" by establishing "social intercourse." Many of the first churches in the Midwest were not single-use buildings, particularly when construction materials were expensive and congregations were small and poor. People often gathered wherever they could find room, in each other's homes, at the local schoolhouse, or even under a large tree. Attendees often led the services themselves until circuit riders could visit their meager settings. Despite the informality, early midwesterners relished the opportunity to socialize and get to know "each other intimately." The church was more than a building or even a religious experience; it was the heart of these developing communities, fostering mutuality and creating cherished social bonds.[27]

During the 1870s, as settlement increased in the Midwest, a host of denominations emerged, often separated by ethnicity. The first groups to establish congregations were mainly evangelical Protestant Yankees, including Congregationalists, Methodist Episcopalians, and Baptists. As immigrants swelled in number, so too did Norwegian and Swedish

Lutheran and German Catholic denominations. Germans were split, however, and some formed separate Protestant congregations. Despite the variety, almost all were Christian, which made Christianity a powerful social organizer. As populations grew, midwesterners used funds raised by women's church groups to construct permanent church buildings with rooms for worship, school, and food preparation. Many times, ethnicity, gender, and religious affiliation went hand in hand. As Robert Ostergren notes, immigrants often acquired land and established communities around a specific church, creating "conscious units of culture" based on denominational or theological association. He argues that religious affiliation, not necessarily land quality or farming potential, determined settlement patterns. Catholics in Minnesota exemplified this trend when they chose religious affiliation over land value. In 1881 Bishop Ireland of St. Paul, Minnesota, organized a Catholic colony in northwest Lyon County. Five townships composed the massive settlement, and large numbers of Belgian and French-Canadian Catholics came to dominate that section of the county.[28]

Church membership was a significant part of a person's identity, and midwesterners spent a great deal of effort defining their faith communities. In the process, conflicts could occur over theology, customs, or mission, resulting in fragmentation among neighbors. In these places, ethnic diversity promoted segmentation among denominations. Despite the presence of Free Baptists in Clay County, Welsh settlers formed their own Baptist church called the Welch Pioneer Baptist Church. The Methodist Episcopal church also splintered among Yankees and German immigrants in Clay County when the Germans created their own Methodist Episcopal church in 1895. Three ethnically distinct Lutheran churches—German, Danish, and Swedish—held separate services in Spencer, the county seat, until combining into one congregation called Bethany Lutheran Church. Religious fragmentation also could occur among members of the same ethnic group, often because of theological differences. Norwegian Lutherans in Yankton County split over religious doctrine in 1882 and 1889, forming four small but distinct congregations.[29]

The pattern of ethnic variety in church formation repeated across the Midwest, providing residents with comfort and cultural affirmation in a confusing place. Churches also allowed newcomers to celebrate their heritages in public ways. Many times, immigrants chose to name their churches after places from the Old Country. When Norwegian Lutherans split in Yankton County, they bestowed the names Meldal and Tronhjem on their respective churches. In 1872, Norwegians in Lyon County named their church Hemnes after their hometown in Norway. Other Lutherans combined religious practices with cultural activities. In 1884, Icelandic Lutherans at St. Paul's Church in Lyon County not only built a structure for church services but also organized cultural activities through the popular "Progressive Society," a gender-inclusive group created to promote Icelandic heritage and community events. Other ethnic groups formed similar associations. In 1901, a large contingent of German Lutherans near Everly in Clay County founded the Unter Haltungs Verein, or "Entertainment Association." With almost 350 members, the society promoted German culture while providing opportunities to socialize. Members enjoyed "entertainments, lectures, and all public meetings" that fostered solidarity among German immigrants.[30]

Politics

Politics was robust during the late nineteenth and early twentieth centuries in the Midwest, and national politics shaped politics at the local level. Campaigns, elections, and political issues were a significant part of midwesterners' daily lives, and they embraced this political culture wholeheartedly. Races for public office were often contentious and were followed closely in local newspapers and the halls of gossip. People discussed politics with fervor on "every street corner in [the] village." Elections were "lively" and sported "numerous candidates in the field." Newspapers followed electoral races closely, and local candidates had frequent and direct interactions with voters. Election days were full of activity, mostly at polling places. As voters approached one polling location in South Dakota, the newspaper reported that "enthusiastic workers" bombarded them in an attempt to promote their particular candidate. Political conversations were open to all residents, and Yankee newspaper editors noticed that women as well as men attended and participated in political gatherings. Midwestern Yankees justified women's involvement in politics by arguing that the home deserved a mother who was well versed in the issues of the day. In particular, economic issues, like tariffs and free trade, were important to the housewife, one newspaper noted, because she was the treasurer of the home. Political participation, just like community engagement, was an expectation for Yankees, regardless of gender and whether or not they could actually cast a ballot.[31]

Ethnicity not only shaped religious practices among immigrants and native-born people, but also influenced politics and political ideology in the Midwest. Historians note that politics often fragmented among a variety of beliefs and practices. General patterns emerged, particularly in terms of voting preferences. Andrew Cayton and Peter Onuf note that middle-class Yankees living in small towns more often supported the Republican Party, while foreign-born farmers typically comprised the Democratic Party. Jon Lauck agrees, explaining that Yankee settlers "embraced . . . a centuries-old republican tradition." They demonstrated these values by promoting the welfare of the republic over individual interests. Public virtue and civic responsibility were keywords for Yankees. Lauck also noted their adherence to agrarian virtues, deriving a strong sense of freedom and individualism from the land. During this period, the Republican Party was the majority party in most places in the Midwest. In South Dakota, 80 percent of voters went Republican in 1880. Early accounts from Minnesota echoed this pattern, as one observer noted that political preference "was about four to one republican" with voters choosing "republican on general issues and important offices."[32]

While electoral victories gave the Republican Party power, the Democratic Party was also a strong political force. Partisanship was intense, and Republicans sometimes won nineteenth-century elections by razor-thin margins. Politicians were active in courting voters, both Americans and foreigners, especially as demographic change and mobility continued to reshape the political composition of local communities. The competition between Republicans and Democrats was fierce, and scholars argue that nowhere was the rivalry more intense than in the Midwest. County newspapers typically divided between Republican and Democrat and spewed vitriolic attacks back and forth without hesitation. As Kathleen Neils Conzen notes, local newspapers were central "to the political campaigns that were often little more than local development projects in different guise." The parties clamored for voters, particularly native-born arrivals and foreigners who gained enfranchisement after completing some part of the residency requirement for citizenship. Cayton and Onuf argue that the Democratic Party remained a potent political spoiler because it was attractive to foreigners and others who felt marginalized by the Republican Party. Democrats often attacked government interference and overreach, serving as an "outsider" party that provided a legitimate platform for dissent and fomented third-party assaults on the political system. By 1890 many people, including farmers, Catholics, foreigners, and other outsiders, had left the major parties for Populism. In such a tight political climate, their departure was a blow to Republicans and Democrats, and they spent much of the decade trying to win them back.[33]

The choppy political waters of the late nineteenth century reveal how much the individuality that midwesterners coveted could upset expectations about political behavior. Political sentiment could swing wildly, and among ethnic groups it became especially difficult to guess a particular party preference. Immigrants certainly did not always vote as an ethnic bloc. They also were some of the first to reject the two-party system and join the Populists. Despite these vacillations, there were trends. Scottish, English, and Welsh immigrants usually voted Republican with Yankees. Scandinavians also typically chose the party of Lincoln, but they also seemed to change positions readily. Irish and German immigrants often supported the Democratic Party because of their Catholicism and anti-temperance position, but exceptions also appeared rather frequently. German Protestants, including Lutheran, Reformed, and other groups, voted Republican, but some strict denominations could also support other political elements. Nancy Vargas found that in southwest Minnesota, Germans, as well as Norwegian and Icelandic immigrants, generally voted Republican while Swedish, Polish, and Belgian immigrants chose Democratic candidates. In some cases, political affiliation was inconsequential when voters banded together to elect a candidate based on their ethnicity. In Lyon County, a large contingent of Scandinavian farmers demanded that the position of county treasurer go to a Scandinavian man regardless of partisanship.[34]

Dissatisfaction with the established political parties fostered new political affiliations and groups, and some midwesterners sought third-party alternatives when they felt abandoned by both Democrats and Republicans. During the late nineteenth century, the economy grew substantially with major industrial development, but farmers felt ignored when railroads, grain elevators, flour mills, and other corporate enterprises held monopolies over rates and prices. In response, farmers turned to groups like the Populists and the Farmers' Alliance for redress. In South Dakota, the Farmers' Alliance formed the Independent Party in 1890 after Republicans thwarted a plan to elect Alliance men to the state senate. Yankton County had a strong Farmers' Alliance, particularly among foreign-born farmers. At one picnic, people strung up flags from their native countries around the American flag to show the duality of their national identities. The Farmers' Alliance stormed state politics that fall, taking a good share of Republican votes even though the Republican state ticket still triumphed. By 1892 the Independents had merged with the Populist Party, which continued to agitate for economic justice into the election of 1896. County-level branches of the Farmers' Alliance also popped up across the Midwest, and they allowed people to air their grievances against corruption and demand reform. By 1890, the Farmers' Alliance had infiltrated county politics in Minnesota. In Lyon County, many farmers left the Republican Party to support the Alliance ticket, and voters chose Alliance candidates for governor, congressional representative, superintendent of schools, and county commissioner. In some precincts the Democrats pulled their entire slate of candidates, deferring to the Farmers' Alliance instead. By 1892 the Farmers' Alliance had fused with the Populists, or People's Party, after the previous legislative session had failed to loosen the grip of the Republicans. The Alliance managed to hold seats for another two years, but by 1894 the momentum of the People's Party had declined. That year Lyon County voted Republican, ending what had seemed a promising moment of unity among farmers and other outsiders.[35]

As Populism faded, Progressivism challenged the two-party system by championing sweeping reform. Progressives sought government intervention to solve complex problems, which brought individuals closer to the state. Unlike Populists, who focused on a more narrow set of issues, Progressives had many concerns. There was no single "Progressive" but many, and what unified them was their desire to rid society of political and economic corruption by eliminating or regulating it. While they disagreed on what to reform, Progressives were certain that active participation in all levels of government was crucial. Progressivism amplified the link between citizenship and community in the Midwest, and most Yankees enthusiastically welcomed the reform movement. It matched the midwestern impulse for civic engagement and built on the region's gender-inclusive political culture. The Progressive spirit electrified both political parties, but Republicans continued to win elections as they adopted Progressive values. Some regional reforms overlapped with national concerns, and midwestern Progressives joined a nationwide effort to regulate corporations, pass health and sanitation initiatives, and adopt measures to protect children. Other reforms were distinct to the region. To assist farmers, midwestern Progressives established state-run businesses that challenged corporate monopolies. They also promoted infrastructure development, including more state highways. As Annette Atkins explains, Progressivism was notable because it energized ordinary midwesterners "to do, make, expand, grow, improve, develop, and beautify." It encouraged a faith in the state to improve society, and it encouraged people previously denied access to government to participate in civic affairs.[36]

While partisanship and reform created a dynamic political landscape in the Midwest during the late nineteenth and early twentieth centuries, certain issues held sustained interest over time. Of all the causes that galvanized people, prohibition had both the longest history and the most direct influence in local communities. The presence of temperance societies, like the Women's Christian Temperance Union (WCTU) and the Anti-Saloon League, did not determine the level of engagement with temperance. In other words, people in the Midwest debated prohibition frequently, usually during political elections but also generally when assessing their community values. Temperance sentiment often mirrored religious and political affiliations, and it meant far more than just opposition to consuming alcohol. According to Republicans, excessive drinking threatened civic virtue, self-discipline, and reputation, and they linked instability to inebriation. Democrats saw prohibition as an overextension of government, and many ethnic groups agreed, arguing that drinking was a fundamental cultural expression. The fervor over prohibition was so intense that in some cases temperance sentiment, not political affiliation, was the determining factor in an election. In Clay County, the 1881 mayoral election in Spencer, the county seat, came down to two candidates, the "anti-saloon" candidate and the "candidate . . . in favor of saloons." While the pro-saloon candidate won by a landslide, he lost two years later. This back-and-forth revealed that prohibition was a contentious issue in local politics.[37]

In many parts of the Midwest, local option laws dictated alcohol restrictions, and these laws created a scattershot pattern of regulations. Sometimes, opposite policies existed in the same county. Not until 1916 did prohibition laws largely ban alcohol in the region, so for most of this period, prohibition was a local decision. In Yankton County conflict over prohibition was intense, especially because Yankton had emerged as a distribution center for alcoholic beverages. By 1870, the town contained twenty-four licensed saloons and two breweries. These breweries served much of the Dakota Territory, providing bourbon, brandy, gin, and wine. In November 1889, statehood and a strong Republican majority gave temperance advocates a victory when voters endorsed statewide prohibition. Yankton County residents opposed the measure by almost a two-to-one margin and lamented the loss of tax revenue from saloons. Prohibition lasted until 1897 in South Dakota, when voters, undoubtedly influenced by Populism and the Farmers' Alliance, repealed the measure. Yankton had lost powerful distribution markets during prohibition, but a number of saloons reopened locally.[38]

By the early twentieth century, local option laws had created a patchwork of regulations in Yankton County, causing problems when some towns went "dry" while others stayed "wet." For example, in 1905 Yankee-strong Gayville voted for prohibition, while Germans and Norwegians in Volin, Mission Hill, and Lesterville elected to keep their saloons. In 1914, a legal battle over alcohol licenses forced saloons to close temporarily in Yankton, so residents flocked to Utica, the closest wet town. While Utica's economy boomed, law enforcement officials struggled to maintain order there. The "drunkenness and disorder got so bad" that Utica's police officers begged Yankton to "keep its undesirables at home." Five months later, the courts ruled for Yankton's saloons, and Utica's time in the spotlight ended. In 1916, the state legislature passed a "bone-dry" law that eliminated local options and reestablished statewide prohibition that lasted through the 1920s.[39]

Prohibition was difficult to secure in Lyon County because large foreign-born populations, including Catholic Germans, Belgians, and French-Canadians, supported alcohol consumption. For only two years, from 1896 to 1898, did voters support prohibition in local elections, forcing a few towns in the county to go dry, including Cottonwood, Balaton, and Ghent. The loss of revenue from alcohol taxes and liquor licenses, however, convinced voters to repeal the restrictions, and so Lyon County remained wet until 1920. Among foreign-born residents there, alcohol consumption was a distinct part of their ethnic cultures, making it difficult for temperance sentiment to gain traction in the county. Small numbers of Yankee women did participate in the WCTU, but their influence was limited. Even the best-known temperance supporters failed to keep their oaths. Charles Whitney, editor of the *Marshall News Messenger,* was an ardent supporter of temperance until his rival, the editor of the *Lyon County Reporter,* revealed that Whitney had been arrested for "disorderly conduct from excessive use of liquor." Prohibition remained a key issue that linked reputation, citizenship, and civic involvement until the ratification of the Eighteenth Amendment in 1919, which ended the manufacture, sale, or transportation of intoxicating liquors in the United States the following year.[40]

Community, Citizenship, and Woman Suffrage

Despite his tendency to exaggerate, Andrew Meek successfully outlined the defining features of community in the Midwest. He praised the land for producing bountiful harvests. He noted how rapid population growth, along with railroads, had transformed the region. He commented on how ethnic diversity shaped relationships among neighbors. He celebrated how much churches had proliferated. He commended his neighbors for their sociability. He left out the "loneliness and hardships," like economic depression, ethnic tension, religious fragmentation, and political anxiety, not because he was unobservant but because they were so evident. Meek wrote in the mid-1890s, a time of dramatic change in the Midwest. Industrial capitalism, coupled with an economic depression, shook up the two-party system, and political wrangling was intense. These problems challenged midwesterners to understand this dynamic change both as individuals and as members of communities. Writing the article was a means of inclusion, and Meek skewed his assessment to show that he belonged.

During the late nineteenth and early twentieth centuries, midwestern communities flourished as people, marked by identities rooted in ethnicity, religion, and gender, engaged in local politics and established networks of sociability. Nineteenth-century regional promoters recruited immigrants enthusiastically, and midwesterners embraced a proliferation of cultural traits. Residents sought unity out of the abundance of diversity. As both place and experience, local communities defined life in the region. In small towns and rural enclaves, individuals negotiated the tensions that complicated the ways people approached civic life. Civic engagement, fostered by a republican notion of civic participation, spurred Yankees to public service, but some immigrants, especially Germans, defined community differently. Despite its contested definition, community, and its connection to citizenship, was paramount to understanding woman suffrage in the Midwest. Residents approached the cause of woman suffrage as members of local communities, which fostered political attitudes based on religious traditions, ethnic expressions, and gendered social lives. They saw female enfranchisement not as a single issue but as one informed by a host of other concerns. Partisanship, religious sentiment, and prohibition were only a few of the many factors that midwesterners considered when weighing their stance on the contentious issue of suffrage for women.

Midwestern women also approached woman suffrage from identities situated in community, which created a range of responses, both anticipated and unexpected. Yankees more often supported the cause while foreign-born women typically did not, but in an era of profound political instability, exceptions could occur. When measures for female enfranchisement emerged in the region, the intricacies of midwestern communities made campaigns difficult. While suffragists struggled—frequently and often painfully—they eventually found a winning strategy at the intersection of community engagement and citizenship. Decades of public service eventually gave women renowned records of civic responsibility. They cultivated unblemished reputations as loyal citizens, which they translated into demands for the ballot.

Chapter 2

HUMBLE BEGINNINGS: HOW MIDWESTERN WOMEN CLAIMED CIVIC ACTIVISM

IN NOVEMBER 1894, the same month it published Andrew Meek's article, the *Lyon County Reporter* featured an upcoming supper in its "Around Home" section. Many small-town newspapers included a section of local news in each edition, and neighbors read this section regularly, catching up on the latest chatter around town. The level of gossip contained in the "Around Home" section was impressive. Usually, the editors listed the current visitors to Lyon County by name, noting for how long and with whom they stayed. In this edition, the local page included news of the sale of a farm, a recent magic show, and a spate of Halloween "mischief." Nestled among these tidbits was an invitation from the Ladies' Aid Society of the Congregational Church to attend an oyster supper on Election Day. The event was open to all regardless of political affiliation, and the organizers enticed readers by claiming that the "election stew" promised to "cheer the successful and soothe the downcast while waiting for returns." Community-wide invitations to church dinners, bazaars, and picnics were common among midwesterners, and attendance at these events was typically robust. In this case, the Ladies' Aid Society combined the reputation of a respected church group with involvement in politics. While no records exist as to the attendance and conversation at the oyster supper, it was clear that the Ladies' Aid Society was blurring the alleged line between propriety and political activism. Women living in the Midwest did not separate their private and public lives; they behaved as full contributing members—as citizens—of their communities.[1]

During the late nineteenth and early twentieth centuries, midwestern women pursued full citizenship through their community-building efforts. They did so because since the founding of the United States, gender distinctions had excluded women from active citizenship. For most of the nineteenth century, citizenship had guaranteed membership in a community, but questions remained about what constituted community, how a woman achieved citizenship, and who defined its requirements. The Constitution did not say whether women were merely residents or actually citizens, and not until 1855 did Congress pass a law that granted women derivative citizenship. Contradictions remained, however, especially after the Fourteenth Amendment, passed in 1868, codified birthright citizenship but failed to elaborate on the rights and responsibilities associated with it. Native-born women faced a perplexing legal and political position. They were disenfranchised citizens, incapable of serving on juries, running for office, and in many states, of owning property or signing contracts. Their legal status was perilous.[2]

Nineteenth-century ideas about gender help to explain the inconsistencies of citizenship. Prescriptive literature aimed at middle-class women insisted that domesticity, rooted in the home and family, was paramount. It envisioned a private household that bound women and children to a patriarch. In the domestic sphere, women's responsibilities were child care, cooking, and cleaning. They were dependents and political outsiders who were neither autonomous nor self-reliant. In contrast, men engaged in politics and business in the public sphere as representatives of their families. Religious ideas supported these gendered domains, and most Americans embraced the notion that domesticity preserved morality in the face of increased corruption and competition in public life. The system of coverture, adapted from English common law, established legal protections that further shielded women from public entanglements. Most midwesterners even agreed that republican ideology, which encouraged civic participation, only applied to men. Engaging in public service was a masculine act for unbound individuals. Since the domestic sphere robbed women of any autonomy, they were unable to contribute to civic life.[3]

While many midwesterners liked the idea of separate gendered spheres, this did not represent their experiences. Whatever line existed between private and public was impossible to distinguish, and gender distinctions disintegrated as men and women moved seamlessly between the two supposed worlds. Nineteenth-century women produced for market, engaging in capitalist economic development. They participated in politics, signing petitions, speaking at political rallies, and even casting ballots, despite their weak legal status. They challenged coverture through court cases because coverture had left them vulnerable rather than protected. Beginning in the mid-nineteenth century, women's rights activists demanded an array of rights associated with citizenship, crafting sophisticated arguments that tapped into enduring American values. They contended that the Constitution granted liberal principles of freedom and independence to all citizens, including native-born women, and they blasted gender inequalities that undermined the Revolutionary promises of liberty and individualism. They simultaneously asserted that republicanism's mandate for civic engagement overrode any gendered disqualifications.[4]

Midwestern women carefully navigated nineteenth-century gender norms and citizenship's contradictions as they participated in community building. Many understood that the powerful rhetoric of separate spheres had shaped their lives, and most did not challenge the alleged gender binary. They neither called themselves feminists nor engaged in overt protests against gender inequalities. On the surface, they accepted gendered language that deemed them wives, mothers, sisters, and daughters in relation to the men who seemed to rule midwestern politics and culture. In practice, however, midwestern women rejected male dominance. While they did not express a desire to thwart patriarchy, they also refused to acknowledge it as a limitation on their burgeoning political identities. They embraced the accepted channels of female authority and then transcended them. In part, their actions reflected the realities of settlement. Lacking local governments, midwestern women, especially Yankees, stepped into the roles of city planners, parks directors, and public works officials. The opportunity politicized Yankee women, and in embracing civic responsibility they challenged gendered limitations on their public activism. In this way, they located their political identities at the confluence of politics and sociability in the Midwest. By encouraging participation from Yankee women, midwesterners had certified that they belonged as full-fledged citizens.

Settling the Midwest offered women an opportune moment to engage in politics, build social networks, and claim civic responsibility. They channeled the public service of the nineteenth century into Progressive reforms of the twentieth century, including woman suffrage, by establishing civic identities. Planning a bazaar or coordinating a Fourth of July picnic were in themselves not political actions, but they gave women public recognition as loyal citizens intent on making their communities better. By turning reputation into responsibility, women contested masculine notions of republicanism. Gender distinctions meant little when community engagement seemed compulsory, and with the obligation to participate came rights, including the right to vote. This line of thinking explains how a ladies' aid society could host a bazaar and invite a national suffrage leader to speak. It illuminates how a branch of the WCTU could strenuously advocate for woman suffrage in the local newspaper. It reveals how members of a federated women's club could lead a petition drive for woman suffrage without blinking an eye. When woman suffrage arrived, it did not turn midwestern women into political activists. They already were.

The manner in which women contributed was most often through collective associations, and women preferred to work cooperatively to achieve a goal or mission related to community enhancement. As historians Anne Firor Scott and Sara M. Evans argue, these nineteenth-century groups anchored women's political participation that emerged during the Progressive Era. Through these volunteer activities, midwestern women became "citizens in training," carving out identities as active American citizens. They became politically savvy, mastering the rules of order, engaging in the electoral process, and working on political campaigns. In the process, they garnered public authority in their respective locales. Despite women's shared commitment to community uplift, ethnicity and religion could splinter their efforts, and the primary division of labor emerged between Yankees and foreign-born immigrants. Religious differences produced further fragmentation, and a constellation of groups, many times with similar aims, provided the mechanism of community building for most women. Most midwesterners did not see this organizational redundancy as a problem; they accepted it as a product of the fissures that distinguished local communities. Despite their differences, women embraced their roles as social organizers. As Michael Goldberg puts it, they were the "glue that held atomized and socially fractured farm communities together."[5]

Because of their ethnic and religious differences, midwestern women took a variety of approaches to building community and claiming civic identities. Virtually all women enjoyed visiting their neighbors and friends, and cultivating sociability through informal neighborhood associations created the first explicit connection between the home and politics. Forging neighborliness was not simple, however, and ethnic and religious differences could dampen or quell friendships. In addition to visiting, nearly all women also joined a ladies' aid society associated with the church to which their families belonged. These societies held tremendous financial, social, and in some cases, political power, and they deserve attention for how they trained midwestern women to engage with political issues while adhering to domestic virtues. Midwestern suffragists eventually borrowed some of their most effective arguments for women's activism from ladies' aid societies, so examining their work is vital. Like they did with visiting, ethnic and religious distinctions influenced ladies' aid societies by segregating Congregational and Methodist, Lutheran and Catholic, and Baptist and Friends groups. Finally, ethnic and religious backgrounds often excluded immigrant women from the most prominent women's groups in midwestern communities, including the WCTU and federated women's clubs. Limiting membership to Yankees created a two-tier system of activism that privileged native-born white women over foreign-born others.

Visiting

Collective relationships emerged initially from informal visits among neighbors, and practically all women engaged in these social interactions. Networks of sociability lessened isolation on the midwestern prairies, and women found comfort and support within patterns of visiting. Social relationships flourished among residents who settled together in rural enclaves and small towns, and neighborliness extended mutuality from the family to the community. Proximity and population density also influenced the frequency and duration of visits among neighbors, and the divide between town and country dictated how often rural people interacted. As historian Mary Neth points out, neighborhood connections created a "system of reciprocity that went beyond the ties of kinship." Neighboring involved both economic and social exchanges, as friends embraced an "attitude of giving and helpfulness" rather than overt obligation. As Neth argues, families enjoyed a host of social events within their neighborhoods, but women typically organized the informal neighborhood relationships that propelled community development. Neighborhoods comprised communities, but rural neighborhoods also enjoyed fluid boundaries that sometimes superseded the geographic border of a community. Many times visiting involved people with shared ethnic backgrounds, particularly in closed enclaves. Other times, proximity and necessity overcame potential ethnic conflicts, and friendships flourished among different ethnic groups. Through informal gatherings like debating societies, school events, box socials, holiday celebrations, and sewing circles, men and women came together to visit and share life's moments. Although it was "just a social thing," as an Iowan from Pocahontas County said, it was a "chance to get together." As one South Dakota settler put it, neighbors knew each other's "sorrows, joys, and troubles—helping each other in bad times as well as good, in every possible way." That local newspapers across the region almost always featured a section on local gossip indicates the strength of informal visiting and sociability in the Midwest.[6]

Visiting occurred informally whenever neighbors met, sometimes to exchange labor or goods and almost always to enjoy each other's company. The residents of Clay County not only developed intimate neighborhood connections as farm families shared recipes, tips about raising livestock, or news from town; they also cultivated a strong network of groups that promoted social relationships. These groups became the formal manifestations of the neighborhood networks that had blossomed since settlement in the second half of the nineteenth century. Between 1900 and 1920 rural people from Clay County, mostly women, participated in upward of thirty clubs and social organizations. Many of these clubs arranged monthly meetings or gatherings with some sort of informal program and plenty of opportunities for conversation, food, and companionship. As the name suggests, members of the Kill-Kare Club of Spencer, the county seat, enjoyed hours of freedom together away from the obligations of their homes. Most of the time, they joined in fellowship and gossip over needlework. Another women's club, the Loganette Club of Logan Township, organized regular picnics for the neighborhood, where attendees could enjoy baseball games and homemade ice cream. Formal lessons also promoted home education, and talks like "How Safe Is Your Water Supply?" often generated strong interest among members. The residents of Logan Township highly valued the Loganette Club. As one person put it, the club "fostered long time friendships and a closeness of the neighbors." Other rural clubs in Peterson Township and Gillett

Grove Township promoted mutuality and sociability when members organized pie socials, plays, and carnivals. With these kinds of events, women played an active role in "creating the social bonds of intimacy" that connected residents. They also raised their status as civic-minded and loyal members of their communities.[7]

Women, Church, and Ladies' Aid Societies

Patterns of sociability and traditional perceptions of gender also influenced the creation of ladies' aid societies in these midwestern communities. Both native and foreign-born women participated in the life of their churches, and they formed ladies' aid societies and other church groups to support the work and mission of their respective religious institutions. Ladies' aid societies were ubiquitous across the Midwest. They arose as churches formed in the late nineteenth century and, as one historian put it, played "essential roles in church organization." Curiously, women who joined ladies' aid societies often claimed to do so not out of a desire to promote female activism or gain public recognition to further a political agenda. The impetus for their membership stemmed from religious devotion, although the opportunity to socialize was also attractive. Ladies' aid societies provide the best example of rural women outwardly defending a traditional separation of gender roles while subverting the alleged patriarchal authority in their community.

Church parishioners knew that the source of the congregation's power—particularly its financial authority—was the ladies' aid society. Women gained this authority in humble ways, beginning with the work prescribed to the domestic sphere. Sewing and baking were transformed from simple tasks into financial influence, and women used the profits from these humble activities to build the church, both physically and spiritually. With public recognition came political power, and in this way, women undermined the constrictions that patriarchy attempted to place on them. They achieved not because they tore down patriarchy in a radical way; they found success because they articulated political identities in line with their domestic ones. Church leadership provided vital experiences in coalition building, community development, and civic responsibility. Women's ability to engage in politics, particularly in the reform movements of the Progressive Era, came directly from their work in these understudied groups. When the woman suffrage movement developed in the Midwest, it was based upon the robust political energy that had developed among rural women themselves.[8]

The extent to which ladies' aid societies embraced political attitudes depended on local leadership, denominational affiliation, and theology. In Protestant churches, most often Congregational and Methodist, the ladies' aid society easily adopted political identities out of their financial power and religious devotion. Among these denominations, theology and practice rejected gender inequality and embraced social justice. The Social Gospel, which sought to elevate society through reform efforts, influenced congregations to engage in community affairs. In other denominations, like Lutheran and Catholic ones, women were less likely to engage in politics, preferring to focus on domestic work. Theological conservatism provoked a stricter adherence to gender norms and cautioned women against engaging in more secular concerns. The denominational divide generally matched ethnic backgrounds, and Yankees typically filled the pews of Protestant churches while foreigners joined the others. Although theology and ethnicity influenced the degree to which women pursued political agendas, all midwestern women found companionship and gained visibility from their contributions to church life. Membership in ladies' aid societies also helped women transcend the borders of class, ethnicity, and culture, even though most rural women chose to join groups with others with shared backgrounds. Individually, then, women enjoyed these associations because they reinforced the boundaries of identity. Collectively, however, rural women found common ground with other ladies' aid societies out of the shared experience of church work. Mutuality dictated that people support the bazaars, socials, and dinners of neighborhood ladies' aid societies, and reciprocity encouraged them to return the favor. These activities promoted sociability across ethnic, religious, and political lines. Ladies' aid societies became the most important presence in the lives of rural women across the Midwest, in spite of their individual missions.[9]

The work undertaken by ladies' aid societies was often quite ordinary, and it began as soon as enough parishioners demanded a permanent church structure. New residents to the Midwest typically arrived with little cash in hand, so fund-raisers were critical to constructing churches. Women almost always led the charge to raise money, and they often did so through ladies' aid societies. Fund-raising took place across the denominational spectrum, and throughout the Midwest, women excelled at creating both spiritual and physical spaces. For example, in Lyon County, the Ladies' Golden Rule Society of the Lynd United Methodist Church, which formed in 1893, swiftly organized a series of social activities, and area residents applauded the women for enhancing sociability among neighbors. Soon members began fund-raising efforts, making quilts, sewing carpets, and mending grain sacks for local customers. The members of the Golden Rule Society conducted their business in each other's homes because the church lacked a permanent structure. Eventually, the small congregation planned to build a church, and male leaders took out a series of loans to pay for construction. Soon, however, the men struggled to make timely payments, and they turned to the Golden Rule Society for assistance. At first the women just paid the interest on the loans, but soon the men pleaded with the women to take charge of the monthly bills. Ultimately, the Golden Rule Society paid off all the loans entirely through simple fund-raisers. Their financial contributions were essential, then, even if the male leaders never admitted it outright. In this case, the women did not request public recognition for their efforts. Instead, they quietly transformed financial authority into support for temperance. Despite strong opposition to prohibition in Lyon County, particularly among the ethnic majorities clustered in rural areas, the members of the Golden Rule Society endorsed temperance and requested that each member pledge lifelong abstinence from alcohol. As one member of the Golden Rule Society wrote, the reason why Lynd township was a dry exception in an otherwise wet county was because of the influence of the Golden Rule Society, which helped "to aid others to a temperate life."[10]

Ladies' aid societies among Congregationalists and Methodists in South Dakota shared remarkable similarities with their counterparts in Minnesota, focusing much of their attention on fund-raising efforts. In 1902, the Ladies' Union of the Congregational Church in Yankton County spearheaded a massive fund drive to construct a new church. The congregation had outgrown the original wooden structure, built in 1869, and now it needed a "suitable church building at a cost not to exceed $25,000." Raising that much money was a substantial undertaking, however, especially with only $110 in the church's coffers. Undaunted, the Ladies' Union set to work and, over the course of two years, secured almost $20,000, which was 80 percent of the intended budget. As one scholar has argued, the financial success of the Ladies' Union alone convinced the rest of the congregation to construct a permanent wooden building.[11]

Like Congregationalists, the Methodists in Yankton County organized social events, such as bazaars, festivals, and dinners, to raise money for their church. As soon as the congregation organized in 1872, the Ladies' Aid Society hosted both a spring and fall bazaar. Preparations were intense. The women secured one of the largest shops in downtown Yankton as the site for the bazaar. Then they canvassed the county for two months, requesting donations from local residents. They also created hand-embroidered quilts to adorn the church's entryway. Patrons to the bazaar could purchase a variety of items, such as artwork, aprons, comforters, dolls, books, canes, and clocks. Each evening the ladies served a hearty supper, with "Jack Horner's pie" as a signature item. As the *Press and Dakotan* noted, the bazaar attracted a "great deal of deserved attention" among community members. Gaining public recognition for routine church work propelled these women into the spotlight, and their civic identities blossomed as a result.[12]

Civic identities forged through church work blurred whatever boundary existed between religion and politics for women at both the Congregational and Methodist churches. In 1890, a proposed woman suffrage amendment to South Dakota's constitution prompted national suffrage leaders, such as Susan B. Anthony, Anna Howard Shaw, and Carrie Chapman Catt, to descend upon the state. In April 1890 Anna Howard Shaw's tour of southeastern South Dakota included stops in Yankton County. On April 11 Shaw gave two lectures in Yankton. Local organizers had prearranged these visits, and they had selected venues that promised sympathetic audiences and lots of space. In the afternoon, Shaw wowed an audience at the Congregational Church in their original wooden church. In the evening she spoke in downtown Yankton, at the bazaar organized by the Ladies' Aid Society of the Methodist Church. As the ladies cut slices of "Jack Horner's pie," they also heard from the future president of the National American Woman Suffrage Association. The *Press and Dakotan* called Shaw "one of the most eloquent and successful speakers on the question of equal suffrage" and proclaimed that all "who can attend should hear her." That Congregational and Methodist women invited Shaw into their religious spaces was no accident. These women had built these structures with their own financial power. They had gained respect among their congregations, and they exploited that authority to embrace woman suffrage. As rural women in the Midwest explained, the right to vote did not offer a radical departure from their respected civic identities. It merely promised to enhance the highly esteemed work that the community already valued.[13]

Like their colleagues in Minnesota and South Dakota, ladies' aid societies in Iowa also spent their early efforts on building the physical infrastructure for midwestern religious life. During the 1870s and 1880s, Methodists and Congregationalists in Clay County worked diligently to raise the funds necessary to construct permanent church structures. In 1875, the fifteen charter members of the First Congregational Church's Ladies' Aid Society organized a bazaar specifically to support a new church building. No records indicate how much money the group collected, but the total was undoubtedly impressive. That same year, the First Congregational Church erected its church, and the Ladies' Aid Society decided to make the bazaar an annual tradition. Soon, the fall bazaar became the flagship fund-raising event for the church, and it was, as one report noted, "always a huge success both financially and artistically." Planning a bazaar was a tremendous undertaking that involved a high level of coordination among participants, but the central concept originated from simple tasks, like sewing and cooking, that were at the core of rural women's domestic roles. At the bazaar, women sold a variety of items, mostly handmade arts and crafts like needlework, quilts, and articles of clothing. They also provided meals, from light lunches to intricate suppers. Patrons could also purchase baked goods, like breads, cakes, and pies, and preserved items, such as jams or cured meats. The annual schedule allowed some women to develop reputations for mouth-watering pies or particularly exquisite quilts, and their contributions often received top dollar.[14]

The members of the First Congregational Church's Ladies' Aid Society soon became civic leaders in their church community, and the group continued its stellar record of fund-raising into the early twentieth century. Between 1892 and 1909, the women gave about half of their income directly to fund projects to enhance the church's physical space, which added up to a whopping $4,000. Their notoriety earned them full-page mention in the first Clay County history book, published in 1909. Not only did the editors provide a brief history of the church, but they also listed in detail the money raised and distributed by the Ladies' Aid Society each year. Financial power clearly mattered to the residents of Clay County, and these women earned public recognition for doing work well within the domestic sphere. Eventually, these Congregationalists channeled their reputations as pious, churchgoing women into support for women's rights like suffrage. Political identities did not materialize overnight but formed slowly, over decades of activism on behalf of one's church. When an amendment to enfranchise Iowa's women went before voters in 1916, the members of the Ladies' Aid Society of the First Congregational Church led the fight for woman suffrage in the county. The same women whose needlework and pies drew crowds to the annual bazaar also attracted multitudes to speeches, open-air meetings, and other public gatherings in support of woman suffrage. The Congregational Church hosted the first lecturers to Clay County, including Ella Stewart, a past president of the Illinois Equal Franchise Society. The local newspaper reported that some residents expected to see a "freak dressed in oddly-fashioned tweeds, a woman with hair askew." Instead, as the *Spencer News-Herald* reported, her address was "sane and clear and her points well taken." In many ways, planning a woman suffrage lecture relied on the same female networks and organizational skills as a church bazaar. Women anchored their work for woman suffrage on their roles in their churches. Civic identities forged in church shifted easily to political activism.[15]

Other ladies' aid societies in Clay County acquired financial authority and public recognition through fund-raisers, and their bazaars, soup kitchens, and social gatherings became beloved traditions that crossed denominational boundaries. Editors of local newspapers followed these activities closely, making sure to announce the next public supper, sale, or event. Not a week went by without some bit of news from one of the ladies' aid societies in the area. For example, in Clay County the *Spencer Herald* praised the Glad Tidings Circle, the name for the ladies' aid society of the Langdon Methodist Church, for their fund-raising efforts. When church leaders decided to add a basement to the church building, the women hosted a bazaar, raking in over $150 in profits. When the church needed more money, the Glad Tidings Circle held a "shower for the basement" to pay for further work. Finally, in 1915 the Circle purchased the church's furnace—which cost over $100—by hosting yet another bazaar. As construction ended, locals did not hold back their praise for the members of the Glad Tidings Circle, noting that "the neighborhood is indebted to the ladies for their good work and great credit is due to" them. Just as the Ladies' Aid Society at the First Congregational Church transformed their church work into political activism for woman suffrage, so too did the members of the Glad Tidings Circle. Just a year after financing the church remodeling with a series of bazaars, the women held yet another luncheon. This time, however, the cause was not a new furnace. Instead, the women held the luncheon on June 5, 1916, the date when voters determined the fate of the woman suffrage amendment in the state. As the newspaper reported, the Circle hoped for large crowds, not only to "help the ladies in this enterprise" but also to give "their vote for equal suffrage." Once again, civic identity shaped by leadership in the church provided a foundation for political activism for the right to vote.[16]

While Congregationalists and Methodists in Minnesota, South Dakota, and Iowa exhibited a great degree of political activism in their communities, other denominations, such as Lutherans, Catholics, and Baptists, did so less often. The ladies' aid society was still the primary fund-raising group, and in church after church they transformed simple tasks into financial power. Although they accomplished the same work, women in these denominations were less likely to transform their religious identities into political ones. Strong theological attitudes and ethnic customs could dictate that women resist political engagement and avoid agitating for reforms like woman suffrage. Moreover, these denominations frequently constructed churches in rural neighborhoods outside of small towns. Most of the parishioners were farmers, which meant that the practical demands of agricultural production, along with distance and rough travel conditions, made sustained contact with woman suffrage campaigns difficult. For many women living outside town, their first priority was not the right to vote. Instead, they spent more time fostering neighborhood sociability within their tight-knit ethnic enclaves.

Many Lutherans were immigrants, and most were Norwegian, although there were some German Lutherans in Clay and Yankton Counties and Icelandic Lutherans in Lyon County. In Yankton County, four Lutheran ladies' aid societies, each comprised of a different group of Norwegians, flourished on the open prairies. At Vangen Lutheran

Church, the women of the Ringsaker's Kvindeforening, or Ladies' Aid Society, transformed simple domestic chores into financial authority. For example, in 1887 the group purchased the first pump organ for the sanctuary, an expensive addition that garnered acclaim from the congregation. The members of West Prairie, the ladies' aid society formed in 1873 by women of the Tronhjem Norwegian Evangelical Lutheran Church, gathered monthly to sew clothing for auctions, the proceeds of which they donated to missions. By 1886 a sister organization, called North Prairie, had been organized among newcomers who lived too far away from West Prairie. Together, these ladies' aid societies promoted sociability and shaped neighborhood interactions. A slew of socials, suppers, and sales raised money for the church and preserved Norwegian culture. The highlight of the year was the annual Fourth of July celebration, complete with a massive lunch and gallons of homemade ice cream churned by hand. While some Norwegians marked Independence Day with festivities, others chose Thanksgiving Day as their blowout event. The ladies' aid society of the Meldal Norwegian Lutheran Church, which was located in a tiny village called Norway, became well known for its Thanksgiving Day bazaar, an annual tradition that regularly served a crowd of 500—double the village's population. At the intersection of sociability and religion, these Norwegian Lutherans gained reputations for their dedication to religious and community uplift.[17]

Records left by Lutherans attest to the hardships that dogged midwestern settlement and the tenacity of ladies' aid societies' efforts to surmount them. Distances were vast and most women had limited options for transportation. Many women walked for miles, with children in tow, to conduct their business. At West Prairie, members took turns hosting one another, usually in sod homes precariously carved out of the earth. Some women rode horseback while carefully protecting their precious needlework, including quilts, pillowcases, and clothing, from the harsh weather. The unforgiving conditions also made feeding large groups a challenge. In Lyon County, the work of Icelandic Lutherans living near Minneota illustrates the extensive planning and backbreaking labor required to host any gatherings. At St. Paul's Lutheran Church the Ladies' Aid Society, which was organized in 1890, demanded at least three days' notice before any meal because the church had no running water and only a small wood-burning stove in the basement. Members recalled the toll of repeated trips down a rickety staircase while carrying heavy jugs of water and boxes of dishes, food, linens, wood, and utensils. Despite the crude kitchen, the women succeeded in raising remarkable sums of money. The society almost entirely furnished the church, purchasing the pews, pulpit, and two stoves. In 1911 the pastor announced that the church was broke, so the Ladies' Aid Society singlehandedly paid the entire budget for the year.[18]

Ladies' aid societies also supported community institutions like schools and hospitals, and among ethnic groups, parochial schools helped to reinforce cultural identities. Midwesterners valued public education, and they financed the construction of one-room schoolhouses through land sales and taxes. Along with churches, schools provided a nexus for community life, and scholars point out that public education involved more than just teaching reading, writing, and arithmetic. Students learned about civics and democracy, and many foreign-born children learned English at public schools. While most midwesterners supported public schools, a number of immigrants resented what they deemed compulsory assimilation through education. Many newcomers sought educational opportunities that upheld their ethnic identities, and ladies' aid societies often stepped in to foot the bill. In Lyon County, Norwegian Lutherans living in Eidsvold Township organized a Ladies' Aid Society to fund a summer parochial school. They paid for the teacher's salary by selling quilts, food, and other home crafts. Catholic nuns in Yankton County established a parochial elementary school in 1878 for the large number of German Catholics who settled there. About twenty years later, a second group of nuns opened a teacher's academy, orphanage, and hospital, which became the premier medical center in the region. Parochial schools instilled ethnic heritage into pupils, teaching them everything from theological traditions to languages from the Old World. In the face of pressure to adopt American values, these schools promoted alternative ones. Their existence was both a religious and a political statement.[19]

Ladies' aid societies allowed midwestern women the opportunity to participate freely in community life. Activities outside the home, like bazaars, holiday celebrations, and other social events, defied the domestic ideal and afforded women a great deal of public authority. In a region where residents clung tightly to prescribed gender distinctions, most people could not acknowledge this power. Instead, it took humor and the passage of time to defuse tensions. By the 1960s many midwestern churches had begun celebrating their centennial anniversaries, including the First Baptist Church of Spencer, the county seat of Clay County. In a booklet produced for the occasion, church leaders praised the Ladies' Aid Society for its financial contributions. They noted that during the 1890s, the group singlehandedly paid for electric lights, a new church bell, and an alcove for the choir. Covering the story, the editor of a local newspaper went even further, cheekily remarking that "it has been a standing joke . . . that the Ladies Aid is the financial bulwark of the church and the men lean heavily on their women folk." All jokes aside, the editor revealed what midwesterners had known all along: women were the unspoken sources of power in midwestern churches, and they turned domestic tasks into social capital and participation in politics, particularly reform movements like woman suffrage.[20]

Auxiliaries to Fraternal Associations

While nearly all midwestern women shared the experiences of visiting neighbors and participating in ladies' aid societies, ethnic differences prevented immigrants from joining elite women's organizations, like women's auxiliaries to fraternal associations, temperance unions, and federated women's clubs. Typically, middle-class Yankee women living in small towns dominated these groups. Many of them benefited from husbands or fathers whose incomes provided plenty of leisure time to devote to activities outside the home. Since these women usually lived in town, travel was easy and regular attendance was feasible. As Yankees, they enjoyed family and financial connections to the east that kept them informed on national matters. Moreover, they had strong educational backgrounds, some at a college level. Many of these women arrived in the Midwest primed for public activism, believing strongly in civic responsibility and volunteerism. They instilled in future generations a spirit of civic engagement that not only promoted community development in the Midwest's vast prairies, but also responded easily to calls for increased political participation in the Progressive Era. For these women, living in a sparsely populated region among a dizzying array of ethnicities did not preclude them from advocating for woman suffrage. The local context did, however, force them to adopt political identities that highlighted republican citizenship and civic engagement. In many ways, what started among neighbors and in churches blossomed into a rich network of women's clubs that were committed to uplifting their communities and—whether they admitted it or not—solidifying their reputations as civic leaders.

In all three counties, some of the first organizations established by Yankee women were the auxiliaries to fraternal societies like the Masons, Odd Fellows, and Grand Army of the Republic. Segregated by gender, these auxiliaries provided a familiar and nostalgic framework that connected women to their lives back east. Since auxiliaries comprised the upper stratum in midwestern small towns, their membership was often exclusive. During the 1880s and 1890s auxiliaries formed at a rapid pace. Seventy women living in Dickens, an unincorporated hamlet in Clay County, became charter members of the Rebekah Lodge in 1890. Not until 1910 did the total population of Dickens reach 280 residents, which indicates the lodge's popularity in this isolated neighborhood. Across the state line in Lyon County, four auxiliaries formed between 1881 and 1896: the Order of the Eastern Star, the Women's Relief Corps, the Rebekah Lodge, and the Minpah Lodge. These organizations promoted sociability among their members, with calendars full of "meetings, dances, and other social events." They also assumed leadership roles in the community. At Marshall, the county seat of Lyon County, the Women's Relief Corps planned massive community-wide celebrations on Memorial Day and the Fourth of July. These events entertained large crowds, and newspapers reported that during the late nineteenth century, over 10,000 people regularly attended the festivities. As one of the first contingents in the annual Fourth of July parade, the Women's Relief Corps was a prominent reminder of the importance of these auxiliaries in community development.[21]

The Women's Christian Temperance Union

Along with auxiliaries, Yankee women also formed local branches of the Women's Christian Temperance Union (WCTU). During the late nineteenth and early twentieth centuries, the WCTU grew tremendously in membership and influence across the United States. Temperance became one of the largest reform movements in the country, and Frances Willard, president of the WCTU, became one of the best-known Americans in the country. By combining women's domestic roles with their political desires for temperance reform and moral uplift, Willard championed the "home protection" ballot. She argued that the vote could protect families from the evils of drink, corruption, and immorality. As early as the 1880s, chapters of the WCTU had emerged among Yankees in the Midwest. Their early activities included social gatherings and lectures, but as the group gained a reputation, its members often found ways to insert themselves into community-building activities. In Yankton County the local branch of the WCTU, which was formed in 1881, constructed the first public restroom facility for visiting farmers and their families in Yankton, the county seat. These restrooms were more like public parlors, providing a vital service to visiting farm women who lacked a place to go while their husbands conducted business in town. The WCTU furnished the rooms, complete with space for children to play or nap, and served refreshments. According to the WCTU, the rooms were "commodious and comfortable" and were "conducted in the coziest possible manner." While the WCTU's work was simple, it garnered praise from community promoters. Yankton's local officials thanked the women for "this practical step . . . [which] deservedly meets with the encouragement of the citizens." Two years after establishing its restroom, the WCTU hosted Francis Willard, president of the national WCTU. Even though Yankton was a county with two dozen saloons and strong anti-temperance sentiment, Willard spoke to a standing room only audience at the Congregational Church. Any signs of a hostile audience did not dissuade her from delivering a nonnegotiable message of total abstinence.[22]

In 1890, the Yankton County WCTU led the fight for female enfranchisement during the first amendment campaign for woman suffrage in South Dakota. Its members did so out of civic identities honed by nearly a decade of political activism. During the 1880s, the group had financed the county's first library and supported the first permanent public school, no small feat when rapid population growth and demographic change threatened Yankee power. In 1890 about 38 percent of the total population of Yankton County were foreign-born individuals. Almost one quarter of all foreigners were Germans, many of whom were notorious in the county for their anti-temperance sentiments. While not every immigrant opposed prohibition, it was not a priority. At the 1890 annual convention, the local WCTU took a bold stand. Not only did it reassert its authority over moral issues, but it also endorsed woman suffrage. While evidence is scant, the members engaged extensively with the suffragist cause at this meeting. They chose "Equal Suffrage" as the topic of their Bible reading. Members presented papers and orations in support of the cause. One woman, Julia King, eventually presented her remarks, entitled "Equal Suffrage a Protection to Purity," at the WCTU's district convention. They even published their meeting minutes, including their names, in the *Press and Dakotan*, the local newspaper. In a county with a notable enmity toward temperance, these women forged ahead, claiming that the right to vote was paramount to their work. Their support was crucial because many of them became leading activists in the local suffrage club formed during the 1890 campaign. The women combined moral purity and sterling reputations as community leaders to justify their stance on woman suffrage. This was an early expression of civic responsibility, and it signaled that they deserved the ballot.[23]

In Minnesota, large ethnic populations and local politics made the work of the WCTU difficult. In Lyon County, almost one-third of the population in 1890 was foreign born, mostly German, Irish, or Belgian. In Marshall, the county seat, a WCTU branch formed among Yankee women in 1886. Temperance meetings also were held in Cottonwood in 1892, and by 1895 the sentiment among residents was strong enough for at least a temporary ban on alcohol. In the rest of Lyon County, women encountered hostility in organizing temperance groups, including at Minneota, Cottonwood, Westerheim, Ghent, Vallers, Fairview, Stanley, and Florence. The residents of these villages were mostly ethnic Germans, Belgians, Norwegians, and French-Canadians with strong traditions of alcohol consumption and local officials who appreciated the taxes and license fees from saloons and bars. When a group of women in Wood Lake attempted to provide "evening entertainment" for young men to "keep them out of saloons," the *Lyon County Reporter* noted that the "low down cusses refuse to be entertained on any elevated plan." At Balaton, the WCTU lamented that the "women support the churches, [while the] men support the saloons." Small numbers of women did participate in the WCTU, but their influence was limited. These temperance advocates were active for only a few years, from about 1892 to 1898, when three small towns went dry. Lost revenue, along with ethnic customs rooted in drink, convinced voters to repeal the restrictions, and Lyon County remained wet until 1920 with the ratification of the Eighteenth Amendment.[24]

Despite these setbacks, at least one chapter of the WCTU in Lyon County publicly endorsed both temperance and woman suffrage. In August 1891 the *Lyon County Reporter* published a series of resolutions recently passed by the WCTU in Marshall, the county seat. In addition to pledges to keep the sabbath holy and teach children about temperance, the group also extolled its members to "use the power of the ballot we hold on educational purposes." In Minnesota women could vote on school bond measures, and they gained reputations for supporting increased taxes to pay for public schools. The resolution indicated that the WCTU endorsed this voting pattern. Soon, the Marshall WCTU publicized another resolution which proclaimed that women voting in school-related elections proved those men wrong who said that "women will not use the ballot if 'tis granted them." A third resolution instructed the Minnesota legislature to expand voting rights for women to "all municipal questions," not just school bond issues.[25]

By June 1892 the Marshall WCTU had embraced its pro-suffrage identity, and it invited Julia B. Nelson, president of the Minnesota Woman Suffrage Association, as the keynote speaker at its annual convention. This was a daring political strategy in an anti-temperance county. While the WCTU did not record the outcome of her visit, it encouraged at least one member to share her pro-suffrage views in public. In November 1894, a member of the local WCTU who signed her name only as "R-----" published a short editorial in the *Lyon County Reporter.* She lambasted the patriarchal notion that righteous men ought to protect meek women. Alcohol consumption had fractured the family, she thundered, and the WCTU had an obligation to "emancipate" men from the evils of liquor. Moreover, she blamed drinking for bringing "utter ruin" to the community. When men could no longer control themselves, women had no choice but to insert themselves into local politics. In other words, civic responsibility mandated the WCTU to act, and with this obligation came political rights, including the ballot. Even though voting was a distant prospect for the Marshall WCTU, they found other ways to assert their political identities. In early 1895, the group circulated a petition to ban cigars sold in nickel slots and gambling in saloons. Since no newspaper mentioned the outcome, the petition probably failed to change the law. But from its high moral ground and strong sense of civic duty, the WCTU proclaimed its actions as necessary to save men from vice. Using political methods, like petitions, was merely a means to an end. Engaging in politics, however, meant that these women were gaining identities that extended beyond the home.[26]

In Iowa, like South Dakota and Minnesota, temperance was a county-level issue, with local option laws that shifted depending on the demographic makeup of the local population. As communities developed, Yankees and immigrants vied for power, and residents recognized that electoral results were anything but certain. Unlike Yankton and Lyon Counties, the immigrant population was low in Clay County, at less than 20 percent. In the case of Spencer, the county seat, a majority Yankee population and a strong WCTU branch were instrumental in tipping the vote to favor temperance. In 1884 the WCTU organized, and it influenced voters to elect the first of a series of pro-temperance mayors. The WCTU enjoyed steady publicity, and newspaper editors covered its meetings extensively and printed its pro-temperance propaganda frequently. The president of the Spencer WCTU, Martha Janes, even received her own front-page column in the *Clay County News*. Almost immediately, Janes turned her attention to woman suffrage. She pointed to the community-building endeavors of the WCTU, and she argued that temperance had improved Spencer's community life. As "responsible individuals" with an obligation "to protect the home," members of the WCTU had demonstrated civic virtue and community service. They had achieved loyal reputations and, consequently, deserved the ballot. The WCTU also flourished beyond Spencer, with chapters at Peterson, Greeneville, Riverton, Annieville, Pleasant Valley, and Barlow and rural townships like Gillett Grove, Lincoln, Freeman, and Lone Tree. An umbrella organization, the Clay County WCTU, orchestrated events across local chapters. Unlike Lyon County, the WCTU prospered in Clay County, benefiting from popular support for temperance. In 1916, most residents in Clay County probably cheered when Iowa adopted statewide prohibition.[27]

National suffrage leaders welcomed the activism of the WCTU but encouraged temperance supporters to limit their work when it came to suffrage. Mixing temperance and woman suffrage was problematic, and it eventually prompted suffragists to question the promise of campaigning in the Midwest. While NAWSA appreciated that the WCTU offered an established network of female activists, especially in places where no suffrage organization existed, leaders like Carrie Chapman Catt feared that voters would not be able to separate woman suffrage measures from prohibition. In particular, they worried about ethnic groups who opposed temperance, and they grew anxious as large populations of immigrants went through the naturalization process and gained the ballot. They also became concerned at community boosters who valued the taxes and fees that came with a booming trade in alcohol. To prevent these conflicts, NAWSA encouraged locals to form separate suffrage clubs to coordinate campaigns and directed the WCTU to serve only as an auxiliary. For many midwestern activists, however, divorcing temperance from woman suffrage was impossible. They embraced the "home protection" ballot as a result of their activism through the WCTU.

Federated Women's Clubs

Suffragists discovered better allies among federated women's clubs, and of all the female collective organizations in the Midwest, these were the most prominent ones. Women's clubs had emerged among middle-class Yankees in the late nineteenth century, and by the early twentieth century they were among the most respected civic organizations in the region. Nationally, the women's club movement had begun in the 1860s among professional women who were upset at their exclusion from men's activities. The clubs' structure encouraged small-group discussions, which appealed to women across the United States. As historian Sara Evans explains, these clubs appealed to a variety of women for their "intellectual stimulation . . . [and] mechanisms for upward mobility." Members engaged in literature, cultural events, and public activities and learned about parliamentary procedure, fund-raising, and public speaking. Moreover, they cultivated civic identities without engaging in radical behaviors. Ultimately, women's clubs allowed women to become political actors within "established traditions of female benevolence."[28]

A well-worn pattern emerged for establishing a women's club, beginning first with a group of women who had developed friendships through visiting and neighborliness. Eventually they would decide to organize formally, electing a slate of officers to oversee club business, run meetings, and determine the subject of study for each year. Many times, the local newspaper published the proceedings of the women's club, as did the *Dakota Herald* for the Nineteenth Century Club in Yankton County. In 1895 elite Yankee women formed the Nineteenth Century Club, and they operated under that name until 1916, when members changed the name to the Woman's Club. The club held weekly meetings devoted to educational and literary advancement, and members took turns preparing lessons or speeches on related topics. In 1904 the club chose English history as its annual theme, and members presented papers like one entitled "England under the House of Hanover." While the club collectively avoided political matters, a number of members participated openly in the agitation for woman suffrage. The club's first president, Flora Swift, directed the local campaign for woman suffrage in 1890. Over two decades later, club president Kathryn Schuppert led the Yankton Universal Franchise League as it coordinated the 1914 campaign.[29]

In Lyon County, middle-class Yankees jumped aboard the women's club movement in 1874 with the creation of the Current News Club. As the club explained in its bylaws, it sought to "awaken and sustain, in the members, an interest in literature, topics of general information and social concern, by means of study, readings, and discussion." During their weekly salons the women discussed a range of issues, but most dealt with matters of the home and family. By the early twentieth century, the Current News Club had begun to expand its scope by advocating for a series of civic reforms, including a curfew ordinance in Marshall, the county seat, and a cleanup crusade for vacant lots in the town. In 1916 the club sponsored a baby welfare week in the county, with members educating their neighbors about how to prevent common infant diseases. By 1917, when the United States entered World War I, the women had developed reputations as community leaders, and they channeled their civic power into work for the American Red Cross and support for woman suffrage. In 1918 Laura Lowe, a member of the Current News Club, spearheaded a woman suffrage petition drive that collected hundreds of signatures across the county.[30]

Like their counterparts in Yankton County and Lyon County, middle-class Yankees in Clay County also embraced the women's club movement. In 1894 the Spencer Woman's Club emerged among a group of "strong-minded women with a look toward the future." Attendance was higher in the summer months, reaching upward of fifty people, and dropped in the winter to about twenty women when cold, snow, and ice hampered their travel. The Spencer Woman's Club also adopted annual themes, with topics chosen in advance and papers presented by members for study and discussion. In 1896 the members voted to join the General Federation of Women's Clubs, and in the next year the women explicitly added community development to their agenda. It was a bold move that positioned them directly to participate in public affairs. In December 1897 the club created the Village Improvement Committee—known later as the Civics and Health Committee—with the charge to uplift civic life, and its members proposed a variety of initiatives. With these projects, Spencer Woman's Club members became de facto public works officials, displaying an impressive range of interests. They built a public restroom for farm families who required a public parlor during long visits to town. They enacted a beautification campaign, purchasing trees to plant on land surrounding local government buildings and flower seeds for public schools. Finally, they bought an undeveloped lot that would become Spencer's first public park. The Spencer Woman's Club demonstrated how women's clubs transformed the opportunity for intellectual stimulation and upward mobility into community development. Their efforts left a physical mark on Spencer, which served as a constant reminder to residents of the civic power these women wielded.[31]

The Spencer Woman's Club easily channeled its members' civic reputations into political activism. Beginning in 1896, the club began a review of library funding laws in Iowa. When a bill to create a system of traveling libraries came before the Iowa legislature, the women publicized a resolution favoring it, sending it to area newspapers and writing letters to their elected representatives to express their approval of the measure. In addition to libraries, the Spencer Woman's Club also supported educational opportunities, and during the first decade of the twentieth century, the group organized a series of lectures and art exhibits for Clay County residents. The spirit of Progressivism also inspired the group, and the members candidly announced their support for child labor laws, the Pure Food and Drug Act, and compulsory education for young adults. In addition to the Spencer Woman's Club, two other women's clubs emerged in Clay County, one at Peterson in 1915 and another at Everly. In Everly, the women organized in June 1916 to "encourage intellectual development, to promote good fellowship and to work for the good of the community." They sponsored a public library for their first project. As one observer wrote, these clubs truly shaped the civic life of their respective communities, and their "breadth of thought, purity of aim, [and] deep interest in all matters pertaining to the welfare of the home" contributed immeasurably to community development. When Iowa held its only woman suffrage campaign in 1916, the Spencer Woman's Club coordinated campaign efforts in Clay County. Its members served as ward and township chairmen, and Mary Cory, an original member of the Village Improvement committee, served as the county chairman.[32]

Community, Civic Activism, and Woman Suffrage

Midwestern women challenged nineteenth-century views on gender that had traditionally confined women to the private sphere. They did not publicly contest patriarchal ideals, and they avoided controversy by pursuing activities in line with their gendered identities. Casually surveying their work, however, mistakenly overlooks how these women built on humble tasks to gain civic identities. Every pie baked, pillow stitched, supper organized, and restroom furnished seemed to match gendered expectations, but further scrutiny reveals the authority accrued by women over time. Midwestern women excelled at fund-raising, and the money they raised built churches, funded schools, opened libraries, and created parks. Constructing these institutions placed women at the forefront of community development, which resonated among midwesterners who embraced republican ideas of civic engagement. By claiming civic responsibility, women echoed American political values which asserted that participation was an obligation of citizenship. With obligations came rights, including the right to vote. Midwestern women came to woman suffrage with political identities shaped by the expectations of community membership. While they did not outwardly refute the nineteenth-century belief in gender inequality, they wove a subtle yet powerful argument that by their actions, they deserved the ballot. They demanded political inclusion as citizens, blurring the line between the public and private spheres and crossing into politics with conviction and ease. There were no separate spheres of influence for rural women in the Midwest. Becoming political and ultimately supporting woman suffrage rested both on their civic work and on their gendered identity as women.

It was not until the second decade of the twentieth century that civic responsibility emerged as the path to woman suffrage in the Midwest, and during nineteenth-century campaigns, suffragists struggled mightily. Their early battles for the cause faltered and ultimately failed because advocates relied on advice from national leaders that claimed women as equals to men. Those arguments were radical, and they gained little traction in the region. Moreover, suffragists struggled to accommodate ethnic diversity as they plotted their campaigns, and they lacked a coherent strategy to deal with immigrants and their children. Campaigning during the early stages of settlement also meant that travel was problematic, which limited the face-to-face contact that suffragists deemed necessary for victory. Defeat fostered resilience among suffragists, however, and with time, they crafted effective arguments. They delicately negotiated nineteenth-century gender norms, midwestern political culture, and ethnic distinctions to bring victory into view in the twentieth century.

Chapter 3

GENDER, CITIZENSHIP, AND THE STRUGGLE TO ACHIEVE WOMAN SUFFRAGE, 1880–1900

IN NOVEMBER 1898, voters in South Dakota defeated a proposed amendment to the state's constitution that would have granted women the right to vote. It was the third campaign for woman suffrage in the state, following unsuccessful bids in 1890 and 1894. Returns indicated that South Dakotans were about evenly split on the measure, with almost 19,700 for it and not quite 23,000 against it. The National American Woman Suffrage Association (NAWSA) claimed that the close vote was a sign that attitudes had shifted in favor of the suffragist cause. Eight years earlier, in 1890, the initiative to enact woman suffrage had failed ingloriously, by a ratio of two to one. The figures from the 1898 campaign seemed to indicate that opposition to woman suffrage had declined. While the vote in 1898 was almost even, the leaders of NAWSA omitted the fact that turnout in 1890 was much higher, with almost 68,000 people casting a ballot on the measure. Although the number of votes opposed to woman suffrage had dropped, no more people voted in favor of the cause in 1898 than they had in 1890. NAWSA ignored these details of the election, however, putting a positive spin on not only a disappointing campaign but also a discouraging decade of activism in the Midwest.[1]

Most nineteenth-century woman suffrage campaigns in the Midwest ended in defeat, and NAWSA came to harbor a grudge against a population it believed to be backward and unsophisticated. Underlying its spite were two related issues. First, suffrage leaders grew hostile toward immigrants, especially Germans, and they increasingly blamed these ethnic voters for the series of defeats the suffragists had sustained in the late nineteenth century. Many of the newcomers also held strong religious beliefs, like Catholicism and Lutheranism, that were rooted in traditional and conservative values. Most midwestern suffragists were middle-class, Protestant, and Yankee, and they struggled to accommodate immigrants whom national leaders eventually wrote off as never being able to support woman suffrage. Second, NAWSA struggled to divorce woman suffrage from temperance, which was a problematic marriage in the eyes of ethnic groups, especially German Catholics, who adhered to customs rooted in drink. Suffragists, from locals to national figures, were never able to divorce the issue of temperance reform from woman suffrage campaigns, no matter how much they attempted to separate the two movements. Across the Midwest, most communities lacked enough support to establish a local woman suffrage club, so woman suffrage agitation often began among women in the WCTU, especially at the local level. The WCTU was a well-respected and relatively conservative group that celebrated women's traditional roles and demanded temperance. When it became the center of woman suffrage campaigning during the last decades of the nineteenth century, it offended many immigrants.

NAWSA members' resentment of Germans, and the latter's resentment of the WCTU, as well as other quirks of midwestern life, produced tensions between local activists and leaders in NAWSA. For locals, adopting the directives of national leaders was problematic. In particular, NAWSA developed a grudge against foreigners, and it eventually ordered local leaders to exclude them from campaigns. Defying national leaders, midwestern activists preferred inclusion, arguing that by ignoring immigrants from Europe who had become naturalized citizens, NAWSA guaranteed its own defeat. Moreover, locals struggled to espouse the arguments from national leaders which claimed that women were equal to men. This rhetoric was ineffective because most midwesterners, including many native-born Americans, venerated women's domestic role. Instead, local advocates eventually contended that civic responsibility, developed out of community membership and republican notions of citizenship, was a better strategy to demand the ballot. Finally, national leaders recoiled at the crude living conditions they witnessed during late nineteenth-century campaigns. What NAWSA saw as an absence of civilization was to locals the reality of recent settlement. Intensive farming dictated work schedules that were devoid of leisure, and rough, undeveloped terrain made traveling difficult and trips to town infrequent. Audiences were small and were sometimes comprised of foreigners who could not understand English, which irritated national lecturers. NAWSA ultimately characterized midwesterners as ignorant and disinterested people who cared little about gender equality. These labels frustrated local suffragists who saw only half-hearted campaigns that failed to account for the political culture of the Midwest.

While the nineteenth-century woman suffrage campaigns in the Midwest ended in failure, there was still an upside to them. Informal and formal campaigns allowed local activists to work through the complexities of ethnicity, politics, religion, and gender. In general, Yankee women took up the woman suffrage banner, although a few exceptional immigrants also joined the fight. These small but fierce groups of women learned to leverage their civic identities as citizens and members of their communities. They marshaled their community-building efforts and the public recognition that followed into demands for the ballot. For these women, it was easy to transition from holding a successful church bazaar to organizing a well-attended suffrage lecture. They also displayed tenacity against a sea of voters who remained unconvinced that women had the ability or desire to vote. For decades, these women worked tirelessly to change rigid attitudes about women's position in society. They faced the tensions that splintered midwestern communities without hesitation, and they discovered civic responsibility to be an effective argument because it embodied the republican virtues that midwesterners cherished while still celebrating women's domestic identities. Although many midwesterners initially opposed woman suffrage, they eventually came to examine it with careful consideration and genuine curiosity.

Why study the failed woman suffrage campaigns in the Midwest during the late nineteenth century? Although they were unsuccessful, the campaigns produced important insights in the fight for female enfranchisement. Activists learned that enshrining woman suffrage into law was a matter of tenacity and patience. This was a long-term fight, and failure shaped the movement as much as victory. If women wanted to vote, then suffragists had to sustain the movement over generations. Repeated defeats also made the Midwest a testing ground, and suffragists retained the strategies that worked and discarded the ones that did not. Eventually, the methods and networks of activism that crystallized in the late nineteenth century became invaluable during the early twentieth century. Finally, studying woman suffrage in the Midwest reveals that much depended on community subtleties. Experiences varied widely, and ethnic, religious, and political identities tremendously influenced the outcome of campaigns. Large ethnic populations or strong chapters of the WCTU, for example, could sway public opinion one way or the other, creating a constellation of ways that people supported or opposed the cause. There was no one-size-fits-all version of woman suffrage.

Of all the consequences of nineteenth-century midwestern campaigns for woman suffrage, the most powerful one was a better understanding of fundamental ideas about gender, marriage, and citizenship. Most Americans embraced gender norms that celebrated two separate spheres, one private and the other public. They assumed that a male head of household served as both the family and political representative, and they believed that marriage bound women to patriarchs as their dependents. Woman suffrage threatened to shatter patriarchal representation, however, making it a danger to the family, community, and nation. Critics viewed female independence as outrageous because it imperiled deeply held American values. Linking civic virtue to autonomy, a state denied to women, most midwesterners considered woman suffrage a radical menace to all that Americans held dear. They deemed it a political minefield that, once entered, promised to destroy the principles that defined the United States. Woman suffrage also attacked Christian theology that upheld gender inequalities, particularly those in the relationship between wives and husbands. Obedience and submission, not defiance, were the traits of Christian women.[2]

To abolish the hostility that dominated nineteenth-century attitudes toward woman suffrage not only required patience, delicacy, and good cheer but also mandated a bulletproof argument. By crafting a sophisticated claim about civic responsibility, suffragists alleviated concerns about female autonomy and employed the language of republicanism to reassure midwesterners that female enfranchisement actually enhanced traditional gender roles. By connecting female participation in community development to woman suffrage, they asserted that women could be better advocates for their families and communities with the ballot. While suffragists eventually achieved victory because midwestern women cultivated respected civic identities, they also found success because they forced people to grapple with the contradictions of citizenship. Suffragists pointed out that denying rights, including the right to vote, was hypocritical if citizens who were disenfranchised met their civic obligations. By highlighting this inconsistency, suffragists sidestepped the contentious issue of female independence and framed their efforts in terms of republican obligation, an ideal that resonated strongly with midwestern voters. The timing of suffrage campaigns also favored the cause. Suffragists asked Americans to open the boundaries of citizenship at the precise moment when nativist suspicions of Germans were increasing and leading to a more narrow interpretation of that citizenship. By the end of the nineteenth century, Americans were beginning to consider citizenship an active status in which the standard for inclusion was a particular set of "American" behaviors.

Comparing woman suffrage in three counties reveals the hostility that initially defined midwestern reactions and the strategies that activists developed to overcome them. In Minnesota, advocates faced substantial opposition, and they struggled to convince large ethnic populations, particularly Germans, to change their minds about enfranchisement. The state's residents were also usually against temperance, which stymied efforts of groups like the WCTU, especially at the local level. When Minnesotans passed new rules for securing constitutional amendments in 1898, the movement stagnated against an insurmountable standard. Crossing Minnesota's southern border produced a completely different set of circumstances, and in Iowa grassroots initiatives brought a slew of informal campaigns. More Yankees there meant that woman suffrage enjoyed a larger cohort of activists, and sometimes those activists incited dramatic debates that exposed how midwesterners struggled with changing gender norms. Iowa also had a stronger state association than Minnesota did, and it worked valiantly, but futilely, for an amendment. To the west, advocates in South Dakota engaged in two campaigns for full suffrage and one for school suffrage. While suffragists employed similar strategies among these campaigns, the dynamics of each campaign were distinct. Whereas NAWSA played an exceptionally strong role in the 1890 campaign, it effectively had abandoned local activists by 1898.

Ultimately, examining woman suffrage in these three places underscores how diverse the experience of woman suffrage was in the Midwest. Local communities could inspire or discourage activism depending on what elements were most prominent, so it is important to account for contextual differences. In spite of these disparities, however, activists in each place eventually adopted civic responsibility as their winning argument. It was the most remarkable consequence to emerge out of decades of defeat.

Minnesota

The movement to achieve woman suffrage in Minnesota stagnated during the late nineteenth century. As historian William Lass remarks, "Minnesota lagged behind national trends in the question for voting rights for women." The deck seemed stacked against the cause from the beginning. The state's population, comprised largely of foreign-born immigrants, seemingly opposed woman suffrage, and piecemeal efforts emerged only where individuals took it upon themselves to advance the cause. In addition, state-level leadership did not stray far from a predictable pattern of campaigning based on speeches and petitions. They ignored the need for widespread local organization, preferring to direct their efforts almost entirely at the state legislature. Collectively, women avoided the cause, and female associations, including the WCTU, found little success in agitating for the ballot. Finally, in 1898, it became nearly impossible to amend the state's constitution, and suffragists realized that amendment campaigns were only dead ends. The paucity of woman suffrage activity in Minnesota confirmed the importance of dynamic leadership sustained over generations as well as organization at the local level.[3]

The first advocates for woman suffrage came to Minnesota as Yankees moved west after the Civil War. During the 1860s and 1870s there was no formal state suffrage organization, so individuals worked independently to agitate for the ballot. They lectured in their small communities or sent letters and petitions to legislators, but their accomplishments were negligible. In 1868, laughter broke out on the floor of the House of Representatives when a measure to strike the word "male" from voting requirements appeared. Not until 1881 did fourteen activists form the Minnesota Woman Suffrage Association (MWSA), of which Sarah Burger Stearns served as the first president. Stearns had moved to Minnesota in 1866 with her husband, an attorney and later a judge. As a self-proclaimed feminist, Stearns believed in women's equality at a time when most Minnesotans did not. Every year between 1881 and 1898, Stearns and her cohort gave the legislature bills aimed at securing woman suffrage. For example, in 1885 suffragists pressed for a measure to allow women to vote for county superintendents of schools. Legislators opposed it. Six years later, in 1891, the MWSA advocated a measure that enfranchised women in municipal elections. While the Senate passed it, it died in the House. Two small victories, one in 1875 and another in 1898, kept hope alive. A law passed in 1875 gave women the vote in school elections, which allowed women to serve on school boards. A similar 1898 law enfranchised women in library elections, and women also gained the right to sit on library boards.[4]

Despite these small victories, the legislature was undeniably unkind toward woman suffrage. Nearly every year, woman suffrage bills languished in committees or died on the House or Senate floor. The MWSA was undeterred, however, and between 1890 and 1896 it sent petitions full of thousands of signatures to elected representatives. In 1898 the MWSA received a crushing blow. That year, the legislature passed a bill that reinterpreted electoral policy. Before 1898, Minnesota had a simple amending process. Once a bill passed both houses of the legislature, all it required was a majority of the votes cast for the single measure. The 1898 law stated that any future amendments to the state's constitution had to receive a majority of the highest vote total cast in any one election. The new law made amending Minnesota's constitution virtually impossible. It cast aside the simple majority and required a majority of "all the electors voting at said election." In essence, this meant that not voting on a measure was the same as a "no" vote. Targeting the legislature for an amendment—the strategy the MWSA had employed for decades—was now almost impossible, and suffragists lamented that women could never "obtain any further extension of the franchise" in the state. By the turn of the twentieth century, only a few senior members of the MWSA continued to press for a state amendment. A younger generation of suffragists, led by Clara Ueland, recognized the difficulty in such a proposition and instead pressed for a bill that granted presidential suffrage, or the right to vote for only the president of the United States, to women without the necessity of a statewide vote.[5]

Woman suffrage struggled to take hold in Lyon County for many of the same reasons it foundered in Minnesota. A strong ethnic population, mainly Norwegians and Germans, seemed uninterested in the cause, and no one stepped forward to lead a sustained campaign in the county. Collectively, rural women eschewed woman suffrage, and the records of women's organizations, including the WCTU, ladies' aid societies, and the Current News Club, the local federated women's club, rarely mentioned the prospect of women voting. In 1891 the Marshall WCTU endorsed school and municipal suffrage, but its resolutions failed to produce long-term activism. In 1895 the MWSA, led by President Julia B. Nelson, sent two suffrage lecturers, Emma Smith DeVoe of South Dakota and Laura Johns of Kansas, to canvass the state. No women's club mentioned their visit in Lyon County, but perhaps their presence led the editor of the *Lyon County Reporter* to publish six articles against woman suffrage. These were reprinted pieces composed by Mariana Griswold Van Rensselaer, a writer from New York. Van Rensselaer ultimately opposed woman suffrage, but she wavered in her assessments. While she believed it enhanced women's domestic sphere, she underscored that women were inherently unequal and unfit for public life. The tone of her articles was generic and diplomatic, and the headlines merely asked "Should We Ask for the Suffrage?" One article pointed out the difficulty female property holders faced without the ballot, but Van Rensselaer explained that she did so only to provide "careful consideration" and a "respectful" appraisal of the situation. Another article argued that each state, not the federal government, ought to dictate voting rights. The articles were neither provocative nor inspiring, and they created no sustained activism either way.[6]

The tepid response of Lyon County residents to support any activity, however benign, on behalf of woman suffrage reveals the radical nature of the cause. On the pages of local newspapers, snide comments and sly remarks indicated outright disdain. One snippet claimed that only a few women actually wanted to vote. The anonymous author commented that if women only demanded the ballot "with practical unanimity," they could secure it, but he surmised that "it will not be thrust upon the many to gratify the few." Sometimes, editors did not hide their contempt. In April 1895 the editor of the *Lyon County Reporter*, Christopher F. Case, lambasted women reformers, vilifying them for their "lack of sincerity," "false credits," and "skin-deep enthusiasm." He argued that women did not have the "proper grit" to engage in politics. Those who did were prostitutes, controlled by despicable masters who forced them to cast ballots for the "worst element in the community."[7]

Despite the rancor with which newspaper editors sometimes treated the prospect of female enfranchisement, the publicity itself—and even the outlandish character of the accusations—reflected an increasing interest in women's prescribed roles. Just because no person in Lyon County gave outright support to woman suffrage did not mean that residents were indifferent. On the contrary, the prospect of women voting enthralled many Minnesotans. During the late nineteenth century, countless editions of the *Lyon County Reporter* featured articles on women. Some addressed issues of comportment, like dress, but many more highlighted the political actions of women, like temperance reform. In one article, a railroad agent remarked, "We are hearing a great deal now about 'the new woman' . . . [and the] 'woman's sphere,' both from strong-minded females . . . and from fusty and musty doctors of divinity." The deluge of written commentary reflected the heightened public presence of women in Lyon County. Women were ubiquitous, hosting box socials, raising money for local libraries, and organizing WCTU conventions. Women were entering public life seamlessly and already had begun crafting civic identities. They had done so through their accepted roles in the family, home, and church. Lyon County residents had to confront the uncomfortable reality that woman suffrage was perhaps neither as radical nor as unattainable as it seemed.[8]

Iowa

Unlike woman suffrage in Minnesota, the cause flourished in Iowa, despite the absence of formal amendment campaigns. NAWSA highly esteemed Iowa, writing that "in probably no State is the general sentiment so strongly in favor of woman suffrage." The WCTU was a well-respected organization there, and it shaped public life tremendously. The Iowa Woman Suffrage Association (IWSA) was also a vibrant group that encouraged local organization. The IWSA formed in 1870 out of an equal suffrage convention in Mount Pleasant. During the late nineteenth century, the IWSA worked diligently to cultivate grassroots support while pressuring the Iowa legislature to put a woman suffrage amendment to the voters. They sent petitions to the General Assembly, like one in 1878 filled with thousands of signatures, and introduced numerous bills to the legislature during the last three decades of the nineteenth century. Almost always, the measures died either in the House or the Senate. NAWSA blamed a rigged political system for these defeats, arguing that "great brewing interests" and "the German vote" controlled Iowa politics, and these were conspiracies that gained traction into the early twentieth century. Expanding voting rights through the legislative process was also slow because amendments required approval from two consecutive legislatures. Since the Iowa General Assembly usually met every other year, suffragists had to maintain support for the cause as political sentiments shifted and turnover occurred between sessions. Amending Iowa's constitution required patience and long-term planning, so suffrage leaders focused on informal grassroots campaigning.[9]

Pockets of sentiment for the suffrage cause existed across Iowa, and individual efforts marked the movement's activities in the late nineteenth century. Usually, a suffrage advocate called a meeting and throngs of neighbors, some supportive and others just curious, attended. Newspapers announced the upcoming gatherings and provided public reports of the proceedings. In 1892 at Doon in Lyon County, suffragists convened a "crowded meeting" that drew "people for many miles." With only forty-six residents, Doon seemed an unexpected place for such an assembly. Remarkably, the people of Doon were ardent suffragists with open pocketbooks. At two successive meetings, attendees collected forty-two dollars for suffrage, almost one dollar for every person living there. The spark for woman suffrage ignited across Iowa, in small towns like Dunlap, Independence, and Charles City. Suffragists from Dunlap in Harrison County secured columns in twelve newspapers published nearby. In Independence and Charles City activists formed clubs, which they cleverly called "Political Equality Clubs." In 1889 nearly 100 women attended the Independence Political Equality Club's first social. Buoyed by the turnout, members of that club ramped up their efforts, organizing a "Woman's Day" at the 1892 Buchanan County Fair and requesting a regular column in the local newspaper in 1893. In January 1892 in Charles City, the county seat of Floyd County, suffragists distributed petitions, submitting 125 names after just two weeks of work. They also coordinated a suffrage lecture circuit in their county, although their records fail to indicate the outcome of that effort. Finally, the Charles City Political Equality Club spoke at area organizations to convince them to support the cause. For example, in February 1892 they addressed the Farmers' Alliance, although they did not report any results of their visit.[10]

During the late nineteenth century, Iowans enjoyed many grassroots opportunities to encounter the cause, and in Clay County woman suffrage emerged in ways similar to those in Floyd, Buchanan, Harrison, and Lyon counties. In coordination with the IWSA, individuals across Iowa brought woman suffrage to their communities, and Clay County was no different. The WCTU largely shaped the movement there, and advocates clamored for both temperance and woman suffrage. In Spencer, the county seat, temperance was a contentious issue until 1885, when pro-temperance forces took control of the city and held it for over three decades. The temperance takeover coincided with the increased popularity of the WCTU across the county. Led by the charismatic but contentious Reverend Martha Waldron Janes, the Clay County WCTU became the locus of agitation for woman suffrage. Born in Michigan as the oldest of seven children to Yankee parents, Martha reportedly embraced woman suffrage at a young age. She was angry at prescriptive gender ideas that provided only limited educational opportunities for girls. She found work as a domestic, saving her weekly pay to fund a semester of school. She also found a voice in the Free Baptist Church, which she joined at age thirteen. Free Baptists espoused more egalitarian views, and Martha eventually "prayed and exhorted" in public. Her "religious zeal" became so "conspicuous" that people considered her "crazy" and "mentally unsound." Undeterred by her critics, Janes began preaching in 1860, supported by her first husband, John Sober. Three years after his death in 1864, Martha married Henry Janes, a Free Baptist minister. In June 1868 she became the first female ordained minister in the Free Baptist conference, and by June 1870 the family had relocated to Clayton County, Iowa.[11] (See figure 4.)

FIGURE 4. Martha Janes. From Francis Willard and Mary Livermore, eds., *A Woman of the Century: Fourteen Hundred-Seventy Biographical Sketches Accompanied by Portraits of Leading American Women in All Walks of Life*, p. 417. Chicago: Charles Wells Moulton, 1893.

Over the next ten years, Martha Janes traveled across Iowa as an evangelist for the Free Baptist Church and even served as the senior pastor of several churches. She raised three children, Eva and Arthur from her first marriage and Charles from her second, while working tirelessly to promote her religious values. By 1880 the family had separated, and Martha followed her daughter, Eva, to Clay County while Henry went to live in Butler County with his widowed daughter, Anna, from a previous relationship. No evidence indicates the nature of the split, and it appears that Henry and Martha lived apart until his death in 1886. In the meantime, Eva had married Malcolm Gilchrist, the son of a prominent pioneer family in Clay County.[12]

When Janes arrived in Clay County, she was already a stalwart activist for woman suffrage and temperance, and she fearlessly championed these twin reforms in as many ways as she could. She was probably behind the circulation of a woman suffrage petition in January 1884, almost six months before she became president of the Clay County WCTU. This petition reflected the arguments offered by national leaders, who advocated for women's independence in a liberal citizenship model. According to the *Clay County News*, the petition claimed that citizenship equally bound both women and men to the state, forcing them to pay taxes and obey the same legal provisions. Gender distinctions, however, revealed the hypocrisy of citizenship. Women had to "abide and live up to all official enactments" just as men did, but they had no say in "determining of what those laws and enactment should be" because they could not vote. The *Clay County News* did not indicate how many people signed the petition, but the editor added his own commentary, probably to the delight of local suffragists. He explained that citizenship without the vote was an illogical, absurd, and outdated idea held by "unthinking and unreasoning" people.[13]

The petition coincided with an informal grassroots campaign enacted in 1884 by the IWSA. In the spring of that year, the association sent out four workers to canvass the state, including two paid lecturers, Matilda Hindman of Pennsylvania and Helen Gougar of Indiana. Hindman reportedly gave 72 speeches and formed 40 suffrage clubs while Gougar distributed 3,000 tracts. No records indicate if or when any of these field workers visited Clay County, but someone likely arrived there in the spring. Shortly afterward, woman suffrage activity increased markedly in the county, with Janes leading the charge. Her work confirms that individual efforts often produced sporadic, but dramatic, campaigns. Janes transformed the Clay County WCTU from a group that merely espoused temperance reform to one that aggressively agitated for woman suffrage. Her powerful oratorical skills combined with her acerbic wit and unshakable convictions for gender equality. As a religious leader, Janes served as a liaison between the church and civic activists. She was a formidable force, one who alienated opponents as much as she converted followers.[14]

At a meeting in May 1884, Janes orchestrated a full-scale takeover of the Clay County WCTU by convincing the group to endorse woman suffrage unanimously. After mundane business matters, the women opened the floor to a debate on woman suffrage, and Janes moved to limit each speaker to fifteen minutes. She then gave a fiery oration that immediately violated her fifteen-minute rule. According to the recorder, her arguments were so "forcible and convincing that the negatives . . . would as soon be caught stealing sheep as to be found trying to defend the other side of the question." The anti-suffrage contingent mustered enough strength to issue a rebuttal, and they listed a variety of well-worn excuses steeped in nineteenth-century gender norms. Women were mentally and physically weaker than men, with smaller and lighter brains that were ill-equipped to vote. Polling places were full of "filthy" men who threatened to tarnish the reputations of respectable women. Voting required women to spend more time in saloons, billiard halls, and bars and less in their kitchens, an unconscionable threat to the family. In response, Janes issued scathing remarks by "reviewing each and every objection separately" and twisting them to support the cause. With the last word and "so many more" arguments to her credit, Janes won the debate. The vote that followed was a unanimous victory for woman suffrage.[15]

While Janes and her supporters celebrated the victory, the results deeply divided the Clay County WCTU. At the WCTU's second annual county convention in June 1884, the president, Sarah Jencks, tried to settle the dispute by "positively refusing to serve" the newly pro-suffrage group. The members moved swiftly to replace her with none other than Martha Janes, effectively purging the WCTU of anti-suffrage leadership. With Janes at the helm, the Clay County WCTU demanded "the ballot for woman, to the end that she may protect herself, her little ones, and her home from the rum power." While Janes sparked a revolution in the WCTU, she had an even bigger agenda. Around the time of her election, she became district superintendent for the IWSA and convinced the editor of the *Clay County News* to give her a front-page column. It eventually appeared in seventeen weekly newspapers, and she spared no one from her provocative rhetoric. In one of her first columns, she lambasted the Declaration of Independence, calling it a "living falsehood," a "standing menace," and a "disgrace." When half of the nation's citizens could not vote, the values cherished by the nation's founding fathers were worthless. Janes also argued that men "unjustly defrauded" women by denying them the vote. She asserted that God had determined women to be equal to men intellectually, spiritually, and legally, and she proclaimed it a sin for men to treat women with contempt.[16]

In her weekly column, Janes wove blistering arguments that resonated at the intersection of nineteenth-century ideas about gender, religion, and politics. She blasted conventional gender norms that relegated women to the domestic sphere and, taking a page from NAWSA, she envisioned women as autonomous individuals. Like most suffrage activists, Janes had not yet cultivated civic responsibility as an effective claim. Instead, she asserted that God had ordained gender equality, explaining that "God created [woman] a conscious, sentient, responsible, intellectual personality, as much as man" who accounted for her actions only to Him. Woman's obligation was to God and the Constitution, which determined her "an intelligent human being" with the capacity to vote. Janes cleverly revealed the hypocrisy of female disenfranchisement. She accused men of denying women their God-given rights, and in doing so, of robbing them of the same liberty and freedom men themselves prized. Giving women the ballot fulfilled both God's and America's promise. For two months, Janes filled the pages of the *Clay County News* with these messages. She saw woman as an individual who ought to enjoy her "rights as a citizen and a person." Individual liberty ought to determine citizenship and the rights associated with it.[17]

Martha Janes produced a series of arguments that threatened nineteenth-century gender norms and ultimately provoked a cascade of opposition. Her columns divided the residents of Clay County, and she spawned a debate that left indelible scars. An anonymous man discharged the first volley in May 1884 when he endorsed the ballot for single women, a remarkable position in a heated dispute. In a letter to the *Clay County News,* he explained that unmarried women lacked patriarchal representation and therefore could engage in civic affairs equally, albeit temporarily. The author confirmed that women ought to lose the right to vote when they married, but he assured readers that husbands always voted to please their wives. Why did a married woman need the vote when her husband did it for her? While the man's letter offered an exception, it still confirmed that marriage defined women's citizenship status, the standard practice for most of American history. As historian Nancy Cott points out, most nineteenth-century Americans considered women to be legal dependents, bound to a patriarch from whom they derived their citizenship status. In 1907, Congress even stripped a native-born woman of her citizenship if she married a noncitizen. When Janes called for individual liberty to determine citizenship, she not only challenged gender discrimination but also criticized the sacred bond, sanctioned by God, between husbands and wives.[18]

Most people who read Janes's columns did not make exceptions or give partial support in specific cases when it came to the question of woman suffrage. They understood the implications of her logic, and it electrified them to express either absolute opposition or complete support. The barrage of responses revealed the deep chasm that split midwesterners over gender, religion, and politics, and Janes could only watch helplessly as the debate spiraled out of control. It began in July 1884 with a two-column article published on the front page of the *Clay County News*. Written by George Coles, a resident of Sioux Rapids in Buena Vista County, the article lambasted woman suffrage. A divorced teacher, Coles loathed the prospect of wives abandoning their husbands. Quoting the Bible, Coles argued that God had made women subordinate to men. Wives served their husbands while husbands protected their wives, and in these roles, wives and husbands enjoyed separate spheres. When each fulfilled the duties of their sphere, they perfected "the whole, as the Creator designed they should." Woman suffrage threatened to upend this relationship, causing "untold misery," including divorce and irreparable harm to the family.[19]

The assaults against woman suffrage continued, building on each other to reveal how midwestern political culture interwove religious beliefs with political ideals. A second person, writing under the alias "Pro Bono Publico," explained the link in a letter published a few weeks later. "Pro Bono Publico" explained that the family was "the germ out of which nations grow . . . [so] the nation['s] character depends upon the character of the home." This character derived directly from wives' submission to their husbands as "keepers of the home." This rationale was common in the late nineteenth century. According to historian Paula Baker, many Americans perceived woman suffrage as dangerous because it promised to shatter the dynamics of the home, the foundation of the nation. It was not the influence of women in future electoral decisions that bothered observers like Coles and "Pro Bono Publico." They feared female autonomy because it upended the very foundation of civic life—the family. For them, the family—and the marriage that created it—bound individuals to each other and to the nation. These institutions cultivated belonging in a region where belonging was paramount.[20]

By August 1884, pro-suffragists were mounting a stunning counterattack that reenergized the conflict and exposed the fragility of nineteenth-century gender norms. Vehement adherence to the alleged gender binary merely concealed how easily men and women defied it. The first to fire was Charles Brooke, a resident of Tama County, and he aimed his remarks directly at Coles. Brooke recalled Coles's religious framework but skewered it, arguing that gender complementarity in marriage sounded great until a spouse strayed from Christ's command. Husbands were particularly susceptible, especially to "the monster of intemperance." When drunkenness threatened the family, wives had no choice but to vote to protect the home from alcohol. Brooke claimed woman suffrage would be a healing balm that could rebuild families, purify the home, and glorify the nation.[21]

More voices entered the battle, and not only did they stage a blistering offensive against Coles, but they also belonged to local women. One woman, who went by the initials "H. M. H.," attacked Coles for his shortsightedness on citizenship. Women were free citizens, not "subjects" or "political slaves," and all they demanded were the same "rights, privileges, and immunities" granted by the Constitution. Another woman, known as "A. N. G.," unleashed her rage at Coles, accusing him of writing "slush, twaddle, and blatant nonsense." She assaulted his character, calling him a "half-baked lunatic" with "not more than a pint of self-esteem." To her, Coles was a deplorable hypocrite who had forgotten that women in Iowa could vote in school bond elections. As a teacher, he regularly courted women's support on these educational measures. "A. N. G." predicted that sometime in the near future, she would hear Coles say: "I trust Mrs. that I can count on your vote and influence at the coming election," proving that even he could not separate women from politics. It was a withering criticism that exposed the fiction of separate and distinct gender spheres.[22]

While the theatrics of the debate were impressive, in the end, the correspondence revealed that a majority of midwesterners could not support an argument for female autonomy. Many midwesterners believed that marriage defined citizenship for women, and they based their analysis on what they saw as immutable Christian theological principles. When suffragists like Janes sought to abolish patriarchal representation, they questioned the very character of the nation. To sever the familial bond was to delegitimize the state. Most nineteenth-century Americans agreed that governments derived their power from the family, not from the individual, so gender-blind citizenship was anathema to democracy. Debates like the one between Brook and Coles played out across the region. In this case, the dispute lasted nine months after Janes started her "Equal Suffrage" columns, until the *Clay County News* stopped publishing rebuttals. By that point, the battle had devolved into a series of personal attacks. To Coles, Brooke was the "antichrist" and woman suffrage was to blame for everything, including intemperance, divorce, heathenism, and murder. Brooke dubbed Coles a blind, dishonest, and ignorant fool. While there was no victor, there were lessons learned. Demanding individual liberty was not an effective argument in the Midwest, and suffragists eventually reconfigured their message to reassure their neighbors that the domestic sphere would remain intact if women voted. Discarding nineteenth-century arguments led activists to adopt twentieth-century ones about civic responsibility.[23]

Iowa suffragists continued to test their arguments throughout the last two decades of the nineteenth century. Their informal campaigning included meeting with legislators, circulating petitions, distributing propaganda, and handing out literature at the annual Iowa State Fair. In 1886 the IWSA established a monthly newspaper called the *Woman's Standard*, and by 1891 the society had rebranded itself as the Iowa Equal Suffrage Association (IESA). The renamed group increased its efforts at local organization, sending out four field workers in 1893 and hiring a Kansas suffragist, Laura Johns, to organize supporters two years later. Eventually, Carrie Chapman Catt, a national leader raised in Iowa, instructed the IESA to secure a woman suffrage amendment.

Despite the legislature's biannual schedule, suffragists believed that Iowans were ready to endorse the cause. In the spring of 1897 lecturers scoured the state, reportedly organizing in 94 of Iowa's 99 counties, including Clay County. Thirteen years had passed since the controversial "Equal Suffrage" columns, and suffragists had learned a great deal. They avoided any claims about individual liberty, asserting instead that woman suffrage purified politics. They noted how the cause brought "new dignity" to politics by harnessing the "moral force" of women, and they embraced politics from within the family, not outside of it. Activists also avoided temperance, preferring to treat the suffrage cause as a single issue.[24]

The message that emanated from the IESA's convention in Clay County in June 1897 was one of community development and civic responsibility. Speakers like Adelaide Ballard, president of the IESA, assured audiences that the ballot was insurance for a better community. With their moral influence, women could protect the interests of the home and purify politics. Suffragists noted that these arguments were effective because they embraced women's domestic role while also celebrating their civic activism. Local advocates noted happily that churches were now some of the first organizations to support the cause. As one speaker reported, "not a church in the United States would open its doors" to suffragists in the early days of the movement. But civic responsibility had resonated with churchgoers, and now congregations welcomed suffragists with open arms and eager audiences. The speaker's comment undoubtedly rang true with attendees who were enjoying the hospitality of the Methodist Episcopal Church in Spencer. By the end of the convention, participants had elected an executive committee and looked forward to a sustained campaign.[25]

When the Iowa legislature voted down the woman suffrage amendment in 1898, suffragists in Clay County struggled to preserve any remaining momentum. They had met a second time, in September 1897, and added additional delegates from suffrage clubs at Meadow, Riverton, Spencer, Gilletts Grove, and Greenville. Local pastors, including Mary Collson of the Unitarian Church and T. M. House of the Methodist Episcopal Church, had given speeches across northwest Iowa, espousing woman suffrage as fervently as they did their regular sermons. Locals even planned to conduct an extensive door-to-door petition drive to coincide with the legislative session. News of the amendment's defeat in 1898 upset activists, however, and although they promised to "unite in a vigorous protest" and "demonstrate their convictions," they failed to act. Twelve months of vibrant advocacy ended with a whimper in Clay County. Another convention held in May 1898 produced no plans for future work, and eighteen years passed before two consecutive sessions of the Iowa legislature approved a woman suffrage measure.[26]

South Dakota

Compared to Minnesota and Iowa, South Dakota experienced two intense nineteenth-century campaigns for woman suffrage. The state had little developed infrastructure and a low population density because it gained statehood late in the settlement period, in November 1889. Scattered settlements helped to physically separate an ethnically diverse population split between native-born Yankees and immigrants who came mostly from Germany, Norway, and Sweden. In addition, these noncitizens could vote on first papers, which were granted with two years' residency. National suffragists were wary of immigrants, especially Germans, whom they felt more often resisted assimilation efforts. Incorporating foreigners into their campaigns became an obvious and troubling problem because campaigns were frequent in South Dakota. Unlike Minnesota and Iowa, South Dakota required only a simple majority in both houses of the legislature to pass on an amendment to the voters. Advocates proposed three woman suffrage amendments in the last decade of the nineteenth century, including one in 1890 and another in 1898 that asked voters to consider amendments for full female enfranchisement. A third measure, in 1894, requested an amendment only for suffrage in school elections. Even though each campaign ended in defeat, failure paved the way for success in the twentieth century.

Although eight years separated the two major campaigns, suffragists campaigning in South Dakota faced the same set of obstacles on both occasions. Distances were vast and travel difficult. Many times, speakers had to ride twenty miles between afternoon and evening meetings. Inexperienced local organizers also struggled with planning, and financial deficiencies made execution problematic. In addition, woman suffrage suffered from an association with temperance. When South Dakota achieved statehood, voters also passed prohibition by a slim margin, and it existed in the state from 1889 to 1897. Many people despised the law, and alcohol consumption remained an important aspect of life in the state, especially among foreign-born immigrants. Officials often did not enforce the measure, and they grumbled about lost tax revenue from liquor licenses and fees. Even though prohibition was a separate issue, secured in 1889 by a majority of voters, many South Dakotans blamed women for putting undue influence on their husbands to force the law's passage. Finally, leadership between national and state suffragists was often antagonistic, and disagreements abounded among workers over tactics and rhetoric. In 1890 the American Woman Suffrage Association (AWSA) combined with the National Woman Suffrage Association (NWSA) to form the National American Woman Suffrage Association (NAWSA). South Dakota was the first campaign for the newly christened group, and NAWSA hoped that victory there would create a domino effect across the West. Instead, they found a disorganized group of local activists whose interests in temperance and third-party politics competed directly with woman suffrage. Eight years later, these competing interests led NAWSA to break with suffragists in South Dakota.[27]

The 1890 woman suffrage campaign in South Dakota opened in January, and tensions between national and state leaders abounded from the start. Antagonisms grew out of organizational ineptitude and a power struggle. Two months earlier, state leaders had begged Susan B. Anthony to give a lecture tour in the Dakota Territory, assuring her that people there were ready to support the cause. Voters had passed prohibition in October 1889 in a separate referendum, and leading advocates took it as a sign of South Dakota's progressive tilt. It was a stretch, and when she arrived, Anthony faced a mix of apathy and hostility. When she disembarked from the train at Yankton County, the station was deserted and no one was there to greet her. Anthony had to wait until a wagon took her to a local hotel. Without a sponsor, Anthony could not arrange any lectures, so she remained "at rest" for the duration of her stay. The remainder of the tour was just as disappointing, and Anthony grew wary of the empty promises of South Dakota's suffrage leaders.[28]

A battle over financial control led to the first major conflict of the campaign. In October 1889, activists in South Dakota had created the South Dakota Equal Suffrage Association (SDESA) to coordinate the campaign, but they lacked experience and cash. In their desperation, two members of the group, Alonzo Wardall, who was also secretary of the Farmers' Alliance, and Alice Pickler, who also represented the WCTU, attended the first convention of NAWSA. They begged national leaders, including Susan B. Anthony, for funds and support. Anthony agreed to help the SDESA, but she demanded absolute control of the campaign. Wardall and Pickler happily agreed, but the intrusion did not sit well with other members of the SDESA. When Anthony successfully raised almost $40,000 for the campaign, some in the SDESA demanded that Anthony give the funds directly to them. Anthony refused, preferring to distribute the money herself. Two members of the SDESA especially resented her decision. S. A. Ramsey, president of the SDESA, warned Anthony to "keep her hands off" South Dakota, expressing "misgivings" about her leadership. Marietta Bones, one of the state's first suffrage advocates, went further, accusing Anthony of fraud. In a series of interviews Bones went on a rampage, calling Anthony a "trickster" who "seriously crippled" the campaign by her "interference in South Dakota affairs." While Anthony deftly downplayed these remarks, she was, at the very least, annoyed. When Anthony established campaign headquarters at Huron in May 1890, she installed new SDESA leaders at a mass convention. Delegates elected a new slate of state officers, including Philena E. Johnson, who was also a member of the WCTU, as president and Alonzo Wardall, a leader of the Farmers' Alliance, as vice president.[29]

Anthony instructed the SDESA to adopt a threefold campaign strategy. She believed the chief obstacles were ignorance and indifference, so educating people through face-to-face contact became essential. She envisioned a team of lecturers canvassing the state, mustering audiences wherever they could. The message was one of individual liberty, and the SDESA, along with national leaders, claimed female autonomy to make their case. In addition to giving talks, lecturers organized local suffrage clubs whose members worked to enroll more supporters and distribute literature. Finally, Anthony sought endorsements from the state's major political parties, hoping to secure a woman suffrage plank from each group. By coordinating a multi-tiered approach, Anthony hoped for a favorable outcome in November. Anthony readily admitted that victory in South Dakota meant a great deal. She hoped to provoke a domino effect, encouraging other western states like North Dakota and Kansas to pass similar amendments. South Dakota was also the first campaign for the newly christened NAWSA. Triumph in South Dakota promised to erase any lingering concerns about merging the AWSA and NWSA, so the 1890 campaign was crucial. Anthony sent her best speakers into the field and directed the campaign herself. For Anthony, it was personal.[30]

Despite these plans, the SDESA faced several complications produced by internal problems and external factors. On paper the tactics seemed sound, but in practice, the strategies required a momentum that did not exist. Local campaigning sputtered into intense but short-lived bursts of activity instead of sustained action. A single visit was not enough to stir up pro-suffrage sentiment when residents expressed deep skepticism and downright hostility. Opposition was strong and, in some areas, organized. One anti-suffrage convention invited all who believed in "the strictly legal subjugation of women" to join in preserving "moral character" and "family purity" by rejecting woman suffrage. While pro-suffrage lecturers relied on thought-provoking rhetoric to change minds, they lacked the sustained contact required to build convictions. For many rural South Dakotans, the 1890 campaign was the first time they had encountered anyone who endorsed woman suffrage. They needed time to consider the cause, discuss its merits, and apply it to their own interests. Moreover, state and national leaders presumed that local leaders, once selected, had the time, talents, and resources to carry on the campaign according to NAWSA's high standards. Small-town suffragists did the best they could, but they often failed to live up to expectations. Finally, most South Dakotans rejected a rhetoric based on gender equality, and most people received calls for female independence with skepticism and fear.[31]

While the SDESA struggled with these internal issues, it also encountered elements outside its control. First, ethnic and class divisions hampered the efforts of local advocates. Most suffragists were Yankees, and they struggled to connect with foreigners who were wary of outsiders and lived in isolated enclaves. Finding common ground with these newcomers was difficult, especially among immigrants who did not speak English. Second, the timing of the campaign was also a significant factor. People were still settling South Dakota, and rural women were in the process of crafting their civic identities. Although women founded libraries, supported schools, and built churches, they had not yet established a long-term record of civic activism. The seasonal timing of the campaign also shaped its outcome. As Anthony remembered, the summer of 1890 was the "hottest and driest summer on record." A twenty-mile train or buggy ride exhausted lecturers, and country-dwelling suffragists, particularly farmers, gave priority to their crops shriveling in the hot sun rather than the suffragist cause. Third, volatility in South Dakota politics influenced the outcome of the 1890 campaign. The creation of a third party shook up the election, and suffragists struggled to gather partisan support. Part of the problem was that suffragists failed to separate woman suffrage from temperance. They appreciated the WCTU's endorsement of the "home protection" ballot and relied on its networks of activism, but they cringed when voters assumed that all suffragists were prohibitionists. Perceptions intensified against suffragists when NAWSA allowed members of the WCTU to hold executive positions in the SDESA, and unfortunately this decision only created further confusion. The best Anthony could do was to advise workers to avoid offense and work with both "license" and "Prohibition men."[32]

In a campaign where the difficulties seemed to outweigh the likelihood of victory, suffragists displayed a tremendous amount of tenacity. Lecturers arrived in the state as early as March 1890, two months before Anthony set up camp in Huron. At least two of these lecturers, Matilda Hindman of Pennsylvania and Helen Gouger of Indiana, knew something about the Midwest, as they had campaigned in Iowa in 1884. Another woman, Emma Smith DeVoe, was from Huron and joined the effort as the state lecturer of the SDESA. Other speakers came from neighboring states, like Minnesota. A future president of the MWSA, Julia B. Nelson, joined the campaign as a lecturer, and she became perhaps its most valuable asset. Married into a Norwegian family, Nelson spoke Norwegian, which meant that she could engage with Scandinavian audiences. That the SDESA hired her revealed that suffragists did not ignore foreigners, despite their prejudices against them. In fact, the WCTU reportedly donated thousands of pro-suffrage leaflets printed in foreign languages to the SDESA. A vote in favor of the amendment, whether it was from a native-born citizen or a Norwegian, German, or Swede, was still a vote. Already at this early juncture in campaigning, Anthony and the SDESA determined that they could not afford to snub ethnic voters when there were so many of them.[33]

In April 1890 the first wave of suffrage activity rolled into Yankton County with the arrival of nationally renowned speakers, including

Hindman, Anthony, and Anna Howard Shaw. It was part of a targeted canvass of South Dakota, beginning in the southeast before moving north and west. Over the course of six days, from April 9 to April 15, Hindman spoke once in Mission Hill, Walshtown, and Lesterville and two times in Yankton. She admitted that she encountered opposition, particularly among German farmers in the county, but she naively maintained that, by November, the amendment would carry "by a large majority." Shaw engaged audiences at the Congregational Church and at a bazaar organized by the Methodist Episcopal Ladies' Aid Society. Hindman and Shaw did more than just thrill audiences; they also inspired local organization. In April 1890 a group of people, mostly Yankees, formed the Yankton County Equal Suffrage Association. Many were members of the Congregational and Methodist Episcopal churches and the local chapter of the WCTU. Officers included both men and women, and most of the meetings took place at the Methodist Church. In addition to the Equal Suffrage Association, the local WCTU supported the cause, devoting its conventions for the year to woman suffrage. In the spring, as a part of its regular program, the WCTU included an "equal suffrage bible reading" and heard an "Address on Equal Suffrage" from a local minister. Unlike the turmoil that divided the WCTU in Clay County, most of the officers of the WCTU in Yankton County supported woman suffrage without provoking conflict. Attitudes toward woman suffrage had softened in the seven months since Anthony had first visited Yankton County. When she returned there in May 1890 she "delighted a large audience," which was a far cry from her visit the previous November.[34]

Woman suffrage activity swelled during the spring of 1890, as lecturers organized clubs and locals took charge of grassroots campaigning. Anthony's threefold strategy seemed sound, and the final element—gaining the endorsement of the state's political parties—promised to complete the trifecta. As spring turned to summer, however, temperatures sizzled and tempers flared. The first blow fell in July 1890, when the Farmers' Alliance and the Knights of Labor held their convention. As alternatives to the Republican and Democratic machines, these groups had attracted voters outside mainstream politics, including foreign-born men, laborers, and farmers. Until that summer, the Alliance had served as a "pressure group" within the Republican Party, and its members typically voted for Republican candidates. Just a month before the campaign, the Alliance had endorsed woman suffrage, unanimously adopting a resolution to demand that no person "be disenfranchised on account of sex." With yellow ribbons on their lapels, the "whole assembly [arose] *en masse* and cheered vociferously" at the news. Anthony saw in the Farmers' Alliance a golden opportunity. Here was a group explicitly in favor of woman suffrage that also held substantial sway in one of the two major political parties. Anthony's biographer later argued that she only took on the campaign because Alliance leaders like Alonzo Wardall assured her that they could compel the Republican Party to endorse the cause. Anthony even placed Wardall and his wife, Elizabeth, in executive positions in the SDESA. She so trusted the Alliance that she called for a mass meeting in Huron on July 8 to coincide with the Alliance's convention there the next day. She expected Alliance delegates to endorse the cause and challenge Republicans to do the same.[35]

At the July 8 mass meeting, suffragists could not hide their giddy anticipation. They boasted at how "thoroughly organized" South Dakota was and claimed that residents supported the cause wholeheartedly. Glee turned to dismay the next day when Alliance delegates voted to form the Independent Party without a woman suffrage plank in their platform. Anthony was crushed. As a third party, the Independents held far less power in the balance of state politics. Anthony also realized that to gain credibility and sway Republican and Democratic voters, the Independents would have to avoid controversial political topics like woman suffrage until the election was over. Anthony was furious. The Independent Party had forsaken woman suffrage, but the reason it did so was maddening. In a private message to fellow suffragist Alice Pickler, Anthony explained that they scorned the cause "for the avowed object of *winning* the *votes* of . . . *Foreigners* among them" (emphasis in the original). Anthony felt betrayed that the Independent Party chose to cultivate support among immigrants over women, since in her vision of citizenship, native-born women deserved inclusion over foreigners. Worse yet, without an endorsement from the Independents, suffragists had no leverage with which to pressure Republicans or Democrats to adopt woman suffrage planks. Infuriated, Anthony dismissed the officers of the SDESA during a final "stormy session" of the mass meeting. She installed new executives—the third set for the SDESA since the campaign began—while retaining her position as head of the executive committee.[36]

Newspaper reports that followed the convention revealed the tur- moil that tore apart suffragists in South Dakota in the summer of 1890. According to one article, the "only thing accomplished was securing the resignation of the officers and executive committee of the State Suffrage association, and electing new officers and committee[s]." These officers were "induced to present their resignation," and the report noted, "the proceedings of the conference committee are being kept as private as possible. Some interesting developments may be looked for within the next few days." In an article published a couple weeks later, an anon- ymous "traveling gentleman" argued that "there was not a ghost of a show for" woman suffrage because the "suffragists themselves were not working harmoniously, and among the church people there was a lack of unanimity in regard, not only to the expediency of the movement, but its effect upon public morals." Woman suffrage was radical because of its threat to the family, a political grenade that was ready to explode all that Americans held dear. Like the Independents, the Democrats and Republicans ignored woman suffrage to focus on the three-way bat- tle for control of the state. The November election tested the power of machine politics. For Republicans, the Independent Party threatened its base, since many Alliance members were also Republicans. For Demo- crats, the Independent Party became an attractive option, since joining it could pull enough votes away from Republican candidates. Caught in the crosshairs was woman suffrage. Politicians from every party wielded it as a bargaining chip rather than a legitimate measure, and previously supportive candidates soon distanced themselves from the cause.[37]

Both Republicans and Democrats snubbed national and state suf- fragists at their state conventions held in the summer of 1890. Dem- ocrats met at Aberdeen a week after the Independents, and speakers spewed vitriolic attacks against Anthony and the SDESA. When E. W. Miller, a land receiver from Huron, took the floor, he declared that "no decent, respectable woman asked for the ballot; that the women who did so were a disgrace to their homes; that when women voted men would have to suckle the babies." While the SDESA called Miller's speech "indecent" and rude, it received "prolonged and vigorous cheers" from Democratic delegates. Reactions were similar among Repub- licans, who met at their convention in Mitchell at the end of August. Factions spent more time jostling over candidates than considering their platform, and when they finally produced one, woman suffrage was absent from it. This omission was not due to a lack of effort from advocates, however. The SDESA had called another mass meeting to coincide with the convention, and suffragists gathered two days before the Republicans in the same skating rink-turned-opera house. When Republicans began their session, they even opened the floor to two suffragist speakers, Olympia Brown and Anna Howard Shaw. Despite their presence, Republicans opted to sacrifice woman suffrage for a platform that gave concessions to farmers, laborers, and immigrants. They did not want to lose the coming election to the Independent Party. Afterward, Anthony assured South Dakotans that the suffragists were not disappointed at the omission. Because of the "mixed condition of politics," suffrage leaders felt it wise that suffrage remain a stand-alone issue, one not wedded to any particular party. It was a lie. Anthony and the SDESA actually longed for an endorsement from a major political party, recognizing that they needed the clout of mainstream political institutions to win in November.[38]

State and national suffrage leaders were heartbroken at their treatment at the Republican state convention. At the time, they claimed that delegates were courteous, but in later recollections they condemned the disrespect they had received. In a speech given two years later, Carrie Chapman Catt listed a series of abuses. First, when the suffragists arrived, officials seated them in the most remote corner of the opera hall. They could neither see nor hear from their position. Second, when a resolution to enfranchise Native Americans passed unanimously, officers allowed three Lakota men to enter the session and sit "honorably," with clear views of the proceedings. Finally, when Republicans finally turned the floor over to Olympia Brown, the chair adjourned the session to allow committees to conduct business at separate locations. Brown spoke to an empty room. Catt declared that the Republicans greatly insulted women that day, choosing "half barbarous Indians" over "moral intelligent women citizens." The suffragists also saw a troubling pattern emerge. Just as the Independent Party had favored the interests of foreigners, so too did the Republican Party endorse the suffrage of Native Americans in preference to that of native-born women.[39]

As fall arrived, suffragists turned back to local organization, moving forward after their disappointing encounters with state politicians. The formation of the Independent Party had taught Anthony that South Dakota politicians were unreliable. In desperation, she quickly revised her plan of attack to focus exclusively on grassroots campaigning. Anthony called on "home talent," or local advocates, to convince South Dakotans to support the suffrage cause. She reinitiated the statewide canvass, sending lecturers with propaganda to the most remote corners of each county. In doing so she opened the campaign to everyone regardless of their ethnic background, religious affiliation, or political sway, and suffragists found themselves catering especially to Germans and Scandinavians. Anthony even instructed state headquarters to provide non-English speakers and literature wherever needed. She directed locals to make everything about suffrage. Tea parties, dinners, bazaars, debate contests, and other gatherings ought to become "yellow tea parties" and "suffrage dinners." Yellow was the official color of the suffrage movement. It referred to the decorations used at the tea, not the color of the tea itself. Anthony dubbed this line of work the "'do-every-thing' policy."[40]

By late August 1890, state and local workers had set the "do-everything" plan in motion, and in Yankton County organizers took the instructions seriously. They received Nettie Hall, a native South Dakotan with a background in farming, as their first speaker. Hall did not let rough terrain impede her canvass of the county, and she rode on horseback to isolated areas. At first, she struggled mightily. Among Scandinavians at Volin, Hall organized a tiny suffrage club, but she could find only a handful of supporters. "There are so few in this place to do anything," she explained. Other stops on her tour were hopeless. At Lesterville, Germans rebuked her, refusing her any place to meet. A few days later, Hall rode more than seven miles in the rain to an enclave of German Catholics, who also directed her to leave immediately. At another unnamed hamlet, Hall wanted a space large enough to accommodate a sizable audience. Unfortunately, all of the local churches refused, and public officials quoted her exorbitant prices for any other spaces. With disappointment Hall wrote to headquarters, claiming that she believed she could "organize and get an audience" in Yankton County but that "every thing conspires against me." After ten days in the field, Hall's persistence paid off. Members of the local Farmers' Alliance welcomed her, and she happily reported that she had "made converts" and had a "splendid audience." A few days later, Hall spoke to Scandinavian farmers at a rural school in the eastern corner of the county. "I heard I stirred them up," she cheerfully reported.[41]

Woman suffrage activity flourished in Yankton County as national speakers and local advocates gained momentum, albeit temporarily. With two months until the election, Yankton resident Julia King, a prominent member of the WCTU, organized a county-wide convention on September 5, featuring the national speaker Anna Howard Shaw, who drew a "good sized audience." King was a Yankee, a member of the WCTU, and was married to a fire insurance salesman. She was an elite who did not share the same background as most rural residents of the county. King agitated for the suffragist cause wherever she could. At the eighth annual convention of the WCTU, King and others decorated the hall with flags, flowers, and banners. One motto read "our future voters," which one correspondent to the *Press and Dakotan* thought was "a trifle premature." King hoped that Shaw's visit would spur widespread interest among all the residents of Yankton County, but King especially targeted foreign-born farmers. She had struggled to reach "that class," she noted, because she was a Yankee with few ties to agrarian life. King praised Nettie Hall's efforts, but she explained that she needed more speakers from diverse backgrounds. State leaders eventually acquiesced, sending three lecturers and carefully staggering their arrivals in a thorough and sustained canvass. As these speakers infiltrated remote pockets of settlement, they had to reckon with a constellation of ethnic identities, religious views, and political sentiments.[42]

Campaigning in Yankton County in the fall of 1890 both confirmed and challenged the assumptions suffragists had about foreigners, and the campaign showed how community dynamics could bend political expectations. In general, suffragists believed that Germans tended to oppose the cause while Norwegians usually supported it. They also contended that religion shaped attitudes, with Catholics typically against woman suffrage and Protestants in favor of it. While Hall's August canvass seemed to confirm these stereotypes, other encounters challenged them. In September Carrie Chapman Catt, in her first national campaign, won converts among German Catholic farmers near Volin, where she sold seventy-two badges. Badges were buttons or pins worn to indicate public support for woman suffrage, which made Catt's sale to a group of German Catholics all the more surprising. In early October Julia B. Nelson, who could speak Norwegian, traveled across the northern tier of the county, encountering a range of responses from Germans and Norwegians living there. At Jamesville, Nelson dared not leave her

buggy when groups of German Mennonites and Norwegian Lutherans threatened her with physical harm. The fourteen-mile buggy ride
back to her hotel was undoubtedly lonely. At Norway, Nelson reported
that Norwegian Lutherans were more enthusiastic about woman suffrage, a notable report considering that the Norway ladies' aid society
had gained a strong civic reputation for its annual Thanksgiving Day
bazaar. Nelson made sure to send leaflets entitled "Jesus Christ the
Emancipator of Women" to the village, convinced the message would
resonate with Lutherans there.[43]

Less than two weeks before the election, Emma Smith DeVoe arrived
in Yankton County and gave a number of lectures in a last-ditch attempt
to enlist support among residents there. Her stump speech reportedly
captivated audiences, and she began it by claiming the Constitution
was "broad enough" to "admit all mankind to a free exercise of all liberties." The Constitution protected the rights of all individuals, including
native-born women, in a liberal democracy. "It says we the people," she
explained, and "if women are not people, what are they?" DeVoe also
critiqued ignorant foreign voters with an illustration that compared
an American girl to a European boy. With an American education, the
girl became a resourceful woman, owning property and paying taxes.
In contrast, the boy moved to the United States with no "property or
knowledge of our institutions." While he became a naturalized citizen
who voted, the American girl never could vote. DeVoe demanded that
voters extend "the same privilege" to native-born women as they did to
foreigners. While DeVoe inspired at least one Yankton County woman
to pledge "to do all that can posibaly [*sic*] be done now," it was unfortunately too little and too late.[44]

Despite the heightened level of activity in the days leading up to the
election, South Dakotans rejected the woman suffrage amendment by
a two-to-one margin. In Yankton County, the tally at some precincts
was not even close. Voters at the Broadway precinct recorded 196
against and 15 for the amendment, a crushing blow to local advocates.
Anthony and other members of NAWSA blamed foreign opposition
and third-party politics for the defeat. They had feared that without the
endorsement of a major political party, especially in a high-stakes election, woman suffrage had no leverage, and they were right. In addition,
national suffrage leaders accused immigrants, especially Germans but
also some Scandinavians, of casting the majority of their votes against

the amendment. The suffragists saw ethnic voters as dim-witted out-siders who were too undiscriminating to distinguish temperance from woman suffrage. Anthony also pointed out that while woman suffrage had failed, South Dakotans had passed an amendment to enfranchise Native Americans. Anthony claimed that poor wording had led vot-ers to mistakenly choose Native Americans over native-born women, although little evidence indicates that the problem was widespread. It was also weak criticism in a state that had rejected gender equality by a large margin.[45]

The outcome of the 1890 campaign in South Dakota haunted suf-fragists for decades. National leaders reveled in swapping horror sto-ries from the field, as if the experience both fascinated and trauma-tized them. Some remembered sleeping in sod homes with only buffalo chips as fuel for the fire. Others recalled rural people who were suffer-ing from incredible drought and poverty, with little food to offer. Audi-ences vacillated between cheers and jeers, and lecturers became anx-ious wrecks. State leaders shivered as they recalled the "dark day" when "all the labor expended and sacrifices made" failed to "touch the hearts and fire the souls" of voters. South Dakota almost broke the resolve of NAWSA, especially when the Independent Party erased woman suf-frage from its platform. While suffragists blamed ethnic voters and third-party politics for the loss, the simple and harsh reality was that most South Dakotans—like most midwesterners at the time—did not believe women ought to vote. They could not envision equal citizen-ship within a political system that perceived gender as a legitimate measure of civic aptitude. By 1890 midwestern women were engaging heartily in community-building endeavors, but they had not yet estab-lished acclaimed civic records. Female autonomy was frightening, and suffragists had not yet discovered an argument based on civic obliga-tion. In the end, the 1890 campaign confirmed that woman suffrage was radical and politically unsafe.

Despite the results, national suffrage leaders maintained an aston-ishing level of hope. They overlooked the overwhelming margin of defeat by casting blame on outside forces. Instead of self-reflection, suf-fragists sharpened their nativist inclinations and deepened their belief that they must separate woman suffrage from temperance. According to historian Wanda Hendricks, by the mid-1890s NAWSA was pursuing a policy of white supremacy when it called for the disenfranchisement of black and foreign-born immigrant male voters by demanding rigid educational qualifications.[46]

Indignant at the outcome of the 1890 campaign, NAWSA developed a certain animosity against South Dakotans and pledged little support for any future suffrage activities in the state. Suffrage leaders cautioned the SDESA against proposing future amendments, believing residents too opposed to the cause. They also grew suspicious of the large contingent of WCTU officers who, by 1894, occupied almost all of the positions in the SDESA. The WCTU's takeover of the SDESA was more practical than predatory, since no other individuals or groups had volunteered to lead the fight for the ballot. The connection between temperance and suffrage frustrated NAWSA, however, and Anna Howard Shaw warned that unless the SDESA divorced woman suffrage from temperance, they had little hope for success. NAWSA did not participate in the 1894 campaign to enact school suffrage in South Dakota, and without funding or organization, the SDESA accomplished little. Few records exist from the campaign, and South Dakotans defeated the measure, although it lost by only about 5,600 votes.[47]

Three years later, NAWSA was horrified to learn that the SDESA planned to petition the legislature for full suffrage once again. Catt and Shaw advised SDESA officials to change their plans, believing that South Dakotans were "not yet prepared" to endorse the cause. The SDESA had no choice but to support the measure, which passed the legislature and moved to a vote at the general election, scheduled for November 1898. Upon hearing the news, Catt was blunt. She refused to allow NAWSA to participate in the campaign, withholding financial support, talented professional speakers, and advice. She estimated that the campaign would cost at least $10,000, but she pledged not even one cent. NAWSA effectively abandoned suffragists in South Dakota, forsaking the 1898 campaign because it believed that temperance and "backward" immigrant voters meant certain defeat.[48]

Suffragists in South Dakota, rejected and forlorn, faced what they saw as difficult odds. The results of the 1890 and 1894 campaigns had hurt them, too, and they lamented the unpopularity of the suffrage cause. State leaders shared NAWSA's fears that voters, especially ethnic ones, wanted nothing more than to sabotage another suffrage measure. The unstable political terrain also continued to skew politics, and after 1896 the Independent Party fused with the Populists. Populism was attractive to South Dakotans, and many Democrats joined the renegade group. While these reformers set ambitious goals to regulate railroad rates and establish the free coinage of silver, they mostly avoided the issue of woman suffrage. Populists dominated the election of 1896, winning the governorship, control of the state legislature, and two seats in Congress. Finally, temperance emerged as a prominent political issue after 1897, when a majority of South Dakotans rejected prohibition. The legislature reestablished a license system, and unrestricted liquor interests, legal once again, moved back into the state.

Changing tides in South Dakota's political culture in 1898 forced the leaders of the WCTU and SDESA to proceed carefully. During the 1890 campaign prohibition has been law, so suffrage advocates could avoid direct agitation for temperance at the local level. In 1898, however, the SDESA—comprised almost entirely of WCTU state officers—explicitly connected the reestablishment of prohibition with woman suffrage. It was a dangerous maneuver in a state where sentiment had shifted against prohibition. Despite these obstacles, the SDESA moved forward with its plans. It had little choice; the legislature had placed the suffrage amendment on the November 1898 electoral ballot. Without NAWSA, state and local leaders took charge, and the absence of NAWSA created a campaign unlike any other in the history of the woman suffrage movement. Eight years earlier Susan B. Anthony had dictated plans personally, but in 1898 a grassroots effort emerged. It relied on a massive force of ordinary but dedicated individuals who dove headfirst into midwestern politics. They were untrained and inexperienced, but as they pressed forward, they developed political identities. The records they left provide a rare look at how midwesterners navigated the intersection of gender, politics, class, and ethnicity.[49]

Victory required sustained and well-managed work, but suffragists in South Dakota lacked the resources to create the campaign they planned. NAWSA's denial of funds was one thing, but its prohibiting trained lecturers from assisting local advocates was devastating. Campaigning fell to regular South Dakotans, and they readily assumed roles ordinarily assigned to veteran field organizers. Planning was the easy part; more difficult was executing those plans. For the first time, activists admitted that their biggest problem was the widespread unpopularity of woman suffrage. Most midwesterners believed that women were dependents, and they found claims of female autonomy threatening.

What arguments could convince these midwesterners that woman suffrage was not radical? How could they shift an entire population's mindset? As suffragists grappled with these questions, they offered a telling piece of advice to local suffrage clubs. "Do not expect too great results at once," they cautioned. "Prejudices die slowly. Keep hammering away." In these lines, the SDESA revealed its vision for the 1898 campaign. Only an inclusive campaign aimed directly at voters at the precinct level could warm those voters to the cause. The SDESA coached precinct chairmen to engage tactfully with voters, cajoling those who were opposed in an effort to change their minds. Transforming political attitudes required personalized attention and persistence. There was no magic elixir—just repeated, sustained interactions with voters that could soften hearts and change minds to favor the suffrage cause.[50]

On paper the campaign plans seemed sound, but in practice, a comprehensive canvass of each precinct was unrealistic. Locals made do with what they had. In many communities, sociability flourished among neighbors, and suffragists could embed a precinct canvass within neighborhood events, like a church bazaar, without ruffling feathers. They also began to shift their rhetoric to favor civic responsibility. By 1898, many rural women had established reputations for their community-building projects. Their public service changed the campaign message to one built on civic activism, although lecturers still argued for individual liberty and claimed gender equality. As one organizer put it, when "a large per cent of women" participated in community development and the "burdens of government," but lacked the "opportunity of expressing an opinion," they could not carry out their obligations. To vote was to resolve this problem and allow women to contribute fully to community life as citizens. Locals also had no qualms about involving immigrants in the campaign. Friendships and neighborliness had grown since settlement began, and foreign-born women understood civic activism, too. Local activists also knew that immigrants with first papers could vote. Ignoring ethnic voters was reckless.[51]

The fate of the 1898 campaign in South Dakota often rested on individuals living in small towns. In some communities those activists simply did not exist. In others, individuals devoted an astounding amount of energy to the cause. In Yankton County, the Vanderhule family largely orchestrated the campaign. At the helm were 59-year-old Matilda Bramble Vanderhule and her 27-year-old daughter-in-law

Adena, who singlehandedly brought woman suffrage to Yankton County in 1898. Born in Vermont, Matilda and her husband, George, had come to Yankton sometime before 1880. They followed her brother, Downer T. Bramble, who was one of the first white men in Yankton County. Adena married Matilda's oldest son, Clarence, who took over his father's pharmacy business after 1900. They were a well-known family. Matilda was a member of the WCTU and Eastern Star while George was a Mason. They were also active in their church. The Vanderhules were civic leaders with social and familial connections that proved tremendously important to the campaign. They reorganized the Yankton County Equal Suffrage Association, defunct since 1890, and under that banner they set to work, focusing on immigrant communities located in rural areas of the county. They also were responding to advice from NAWSA to target farmers. As Catt wrote, it was not that farmers were less "intelligent as the people in the towns, for I do not think this is true." She believed, without explaining why, that the "country people are more favorable."[52]

Late-nineteenth-century political campaigning in South Dakota required copious correspondence, and Matilda and Adena spent most of their time writing letters to officials in the SDESA. Securing a speaker or requesting literature meant a flurry of papers sent back and forth among a variety of advocates, and the duo relied on patience and good memories to keep track of conversations spread out over many days. Matilda spent much of her time arranging speaking engagements and pleading for organizational support. In particular, she demanded German- and Norwegian-speaking lecturers to canvass the county, but lacking one, SDESA never sent a German speaker to Yankton County. In late August, Matilda learned that the SDESA planned to send Emma Cranmer, a lecturer from Aberdeen, to southeast South Dakota, traveling into Yankton County from the east after organizing Clay County. Cranmer only spoke English, but as a South Dakotan, she showed proper deference to ethnic customs and highlighted her shared rural background to ethnic audiences. Matilda arranged a "schoolhouse campaign," with thirteen lectures in fifteen days. It was an intense canvass, but Matilda recognized that if Cranmer were to reach the most remote enclaves, she needed to make every date.[53]

The logistics of a rigorous schedule were complicated, and Matilda relied on social connections to assist her efforts. Her civic power proved incredibly important as she delegated tasks to friends, family, and others she knew in the community. Personal relationships advanced political ambitions. Despite her public reputation, in dozens of letters to state headquarters, Matilda grew frustrated at how difficult it was to arrange Cranmer's tour. At each stop, Matilda had enlisted someone to host Cranmer, and the responsibilities were numerous: secure a large space with enough seating, lighting, restrooms, and refreshments for a large crowd; advertise Cranmer's arrival with posters, newspaper articles, and announcements at social gatherings; coordinate all travel from place to place; provide lodging, including meals and a warm bed; and entertain Cranmer by throwing a party and inviting friends and neighbors. When Matilda had to reschedule—which she did twice—it meant that thirteen people had to revise these elaborate plans. Cranmer had no idea of the behind-the-scenes twists and turns, and she cheerily reported to the SDESA that Matilda "makes things come to pass." Cranmer also did not realize that, on top of all the work of orchestrating her visit, Matilda also was directing dozens of precinct chairs to canvass their neighborhoods. Precinct chairs had little experience at political campaigning, but they did the best they could. At "precinct no. 7," located at Mayfield in the northwest corner of the county, farmer Fred Richter reported that the "chances of victory" were "very good." Since he provided no figures to prove these assertions, it seems he derived his assessment more from a general sense than from actual interviews.[54]

Cranmer had a successful visit to Yankton County in August 1898 because of the tireless work of Matilda and Adena Vanderhule. For example, at Mission Hill, Cranmer spoke at the Congregational Church. She wrote that the church was "splendid" with a full audience, and she collected nearly eighteen dollars for the cause. Meanwhile, Matilda continued to badger SDESA leaders to provide resources tailored to ethnic communities. Falling through the cracks were immigrants who could not speak English and who were a large portion of the population in the county. Despite the work that Cranmer accomplished on her "schoolhouse campaign," no independent suffrage groups organized outside of Yankton, the county seat. Both Matilda and Adena begged the SDESA to send Norwegian and German speakers. While the state association sent a "Scandinavian Lady Speaker" in September, it could not supply a German one. By October, Adena reported that the Yankton Equal Suffrage Association had received voter lists from each precinct, and it used the lists' names to continue to canvass each precinct. Her letter also revealed that two Norwegian-speaking suffragists had come to Yankton County to lecture, but apparently they had to leave before finishing their tour. Adena expressed her disappointment but promised to send literature instead. Pamphlets and leaflets were a sad substitute for lecturers, however, since suffragists had not translated most of their propaganda into German and Norwegian. It was also doubtful how many immigrants could read. This was a far cry from the personal interactions that the SDESA had planned, and it meant that local advocates had failed to engage a large portion of the non-English-speaking foreigners who could vote.[55]

While Matilda and Adena struggled to surmount the barriers of language, talent, and time, they also faced unforeseen problems. Mail service was slow, and the Vanderhules rarely received a swift response from the SDESA. Sometimes the women could not conceal their frustration. In a letter dated October 4, 1898, Adena repeated her sustained request for more speakers. She asked for more literature and reminded state officials that she was still waiting to hear about a proposed meeting of the county association. She could not hide her sense of urgency. "Please answer right away. . . . Please write directly. . . . When are you going to send the literature? . . . I wrote you in regard to our county association annual meeting but have rec'd no reply." Timing was everything in this campaign, and any delays created problems in what was already a difficult effort. Adena also noted that some anti-suffragists were scattering literature, stirring up opposition, and spreading lies. She was especially perturbed by attacks on her reputation, including slanderous accusations that she was an atheist and immoral woman for being a suffragist. In the face of all these troubles, the Vanderhules did the best they could, but speakers still missed their engagements, audiences failed to appear, and literature never reached its destination. NAWSA's absence was most palpable in these moments, when the SDESA faltered and local advocates had nowhere else to turn.[56]

The 1898 campaign in South Dakota was both an impressive display of tenacity and an abysmal failure of leadership. The dedication displayed by local advocates like Matilda and Adena Vanderhule was amazing, and it demonstrates their convictions with regard to gender equality. They believed in female enfranchisement enough to put their civic and social reputations on the line. Their devotion was commendable in a situation where the odds were never in their favor. The SDESA raised $1,500, but this was only a fraction of the estimated $10,000 that national suffragists determined necessary to achieve victory in the state. In addition to financial woes, suffragists also faced a dearth of talented lecturers and trained field organizers, leaving it up to ordinary South Dakotans with no experience to canvass precincts. This particular difficulty often overwhelmed even the most resolute advocates. Most counties did not have people like Matilda and Adena Vanderhule who could devote almost all their time and energy to the cause. For a people with livelihoods rooted in agriculture, the late summer and early fall were times of intensive labor. Harvests required long periods spent laboring in the fields, away from a desk and pens and paper. Speakers often arrived to discover that local advocates had failed to publicize their lecture schedules. Audiences did not appear, and local clubs never formed. Disappointment grew, and complaints abounded among members of the SDESA. Lecturers grumbled about "hours of tedious waiting" and "monotonous indifference." Ida Hazlett, a lecturer hired by the SDESA, reported that most meetings ended in disappointment. "It will be just like all the other meetings so far, none of the general public knowing anything about the meetings, not a voter reached to amount to anything, just a few old women out and three or four men who mean to vote that way anyway." Speakers and precinct canvasses were useless when farmers spent long days in their fields.[57]

When reports from South Dakota reached NAWSA, its leaders offered tepid condolences that only added salt to the SDESA's wounds. In a moment of pity, Carrie Chapman Catt sent the nationally renowned organizer Laura Gregg to South Dakota, agreeing to pay for her expenses for a month. Catt's generosity was short-lived. Gregg soon reported that over a seven-day period she had spoken to only thirty-seven people at six separate locations, collecting a paltry $1.17 in donations. Catt demanded that the SDESA release Gregg from her contract, explaining that it was an "imposition upon us to expect us to pay expenses and salary of a valuable woman in a doubtful campaign." Catt was careful to avoid blaming South Dakota suffragists for the organizational snafus. She recognized the difficulty in making arrangements without "the benefit of previous campaign experience," and she alluded to "mistakes" that had occurred "farther back" in time as the real culprits. She ended her note with the "hope" that "a miracle may be wrought in South Dakota and a victory come to you." Apparently officials in the SDESA did not appreciate Catt's sentiments, for in her next letter Catt pledged to continue to "hope and pray for the miracle," although she admitted that they seemed "rather resentful at me for calling it so." South Dakota suffragists clearly did not appreciate it when Catt revealed that she believed miraculous intervention, rather than their hard-fought efforts, would determine the outcome of their campaign.[58]

The 1898 campaign was a watershed moment in the history of woman suffrage in South Dakota. In November 1898 South Dakota voters defeated the amendment. Some suffragists took heart from the fact that the totals were remarkably close, with 19,698 in favor and 22,983 opposed. Despite these results, the loss still stung. The suffragists had failed to attract enough voters because they lacked a sustained campaign with sufficient resources and talent. They particularly struggled to accommodate foreigners with speakers and literature in their native languages. It was the last campaign the SDESA ever directed. In late 1898, Catt severed NAWSA's relationship with the SDESA. On December 15 she wrote directly to local advocates, asking them to pledge their allegiance to NAWSA. She commanded them to correspond only with the national association, requesting the names and contact information of the suffragists in each county. Catt effectively blacklisted the SDESA by denying them crucial information about the suffragists in their state, and state officers were crushed. It was a shrewd maneuver, done less out of spite and more because Catt believed that as long as the SDESA and WCTU shared the same officer corps, South Dakotans could not disentangle temperance from woman suffrage. In 1900, the SDESA confirmed that it had no intentions of cutting ties with the WCTU when it elected Alice Pickler, former head of the WCTU franchise department, as president.[59]

NAWSA ignored the SDESA for ten years, from 1899 to 1909, coordinating any activities directly with local clubs. Keeping track of every suffragist in South Dakota was a monumental task for NAWSA, however, and without coordination with the state association, the momentum for woman suffrage stopped. The SDESA dared not risk another amendment campaign, and without a specific objective, local clubs disbanded. Even the stalwart Vanderhules struggled to engage with people, and interest in the cause dissolved. In her last report, Matilda lamented, "I find the county people slow to move." By 1902 NAWSA began to demand that the WCTU officially separate from the SDESA. A few years later, national leaders selected a new crop of state workers for South Dakota, replacing the embattled SDESA with the South Dakota Universal Franchise League (SDUFL). Although senior activists were upset at the takeover, they accepted it. They did not want to repeat the 1898 campaign. NAWSA was a better friend than enemy.[60]

Lessons from Nineteenth-Century Campaigns

While the late-nineteenth-century campaigns in the Midwest ended in defeat, their outcomes shaped the woman suffrage movement in profound ways. They forced suffragists to remove the barriers that blocked the path to victory. They also helped the leaders of NAWSA, especially its new president, Carrie Chapman Catt, to clarify their goals and hone their political and organizational strategies. The campaigns in the Midwest helped Catt develop strong organizational skills that she used to cultivate a clear hierarchy with explicit instructions for achieving suffrage. Divorcing woman suffrage from temperance was also essential because it remade woman suffrage into a separate and single issue. Issue-based political campaigning brought disparate constituencies together and reenergized the movement. By the early twentieth century, a broad coalition of working-class, immigrant, elite, urban, rural, educated, and poor women had formed to advocate woman suffrage. As more women joined the effort, woman suffrage shed its radical label and gained currency with existing voters and established political parties.[61]

Not only did the suffragist cause benefit from its status as a single issue, but it also gained traction as nativist sentiment intensified in the United States. Millions of immigrants came to the United States in the late nineteenth and early twentieth centuries, and many Americans, including leaders in NAWSA, questioned their fitness for citizenship. These foreigners perplexed NAWSA, especially those living in almost two dozen states that gave them the right to vote on first papers. Their votes mattered in elections, so ignoring them seemed an unwise political move. Immigrants opposed the suffragist cause in overwhelming numbers, however, so NAWSA wondered if it made sense to include them in its work. Key figures like Susan B. Anthony detested foreigners, believing that the "ignorant vote" was "solid against women's emancipation." She thought that foreigners recklessly abused their power when they denied the ballot to native-born women who, unlike immigrants, enjoyed indisputable birthright citizenship.[62]

While Anthony and other leaders wrote off foreigners, a few voices paused to consider the ramifications of that decision. Carrie Chapman Catt waited to pass judgment, using the 1898 campaign in South Dakota as her test case. The day before the election, Catt wrote to the SDESA, requesting detailed records of voter turnout. She explained that she wanted to know whether "it paid best to let the foreigner alone or to work with him." Catt intended to build a major component of NAWSA's twentieth-century campaign strategy on the outcome of South Dakota's election. When the results of that election revealed that foreign opposition was high, Catt confirmed what others had suspected, and so she steered NAWSA toward nativism as a powerful rhetorical weapon. Left out of the decision-making process were local advocates like the Vanderhules, whose efforts during the 1898 campaign had centered on the inclusion, not the exclusion, of immigrants. For them, condemning foreigners was difficult when those very foreigners were friends, neighbors, and partners in community development. They were also voters. The Vanderhules could have challenged Catt's assumptions about why foreigners opposed the suffragist cause. They did not immediately dismiss the cause out of a deep-seated antagonism or hostility toward gender equality. Instead, the problem was ignorance. Suffragists had failed to mount effective campaigns that exposed foreigners to the merits of woman suffrage.[63]

The blaming of foreigners emerged as suffragists discarded arguments about individual liberty and adopted ones that highlighted women's civic responsibility. Nineteenth-century arguments that cast woman suffrage in terms of female autonomy threatened the family and its position as the "germ" of good government. Assertions of civic activism were effective, then, because they relied on well-regarded notions of republicanism while reassuring voters that women could maintain their moral position in the home. Gender became superfluous when the essential issue was citizenship and its obligations. By linking civic responsibility and the vote, midwestern suffragists could claim that actions, not words, set the standard for citizenship.

Chapter 4

WOMAN SUFFRAGE AS AN OBLIGATION: CIVIC RESPONSIBILITY AND CITIZENSHIP, 1900–1916

IOWANS VOTED FOR WOMAN SUFFRAGE only once, on June 5, 1916. For months, suffragists had cultivated an impressive ground game, and in Clay County their activities were numerous. On May 24, 1916, the editor of the *Spencer News-Herald* noted that with less than two weeks to go until the primary election, local advocates were pulling out all the stops. The county campaign committee had invited Ella Stewart, former president of the Illinois Equal Franchise Society, to address the public. Inspired by her talk, "several clubs and one or two organized Sunday school classes" held informal discussions on woman suffrage, and the Methodist, Congregational, and Baptist churches hosted other campaign events. Mary Cory, chairperson of the Clay County campaign and member of the Spencer Woman's Club, a local federated women's club, explained that because of these efforts, residents were "fully awake" to woman suffrage. While the level of campaign activity was remarkable, the argument put forward by Cory was also noteworthy. She claimed that the ballot enhanced her civic responsibility. She had come to support woman suffrage "slowly, but with conviction . . . based not so much on the right of women to vote" but on her "long experience of woman's work." As chair of the Civics and Health Committee of the Spencer Women's Club, Cory had spearheaded many community development projects aimed at keeping "the home pure, sanitary, and morally clean, a fit place to rear children to become citizens of our great republic," including a birth registration program and a garbage removal service. While these endeavors were successful, many others were not because "the sympathies of men" in local government often changed on a whim. Only the ballot gave a woman the power to protect her home and community.[1]

In the opening years of the twentieth century, middle-class Yankee suffragists in the Midwest began to respond to the changing rhetorical approaches offered by national suffrage leaders. These suffragists began to recast the home as a site for politics, calling for government intervention on matters related to the family. While they claimed the ballot to protect their families, these leading figures more often situated themselves as mothers, wives, and caregivers. In this way, they shifted away from nineteenth-century rhetoric that argued for individual liberty and female autonomy. Instead, they played up their domestic identities, asserting that their interest in the vote was out of concern for the home. At the same time, state and national suffragists addressed women's role in public affairs, arguing that their morality and virtue made them especially well positioned to clean up politics. They dubbed this argument "municipal housekeeping," explaining that just as women sought to purify the home, so too did they aim to eliminate corruption and purge vice from public life.

Midwestern suffragists, who were mostly Yankees with ties to the Northeast, embraced the politicized home and "municipal housekeeping" as they developed their ideas about civic responsibility. Like national leaders, they claimed the ballot in order to protect the home and their interests in it. They deviated, however, when they emphasized civic virtue and the social obligations of community membership. To Yankees living in small towns and rural neighborhoods, voting was an action taken by citizens who belonged to a community. It was the "recognition that they too were endowed with . . . the capacity for social responsibility." Casting a ballot was not about individual self-interest; it was about mutual uplift and civic duty. Suffragists also linked civic responsibility to foundational democratic principles that most midwesterners understood and cherished, like civic virtue. When World War I erupted out of nationalistic rhetoric inflamed by authoritarian regimes, it threatened these democratic values, and midwestern activists argued that woman suffrage would safeguard promises made at the founding of the United States to be the land of the free. They asserted that American independence in the face of the rise of German aggression rested on the unfettered participation of all its citizens in government.[2]

As Yankee midwestern suffragists transformed their arguments, they responded to Progressivism, which created profound changes in the political landscape of the United States. From about 1900 to 1920 ordinary people took up reform, attempting to eliminate a host of perceived corruptions and injustices in American society. Progressivism was not an organized movement but rather a nebulous impulse that lacked specific goals. In general, Progressives sought to regulate business by breaking up trusts and imposing regulations on corporations; clean up political corruption by removing crooked officials from government; and restore power to ordinary people by removing control by special interests. Like most Americans, many midwesterners became caught up in the spirit of Progressivism. They did not worry that Progressive reforms meant many different things to many different people. What counted was active engagement with society's problems and a reliance on the state to solve them.[3]

Progressives reshaped assumptions about gender and politics. Direct involvement with the state privileged the relationship of the individual to the government, which decreased the importance of patriarchal representation. Not all Progressives were suffragists, but many saw the cause as a "way to empower women to improve their working and living conditions." For Yankee suffragists in the Midwest, the Progressive impulse freed them to engage in politics as community members and citizens by providing "strong credentialing for [the] participatory thread of citizenship." In the process, women realized that they could not fulfill their civic obligations without the right to vote. They could not protect the home, clean up political corruption, or uplift their communities without a voice in policymaking and governing. These were practical concerns that trumped abstract liberal arguments. As Jo Freeman writes, Progressivism "legitimated political work as an expansion of women's duty to maintain the home, and women moved into political life" in new and exciting ways. It gave Yankee suffragists in the Midwest new energy during the early-twentieth-century suffrage campaigns by enhancing the rhetoric around citizenship and community. Armed with records of civic activism and moral virtue, suffragists asserted that they were ready to defend their families, their communities, and their country. The Progressive desire to act encouraged midwestern suffragists to argue for the ballot as their civic duty.[4]

Midwestern suffragists refashioned their rhetoric at the same time that Americans were reconsidering ideas of citizenship. For most of the nineteenth century, Americans had assumed that citizenship was a status enjoyed by white, Protestant, native-born men, thus tacitly endorsing the exclusion of women, African Americans, and other underprivileged and minority groups. The arrival of millions of immigrants from southern and eastern Europe in the late nineteenth century tested this notion, however, especially since many of the newcomers were neither Protestant nor Anglo-Saxon. Initially, poor enforcement of simple naturalization requirements allowed foreigners to join the republic with ease. By the early twentieth century, however, federal officials began to question these immigrants' fitness for political participation in a democratic system. A few even argued that their perceived genetic differences made them categorically unfit. By the early twentieth century nativism had begun to percolate, and legislatures and courts began to codify nativist fears into law. With the Naturalization Act of 1906, Congress passed the first comprehensive reform to naturalization since 1802. It established federal control over naturalization, unified the naturalization process, and created the Division of Naturalization, part of the renamed federal Bureau of Immigration and Naturalization. As a result, the federal government ended local irregularities that made naturalization inconsistent, and it increased the rigor with which the government regulated the process of becoming a citizen. Innate characteristics, along with moral attributes, now had as much to do with citizenship as residency.[5]

The national debates about immigration and citizenship also played out in the Midwest in the early twentieth century. Yankees slowly developed prejudices against the foreigners living in their midst, setting their sights not only on recent arrivals but also on ethnic outsiders, especially Germans, who had lived for decades in the region and had managed to preserve their cultures in isolated enclaves. By 1914, World War I had begun to encourage ethnic paranoia as many native-born Americans bristled at the number of German Americans who aggressively defended the military actions of Germany. The native-born eventually positioned themselves against foreign "others," whom they began to label "unfit" and "un-American." In doing so, they endorsed a narrow standard of citizenship that privileged behavior over words. Citizenship became an active status determined by how well a person demonstrated his or her civic obligations. Those who bore their civic responsibility deserved the ballot, while those who refused to assimilate, and thus failed to participate in civic matters, were suspect.

NAWSA struggled to secure effective leadership amid early-twentieth-century demographic and political change. In 1900 Susan B.

Anthony relinquished the presidency to Carrie Chapman Catt. Since 1890 Catt had risen through the ranks, demonstrating her impressive organizational skills. They were desperately needed. Poor management had plagued NAWSA, and it struggled to maintain accurate membership records and codify long-term financial plans. From 1900 to 1904 Catt served NAWSA well, creating systems and hierarchies out of half-formed procedures. She vacated her post, however, when her second husband fell ill. Catt's departure opened the presidency to Anna Howard Shaw, a peripatetic suffragist who made her living as a lecturer. While renowned for her oratorical skills, she could not replicate Catt's knack for planning. The death of Susan B. Anthony in 1906 also placed a cloud over NAWSA, and Shaw struggled to rebuild the momentum that Anthony and Catt had built.[6]

NAWSA struggled through the first decade of the twentieth century. Competing factions splintered the organization, and Shaw's distrustful leadership style divided members. For ten long years, from 1900 to 1910, no states held elections on woman suffrage amendments. While some historians describe this period as the "doldrums," others characterize it as a time of rebuilding. Suffragists used the interval to reevaluate their plans and reconsider their strategies, shedding their controversial past and de-radicalizing their demands to vote. They linked the vote to "municipal housekeeping" and civic responsibility. They raised funds to train and send field organizers to distant campaigns. They recruited people, especially ministers, influential clubwomen, and politicians whose reputations lent respectability to the cause. They participated in efforts for Progressive reform, which amplified their claims for civic responsibility.[7]

By 1910 NAWSA no longer resembled its nineteenth-century version. A younger generation of activists swelled its ranks, and these people brought complex political identities and new networks of activism. Many encountered the suffragist cause while participating in voluntary associations, and they learned to balance their domestic identities with political ones. A variety of others, including working-class, urban, single, educated, and elite women, joined for practical reasons ranging from economic concerns to improving working conditions and advancing social justice. In the Midwest youthful energy rejuvenated woman suffrage, and fresh leadership reorganized state associations. In Minnesota, Clara Ueland electrified a state that had seriously lacked woman suffrage sentiment. Flora Dunlap, a settlement house worker living in Des Moines, took charge in Iowa and eventually directed the monumental 1916 suffrage campaign. South Dakota's Mamie Pyle took the helm of that state's revitalized organization and persevered through three campaigns spanning five years. The suffragists relied on professionally trained field workers who encouraged grassroots mobilization, sometimes in places where it had never before existed. In 1916 field workers canvassed all three states, and one organizer, Maria McMahon, visited Clay and Yankton counties only months apart. McMahon hailed from Virginia and served as a field director of NAWSA. During that time McMahon's counterpart, Rene Stevens, spent time in Lyon County. Their goals were to invigorate ineffective clubs and start new ones, using open-air meetings, parades, conventions, and posters to attract leading individuals in each community. Field organizers especially targeted federated women's clubs to fight for the ballot. These had proliferated across the Midwest, and their members had established sterling civic reputations. By 1910 over 1,000,000 women enjoyed membership in the General Federation of Women's Clubs (GFWC), which made it a powerful political coalition.[8]

As NAWSA reorganized itself, suffragists in western states achieved a series of stunning victories, including ones in Washington in 1910, California in 1911, Arizona, Oregon, and Kansas in 1912, Alaska and Illinois in 1913, and Nevada and Montana in 1914. Galvanized by these victories, NAWSA courted Carrie Chapman Catt to return to the presidency to continue her coalition-building efforts. The move was intended as much to channel growing support as to concentrate the association's power in a central figure. Shaw's inability to lead had allowed others, like Alice Paul and the Congressional Committee, to chart alternate paths to victory. Paul demanded that NAWSA discard its state-by-state strategy and focus solely on obtaining an amendment to the U.S. Constitution. By 1915 the Congressional Committee—renamed the Congressional Union—was openly attacking the main political parties for failing to endorse woman suffrage, a line that Anthony, Catt, and other "old guard" leaders had refused to cross. When Catt returned to the presidency, she reestablished NAWSA as a nonpartisan pressure group, edging Paul out. Paul organized her followers into a militant group called the National Woman's Party (NWP).[9]

While NAWSA had rebuilt and rebranded itself in the second decade of the twentieth century, there were still nineteenth-century points of tension that lingered. Even though Populism had waned and the old coalitions between farmers and industrial laborers had ended, Progressives absorbed many Populist initiatives and continued to serve as a third-party foil for Republicans and Democrats. Political expectations were not certain while Progressives challenged the two-party system. Immigrants continued to enter the United States in high numbers, and suffragists remained suspicious of ethnic groups. In places where the foreign-born population was high, suffragists faced a perplexing problem. While most immigrants seemed to resist woman suffrage, many of them could vote. Devoting resources to foreigners who stubbornly rejected the cause seemed silly, but ignoring them also seemed unwise. Not until World War I inflamed nativism did suffragists finally shun foreigners. Temperance remained another thorn in the side of suffragists. While younger suffragists approached the cause from outside the WCTU, in the Midwest the WCTU still provided important networks of activism. Even though suffragists turned to federated women's clubs, the WCTU remained crucial, especially in communities where it was the only female voluntary association.

South Dakota Comes of Age, 1910–1914

Of the three states under scrutiny, South Dakota experienced the first official twentieth-century campaign for woman suffrage. Just over ten years had passed since the last one, and the context had shifted dramatically. In 1898 Carrie Chapman Catt had undermined the South Dakota Equal Suffrage Association (SDESA) by demanding that local clubs correspond directly with NAWSA. The blacklisted SDESA sputtered along until 1909, when NAWSA demanded that all of its current officers resign their posts, thereby purging the SDESA of its ties to the WCTU. When they learned of their demise, members of the "old guard" were furious. With their years of devoted service, the news felt like a betrayal. Philena Johnson, who had worked alongside Susan B. Anthony as president of the SDESA during the 1890 campaign, complained bitterly. "I have been fairly *boiling* with indignation," she proclaimed. Her demotion was crushing, and she raged at the prospect of taking orders from inexperienced activists. In the end, Johnson grudgingly relinquished her post, choosing the cause over her hurt feelings.[10]

As NAWSA attempted to revitalize the SDESA, new recruits faced a political climate in flux. Progressivism had infiltrated state politics, where the Republican Party had continued to enjoy an electoral advantage but had split into two factions, the Progressives and the Stalwarts. In 1907, Progressive Republicans in the South Dakota legislature won support for a series of measures designed to curb corruption, including anti-lobbying, direct primary, and campaign finance laws. They also regulated railroad rates, created a food and drug administration, and provided free textbooks in public schools. While South Dakota's Progressive Republicans embraced this active agenda, Stalwart Republicans were less enthusiastic. The dilemma intensified in 1912 when William Howard Taft won the Republican nomination for U.S. president. Most Progressive Republicans supported Theodore Roosevelt, but they refused to abandon their party when Roosevelt joined the Progressive Party. Roosevelt's departure fractured South Dakota Republicans, who were torn between supporting him and Taft. The schism ended in 1916, when Peter Norbeck became the state's governor. Norbeck skillfully united Republicans under a Progressive mandate, and during the 1917 session, the legislature enlarged the state bureaucracy. It created offices for state highways, industrial development, workmen's compensation, and mothers' pensions. The state even got involved in the banking industry, giving loans directly to farmers through a rural credits law. Out of 545 bills, the legislature enacted 376 laws. It also submitted twelve amendments to the state constitution to voters, including four that established state-run businesses, including a hydroelectric project, cement plant, grain elevators, flour mills, and meat-packing houses.[11]

While Progressive reform gave woman suffrage a much-needed boost in South Dakota, the cause faced political uncertainty during the 1910 campaign, the first of the twentieth century. Voters had not yet settled the temperance question, and the remnants of the SDESA struggled to cultivate new networks of activism. When the WCTU agreed to work for the cause independently through their own franchise department, suffragists new to the cause formed the State Political Equality League (SPEL). While separating temperance from woman suffrage was a wise move, inexperience plagued the SPEL, and the 1910 campaign passed with little fanfare. From her position in the WCTU, Philena Johnson watched as the officers in the SPEL "did nothing but quarrel." Six months before the election, Johnson and other "old guard" leaders in the WCTU stepped in to salvage what they could, but the campaign was a debacle. Only one trained field worker, Mary Craigie of New York, visited Yankton County, and she arrived on November 1, about a week before the election. Only one local newspaper, the *Dakota Herald*, covered her visit. Edited by Mark M. Bennett, the *Dakota Herald* was the only source of printed propaganda for the entire county. Bennett and his wife, Harriet, probably wondered if they were the only suffragists in a sea of anti-suffragists. Craigie reported that her message was one of Progressive values, and she warned that "until the ballot is put in the hands of women," the country faced threats of "vices and crime." A few days before the election, she called for a mass meeting at City Hall. Craigie opened the assembly with "convincing" remarks, but what happened next was significant. Eight influential local leaders voiced their support of woman suffrage, including four clergy, a female physician, a railroad agent, and a city commissioner. Although no one recorded their remarks, their presence alone was profound. With their reputations on the line, these respected community leaders stood up and explained why they favored woman suffrage. While South Dakotans handily defeated the 1910 amendment, 35,290 in favor to 57,709 opposed, the campaign was not in vain. It gave ordinary people a chance to test the political waters. It also killed the SPEL.[12]

The defeat of woman suffrage in 1910 convinced NAWSA to form a new state association called the South Dakota Universal Franchise League (SDUFL). While activism did not flourish overnight, with determination and patience, the new organization secured allies, gained resources, and began grassroots mobilization. Leading the charge was Mary "Mamie" Shields Pyle, a suffragist whose civic activism began as a schoolteacher. (See figure 5.) Born in New Jersey in 1866, she moved with her family to Minnesota as a child. Teaching took her to the Dakota Territory in the 1880s, and after a few years she married John L. Pyle, an attorney from Huron. She bore four children, and after her husband died she raised them as a single mother. Her dedication to education spurred her activism, and with her husband she helped establish Huron College. Like other activists who came of age at this time, she drew on her experiences in community development to cultivate a respectable civic reputation. When she became president of the SDUFL, she followed the directives of NAWSA, implementing desperately needed organizational and hierarchical strategies.[13]

While Pyle was "politically wise" and "firm, but sympathetic," she was able to steer the SDUFL to victory because she refused to align the group with temperance. Debates about prohibition had increased as Progressivism reshaped politics in South Dakota. It remained a potent issue between Yankees and immigrants who disagreed about the cultural value of alcohol. It also provoked conflict because regulating liquor was problematic. Local option laws had created a kaleidoscope of competing regulations, many times in the same county. Demographic or political change could reverse decisions created only a few years earlier, which made the enforcement of prohibition a challenge. Progressivism reenergized pro-temperance sentiment, however, and many South Dakotans endorsed prohibition as another way to curb corruption. In 1916 South Dakotans voted to enact statewide prohibition. Suffragists

FIGURE 5. Mamie Pyle. South Dakota State Historical Society.

welcomed prohibition not necessarily because they supported temperance, but because it allowed them to advocate for woman suffrage as a single issue.[14]

Activity stalled for four years until 1914, when the South Dakota legislature endorsed another woman suffrage bill. During that hiatus, NAWSA had trained numerous field workers, standardized its propaganda, and gained powerful allies. Pyle relied heavily on these resources as she planned. From her state headquarters in Huron, Pyle hired paid lecturers to canvass the state, implemented a hierarchical strategy, and selected local representatives at the district and county levels. She charged local activists to coordinate speaker schedules, directing organizers to start new suffrage clubs and stir up sentiment at each stop. Even though the SDUFL had distanced itself from temperance, it still allowed the WCTU to agitate in local communities. It had no choice.

The WCTU was a vibrant organization with a proliferation of local chapters. Engaging with already established networks of female activists was much easier than creating them from scratch. In the spring of 1914, the WCTU franchise department also sent lecturers across South Dakota. Rena Bowers, a Congregational minister from Sioux City, Iowa, went to the southeastern district. Bowers arrived in April, ready to gain converts.

Despite their long history with it, most South Dakotans still opposed woman suffrage. Although some people had warmed to it, it remained controversial. The lack of sustained agitation over time had also limited efforts to gain widespread support. Consequently, a long, grueling campaign awaited suffragists, and changing indifferent or ignorant minds required a bulletproof message. During the 1914 campaign activists spent the most time on rhetoric and argument, tinkering, experimenting, and revising until they landed on a sophisticated claim that civic responsibility was their ticket to obtaining the ballot. Arriving at this conclusion took months, however, so initial efforts were limited. In addition, in many communities the WCTU reached voters first, which confused temperance and woman suffrage. WCTU lecturers, including Bowers, faced an uphill battle.

In Yankton County, the 1914 campaign began with a whimper as suffragists struggled to build grassroots activity. In many cases, they faced dire circumstances. Confirming Bowers's final itinerary was a nightmare because many advocates refused to host her. The litany of excuses was impressive. One local WCTU club claimed they had no place big enough to host Bowers. Others warned that no one cared enough to attend a meeting. Some lamented that they had no money. Bowers was undeterred, and she gleefully explained her plans. At each stop she would form a "campaign club," and with local leaders she would hold a rally and parade, complete with banners with mottos like "Our Mothers Are Citizens." Bowers's confidence turned to dismay after only four days in South Dakota. When she returned to Iowa, she nearly quit the movement altogether. "You guessed right," she wrote, "that I would come home when I reached the end of my rope." Most locals were unenthusiastic, she explained, and if anyone showed up to hear her speak, they usually refused to join. In response to strenuous encouragement, Bowers returned to the campaign trail ten days later, although now uninspired. Cancellations at Gayville and Yankton were disappointing, but

Bowers met with a Mother's Club in Mission Hill and the Volin chapter of the WCTU. At Volin she addressed a full house, which boosted her spirits. If only Bowers had read the *Volin Advance*, the local newspaper, four days after her speech. The editor printed a short article that explained how woman suffrage incited divorce when couples disagreed over which candidate to support.[15]

The 1914 campaign began slowly, achieving only mixed results until the summer, when the SDUFL began a massive offensive. It combined a press blitz, orchestrated at the district level, with the formation of county suffrage clubs. By June, field organizers were sweeping the state and locating pockets of supporters to turn into suffrage organizations. In Yankton County, workers tapped the members of the Nineteenth Century Club, the local federated women's club, to form the Yankton Universal Franchise League (YUFL). At the helm was 38-year-old Kathryn Schuppert, a native of New York. She had arrived in Yankton only four years earlier, when her husband, William, took a job at Yankton College to teach history and political science. Despite her best intentions, Schuppert offered no plans for work at the YUFL's first meeting, and this stalled efforts for a month. She mentioned that Flora La Follette, the daughter of Belle and Robert La Follette, planned to give a woman suffrage address as part of the upcoming Midland Chautauqua Circuit, an outdoors series of speakers and entertainments. Belle was a well-known suffragist while Robert had made a name for himself as a Progressive, first as governor and later as a senator from Wisconsin. He opposed corruption in government and business and supported consumer protection legislation, minimum wage and child labor laws, and woman suffrage. He was one of the best-known and popular politicians at the time, and a visit by his daughter promised to garner large crowds in South Dakota. The YUFL looked forward to Flora's arrival not only because of her parentage; they desperately needed her to ignite their campaign.[16]

Between July and September 1914, three major turning points helped suffragists to crystallize their message on civic responsibility. Flora La Follette's speech was the first transformative moment, and she convinced voters with the claim that women's performance as citizens, particularly through community-building endeavors, demonstrated their fitness to vote. Pomp and circumstance greeted La Follette, and after a social, luncheon, and meet-and-greet, she gave a long address on Yankton's Chautauqua stage. Mark Bennett, the editor of the *Dakota Herald,* had advertised her lecture for days, and afterward he used four full-length columns to describe the occasion. Although La Follette was exhausted from a whirlwind day, she gave a rousing speech. Her two-tiered argument was compelling. She began by explaining how Progressivism obligated women to "clean up" corruption. She was careful to praise the domestic virtues of women while demanding for them a political identity that was fully integrated into the state. Progressivism obligated people to action, to cure "social ills" and combat "industrial evils." Solving these problems inspired individuals, no matter what their gender, to use the government to enact legislation. At this juncture, La Follette introduced woman suffrage. She asserted that Progressive reform confirmed that women were citizens. They shared equally in the mandate to fight corruption, and they took their civic responsibility seriously. Enfranchised women protected their families and communities by fulfilling the mandate of Progressivism. Crafting her argument in this way allowed La Follette to speak deliberately to a midwestern political culture rooted deeply in belonging. At its core was a "real social democracy" of people who shared a "common cause" of community development. La Follette recalled her own upbringing in Wisconsin when she argued that activism on behalf of the community trumped gender inequalities.[17]

Two months later, suffragists added a second element to their argument about civic responsibility by incorporating anti-immigrant sentiment. This turning point allowed suffragists to accentuate their claims to the ballot. In September 1914 Anna Howard Shaw, the president of NAWSA, returned to Yankton County. Almost twenty-five years had passed since her visit to the Methodist Ladies' Aid Society's bazaar, and although her commitment to woman suffrage had not wavered, the times had changed. Only a month earlier, World War I had erupted in Europe. Newspaper coverage revealed that Americans were growing increasingly hostile to Germany, and midwesterners were nervous. Germans were the largest immigrant group in the Midwest, and their presence stoked nativism and paranoia, especially among Yankees. With the conflict on their minds, Yankton County residents gathered to hear Shaw speak at the Congregational Church. To her credit, Shaw sensed a golden opportunity to situate woman suffrage within the growing concerns of the First World War. As the *Dakota Herald* reported, she argued that because women were citizens whose morality uplifted democratic principles, they held an inherent interest in the outcome of the war. This was a brilliant maneuver.

While Shaw repeated many of La Follette's points about women and civic responsibility, she also lambasted immigrants, asserting that foreigners, especially Germans, misunderstood democracy and rejected responsible citizenship. According to Shaw, part of the problem was the naturalization process itself. Lax enforcement meant that some immigrants never completed it. Worse still, almost two dozen states gave "alien suffrage" to foreigners when they secured their first papers, after only two years of residency. South Dakota and Minnesota were two of those states, and in her remarks, Shaw insinuated that foreigners, especially Germans, took out first papers only to sabotage democratic policies. She warned the audience that the war, not loyalty to the United States, was prompting millions of ethnic Germans, many of whom had lived illegally in the country for years, to petition for citizenship. And when they did, they revealed just how unfit they were. According to Shaw, foreigners were astonishingly ignorant about civic matters. She whipped up the crowd with a story of a citizenship hearing. When the judge asked the immigrant to name the president of the United States, the man replied "Charles Murphy" without skipping a beat. Shaw's anecdote was not only shocking; it also positioned uninformed and irresponsible immigrants who were not citizens against educated and responsible women who were. Shaw saw a fatal flaw in a political system that enfranchised potential alien enemies while denying the ballot to its native-born women. Woman suffrage was not only about equal citizenship for women; it was also a shield against the evil schemes of foreign traitors.[18]

La Follette's message and Shaw's warning inspired suffragists in Yankton County to implement a series of dramatic campaign activities. The third and final turning point occurred when the YUFL secured a weekly newspaper column in two local newspapers, the *Press and Dakotan* and the *Dakota Herald*. Edited by Edith Fitch, the press chairman of the southeastern district, the articles provided persuasive arguments and updated readers on the work for woman suffrage. Fitch readily interwove competing arguments. Sometimes she venerated women's domestic roles as wives and mothers. At other times she demanded their equality with men, asserting that the ideal of liberty within a democracy gave them the right to vote. While Fitch switched her stance to fit her audience, she consistently framed her contentions within women's civic responsibility. As she explained, women's civic contributions had enlightened people to the integral role they played in community matters. She recalled how women created churches, libraries, schools, and other public institutions, which served as proof of their active citizenship. The contradiction emerged around their citizenship status. Midwestern women had all the "duties and responsibilities" of citizenship but none of the rights, particularly the vote. They were "half" citizens, unable to act in a political culture that venerated participation. As the election neared, Fitch also linked woman suffrage to the war in Europe. Nations like Germany and Austria-Hungary, corrupted by untrammeled autocratic power, threatened the ideals of democracy. Armed with the ballot, women could revitalize democratic principles like "the consent of the governed," the "voice of the people," and "life, liberty, and equality." These axioms upheld freedom and liberty in the face of autocratic enemies who threatened to destroy American political life.[19]

The 1914 campaign in South Dakota saw the collision of woman suffrage with World War I, which forced midwesterners to wrestle with the meanings of citizenship. Unfortunately, decades of contradictions clouded the process. Nineteenth-century Americans held vague definitions of citizenship, which included some people while excluding many others. With the Fourteenth Amendment (1868) citizenship had become a constitutionally recognized birthright, but the amendment failed to spell out the rights associated with it. Twentieth-century Progressive reforms refocused citizenship on republican notions of civic participation, but some citizens still could not exercise their political rights. Inconsistences emerged as gender, race, and ethnicity imperiled citizenship status. In this case, gender discriminated against women, denying them rights like voting or serving on juries, but allowed immigrant men to secure the ballot with only their first papers. When suffragists pointed out this contradiction, as they did in 1914 in South Dakota, they unlocked the door to victory in future campaigns. They crafted a stunningly effective strategy that exploited ambiguities about citizenship and reconfigured them to stress loyalty, a measure of belonging that favored native-born women over foreigners. Yankee suffragists gained powerful rhetorical leverage when they positioned themselves against immigrants. They continued to celebrate women's civic responsibility, but the way they constructed their political identities began to shift. Advocates still claimed that they engaged in politics to protect the home and community, but as loyal citizens, their duty was also to the nation. World War I turned civic responsibility into patriotism.

Although the United States was three years away from entering World War I, national suffragists campaigning in 1914 sensed the opportunity to connect citizenship, loyalty, and woman suffrage. NAWSA had blamed immigrants for their defeats for decades, so the narrative was a familiar one. While most midwestern suffragists were eager to follow the lead of national figures like Flora La Follette and Shaw, they paused to consider its implications. Like nineteenth-century advocates, twentieth-century activists also celebrated sociability at the heart of midwestern community life. They appreciated the contributions of their foreign-born neighbors, and they sought alliances with them, not division. While NAWSA was eager to sow the seeds of suspicion of foreigners, midwestern leaders were less enthusiastic. Eventually midwestern suffragists adopted these arguments, albeit with reservations. They recognized that nativism was a powerful political strategy. They also grew impatient when defeat continued to stymie their efforts.

Despite all their work, suffragists were downcast when South Dakotans rejected the 1914 amendment by about 12,000 votes: 39,605 ayes and 51,519 nays. In Yankton County the election was a blowout, with the amendment losing by a two-to-one margin. Newspaper coverage revealed skepticism and hesitancy, but not outright opposition, which gave suffragists some hope. In fact, people scrutinized woman suffrage carefully, even admitting that it was inevitable given the marked increase in support for it across the nation. Two issues continued to produce resistance, however. Voters still connected woman suffrage with temperance, either because of an ethnic custom or because of the money made from alcohol sales. Despite suffragists' attempts to separate the two reforms, midwesterners assumed that prohibition would follow female enfranchisement. The presence of the WCTU in the campaign had done nothing to assuage these fears, but suffragists refused to exclude the WCTU on account of its valuable networks of activism. In addition, while civic responsibility had gained converts, South Dakotans reported that woman suffrage still remained radical and unpopular in some quarters. In one article, anti-suffragists acknowledged that women purified politics by advocating for the home, but they contended that women did not require the ballot to accomplish their work. The ballot was not merely an extension of their familial roles; instead, it corrupted women because politics was inherently undignified and crooked.[20]

Minnesota Wakes Up: 1910–1916

While South Dakotans wrestled with the meanings of women's civic responsibility, in Minnesota the silence that characterized woman suffrage in the nineteenth century had become deafening in the first decade of the twentieth century. The Minnesota Woman Suffrage Association (MWSA) struggled with limited resources and ineffective leadership. Not until 1914 did Minnesotans display an interest in the cause, but most of the efforts remained concentrated at the state level. Part of the dearth of activity stemmed from the 1898 law that required a majority of the votes cast at an election for each individual amendment. Not voting on a measure was the same as a "no" vote. In addition, large numbers of ethnic voters continued to oppose woman suffrage, mainly because of their suspicion of temperance. While many suffragists recognized that a suffrage amendment faced impossible odds under these circumstances, some continued to petition the legislature. In 1907 and 1909 suffragists in the MWSA lobbied members of the legislature, but in both cases the Senate killed the intended amendments. In 1911 suffragists planned a huge celebration for Susan B. Anthony in downtown St. Paul, but it was no match for Senate opposition, which defeated the latest suffrage bill by two votes. Proposed measures also failed in 1913, 1915, and 1917, so suffragists considered alternatives to full suffrage. In 1915 and 1917, the MWSA also submitted resolutions for presidential suffrage through legislative decree, hoping to weaken opposition by making a limited request. The presidential suffrage resolutions were also part of Catt's "winning plan" in which she directed Minnesota's suffragists to bypass the difficult amending process and follow the example of Illinois, which had granted presidential suffrage by legislative action in 1913. In both cases, however, the bills failed by a handful of votes, leaving suffragists increasingly bitter.[21]

Suffragists found little support in the Minnesota legislature, but to make matters worse, they faced turmoil in their own organization.

By 1910 instability and mismanagement were plaguing the MWSA, and in 1912, at its annual convention, the organization fractured. The drama emerged along a generational divide. Younger suffragists blasted the MWSA for its tired formula of legislative action. They demanded widespread organization at the local level. Those who left the MWSA formed the Minnesota Equal Franchise League (MEFL). It remained an autonomous group until 1914, when it agreed to become an auxiliary of the MWSA. During the schism, a handful of suffragists undertook a limited campaign to organize clubs in small communities. Twelve clubs formed in 1912, bringing the total number of suffrage clubs in the state to twenty-four. One of the clubs emerged in Marshall, the seat of Lyon County. While MWSA staff failed to list this club's fifteen members, they named Fannie I. Hand as the secretary. Hand belonged to the Current News Club, the local federated woman's club, so the suffrage club probably derived its membership from that organization. Curiously, the Current News Club never recorded its involvement in any suffrage activity. The Marshall suffrage club, like most of the others in the state, probably disbanded soon after its formation, but its existence confirmed that at least a few women in Lyon County supported the cause.[22]

Successful organization came to the MWSA in 1914, when its members elected Clara Ueland as president. (See figure 6.) Ueland had gained fame as a skillful organizer, especially after the public applauded the 1911 Susan B. Anthony parade that she orchestrated in St. Paul. Ueland instituted a number of reforms to energize the beleaguered MWSA. She enlarged its base, bringing in younger women, working-class women, and men. She also raised large sums, recognizing that political action cost money. She divided the state into districts, targeting the constituents in districts with legislators who opposed the cause, and she emphasized work at the county level to supplement district organization. Ueland rightly asserted that the way to win in Minnesota was to mobilize public opinion in favor of woman suffrage, especially through direct interactions at the grassroots level. Finally, she ran the MWSA like a business, with clear organization, efficient operations, and paid staff. By early 1916 Ueland had hired two field workers, Maria McMahon and Rene Stevens.[23]

Minnesotans had gone decades without any targeted county-level agitation, and initial attempts at organization were frustratingly slow. Not only were people hesitant to act, but campaigns in Iowa and South

FIGURE 6. Clara Ueland. Minnesota State Historical Society.

Dakota also interrupted work and created piecemeal efforts. In March 1916, Ueland sent McMahon and Stevens to the southern and western edges of Minnesota to coincide with the amendment campaigns across the border. Stevens worked in the counties bordering Lyon County. She had planned to identify a prominent person in each county to lead a suffrage club, but instead of enthusiasm, she received excuses. Most of the people she encountered had little knowledge of or willingness to work for the cause. A farmer in Nobles County promised to organize her township, but she admitted her work was temporary because she planned to move to Montana. A Swedish pastor and his wife in Lincoln County professed their allegiance to woman suffrage, but they quieted their activism when they discovered that most of their congregation opposed it. In Rock County, a woman's club voiced interest in the movement but admitted that "family duties" and "the family attitude toward suffrage" had prevented them from following through. At each stop, Stevens heard about how "unenlightened" people were, how there was a "crying need" for more information, and how "stumbling blocks" kept advocates from doing work. Most people were sympathetic, she explained, but were unwilling to devote enough time and energy to the cause. Stevens traveled to the counties bordering Lyon County, but unfortunately, she never stepped foot in it. The Iowa campaign called, cutting short her efforts in Minnesota. In April 1916 Stevens went to Dubuque in eastern Iowa while McMahon took up work in Clay County.[24]

Woman Suffrage Consumes Iowa: 1916

In Iowa, woman suffrage emerged at the height of Progressivism and after decades of grassroots mobilization. Progressivism had roiled state political leaders, creating a climate that prized reform. Like their counterparts in South Dakota, Iowa's Progressives did not create a third-party alternative. Instead, they sought reform through established party politics, especially the Republican Party. By 1900 the Republican Party in the state had split into two factions, the conservatives, or "stand-patters," and the Progressives, or "insurgents." Albert Cummins, a Republican elected governor in 1901, rallied the party to pass a wide range of reform measures that, among other things, regulated excessive railroad rates, combatted insurance fraud, and implemented a direct primary. While Cummins found consensus in some cases, divisions still paralyzed work in others. Woman suffrage and prohibition remained controversial, failing to gain enough traction among legislators. While these reforms stalled in state political circles, popular support for suffrage increased among ordinary Iowans. Dorothy Schwieder notes that as more newspapers published articles in favor of woman suffrage, politicians, including Governor Cummins, offered their public endorsements of it. By the mid-1910s attitudes had shifted, and the legislature finally delivered a woman suffrage amendment.[25]

The Iowa Equal Suffrage Association (IESA) celebrated in 1915 when the Iowa legislature passed a measure calling for a woman suffrage amendment to the state's constitution. It was the second resolution, following a successful bid in 1913. With two consecutive victories in the legislature, the fate of woman suffrage fell to Iowa's voters. Members of the Senate and House acted quickly to allow women to vote in the November 1916 election, passing a "special election bill" that included the amendment on the primary ballot, scheduled for June 5, 1916. The IESA acted swiftly, making plans at its annual convention in October 1915. Its president was Flora Dunlap, a Progressive reformer and settlement house worker living in Des Moines. (See figure 7.) Following the lead of NAWSA, Dunlap articulated a strategy reminiscent of other midwestern campaigns. Experienced organizers were to canvass each county while a propaganda blitz supplemented face-to-face agitation. As Dunlap proclaimed, "Iowa should be strewn knee deep with literature." Her preparations were telling, as she explicitly targeted rural voters, and she made her reasons clear when she read a letter from the Nebraska Woman Suffrage Association. In it, Nebraska's suffragists implored the IESA to focus on residents on farms and in small towns. Their advice came from experience, and they explained that their most devastating mistake during a recent initiative campaign had been "failing to reach the rural voter." Dunlap's ambitious strategy demanded intense fund-raising efforts, and the IESA worked with NAWSA and its returning president, Carrie Chapman Catt, to solicit donations from across the country.[26]

Just as Susan B. Anthony had approached the 1890 campaign in South Dakota with personal interest, so too did Carrie Chapman Catt care deeply about the 1916 campaign in Iowa. Victory meant a great deal

FIGURE 7. Flora Dunlap. State Historical Society of Iowa.

to her because Iowa was her home state. The campaign also coincided with a presidential election, and Catt hoped to achieve a win despite the reluctance of Republicans and Democrats to endorse woman suffrage. She believed that a convincing triumph in Iowa in June 1916 could sway national party leaders to include a plank for the cause in their platforms for the presidential election that November. In December 1915 Catt met privately with Dunlap. Catt not only promised to give financial support to the IESA, but she also personally selected a group of trained field workers. She even paid the salary of one worker for five months out of her own pocket. Catt planned to make three trips to Iowa, spending a full month on a county-by-county speaking tour. With Catt's guidance, the IESA distributed a revised "Plan of Organization and Work." It directed workers to adopt a hierarchical structure, with national, state, county, township, and ward levels. At each level a chairperson organized activities, but at the heart of campaigning were suffrage clubs that were charged with scheduling mass meetings, collecting pledge cards, and entertaining speakers. Chairpersons also coordinated propaganda distribution, circulating pamphlets and flyers and soliciting newspaper editors to publish pro-suffrage articles. They also orchestrated a massive door-to-door canvass, coaching suffragists in giving stump speeches. The size and scope of the campaign were astounding, and it mirrored Anthony's 1890 "do-every-thing" policy. Nothing was off limits; any place where women could introduce the cause was fair game.[27]

In Clay County activists embraced these demands wholeheartedly, transforming their work on behalf of their communities into demonstrations in support of woman suffrage. By April 1916 the members of the Spencer Woman's Club, a federated woman's club, had emerged as local leaders. They built their support for woman suffrage on an impressive record of civic improvement that spanned nearly two decades. While Progressivism had encouraged them to explore civic interests, they also pursued activism as community members who took the midwestern impulse for civic uplift seriously. Under the leadership of its Civics and Health Committee, led by Mary Cory, the club pursued a variety of issues, mostly related to healthy living and sanitation. In 1912 the club's members had arranged a publicity blitz in local newspapers, encouraging farmers, storekeepers, bakers, creamery workers, and others who handled food to maintain sanitary conditions. That year they also sponsored a series of films on sanitation and disease prevention at the local Farmers' Institutes. Members of the club gave talks at the event, like one entitled "The Menace of the Fly." They also instructed rural women to inspect food service operations and report any infractions to the club. "Women direct a large percent of the buying" for the home, the club explained, so clean food was a "woman's cause." While these public education campaigns changed attitudes, the Spencer Woman's Club realized that health initiatives required collective action. In 1914 the club enacted a sweeping reform agenda, spearheading a number of projects that included a garbage collection service and a birth registration program at the hospital. The women purchased the lot for Spencer's first public park and directed a beautification crusade to plant trees and flowers in numerous municipal spaces.[28]

As the Spencer Woman's Club embraced civic responsibility, which plunged them into the heart of local politics, they also began to study woman suffrage. Their initial efforts were inconspicuous and informal, such as a series of short debates beginning in 1911. A year later, a few individuals presented formal papers on the topic for serious consideration. Perhaps the club had reached an impasse in October 1912, because members held an unofficial vote to gauge their feelings on the cause. The meeting minutes revealed a club divided, with eleven women in favor of suffrage and seven opposed. Unlike the acrimony that rankled the WCTU under Martha Janes, the Spencer Woman's Club did not fracture. Instead, increased involvement in community development kept woman suffrage in the forefront of discussions, and respected leaders like Mary Cory, the head of the Civics and Health Committee, slowly won over their friends.[29] (See figure 8.)

FIGURE 8. Mary Cory. "Two Ardent Suffragettes," *Spencer News-Herald*, May 24, 1916.

Like many midwestern women in the early twentieth century, the members of the Spencer Woman's Club became suffragists to protect their homes and uplift their communities. Woman suffrage was neither radical nor dangerous because it enhanced women's domestic roles. Moreover, voting was the civic duty of respectable citizens, and the Spencer Woman's Club had demonstrated decades of responsibility and propriety. In October 1914 the club made its stance on woman suffrage public when Mary Cory invited Flora Dunlap to speak at the Methodist Church in Spencer. Newspapers reported how eager people were to hear her, and Dunlap spoke to a large audience. The *Spencer Herald* noted that Dunlap was a "rapid-fire talker" and a "talented" woman who gave a "very interesting address." She underscored how woman suffrage promised to "influence for the good of the home and the state." According to the *Spencer Herald*, the audience approved of this "sane interpretation" of the suffrage movement.[30]

When the Iowa legislature placed the woman suffrage amendment on the ballot for the June 1916 primary election, the Spencer Woman's Club was ready. In January 1916 the group publicly endorsed the cause, couching their sentiments in the same claims that resonated across the Midwest. The women asserted that because of their record of civic projects, they had ensured the future of their homes, families, and community. Securing the right to vote allowed the club to serve "as an aid to civic betterment." The club also argued that woman suffrage was the "next logical step in the progress of democracy," an assertion that tapped into growing concerns about international chaos. After two years of destructive fighting with no end in sight, World War I now threatened to engulf the United States. Anxiety over the war prompted midwesterners to articulate enduring principles like liberty and equality, which stood in contrast to the militarism that was decimating Europe. The women undoubtedly hoped that a patriotic undertone could boost the popularity of woman suffrage. By framing their resolution in these terms, the members of the Spencer Woman's Club articulated a political identity that was firmly rooted in patriotism and civic responsibility.[31]

By April 1916, when the woman suffrage campaign erupted in Clay County, the members of the Spencer Woman's Club had become veteran political organizers and stalwart suffragists. The club followed the "Plan of Organization" closely, naming ward, township, and county chairpersons. In sum, sixty-four women participated in the elaborate local campaign. Mary Cory became the county chairperson, and she set to work securing speakers. The first to arrive was Ella Stewart, a former president of the Illinois Equal Franchise Society, who gave a lively address at the Congregational Church in Spencer. A few weeks later Gertrude Foster Brown, a former president of the New York Woman Suffrage Association, delivered a lecture on woman suffrage. The club also orchestrated a propaganda blitz, hanging posters in store windows, disseminating literature through the mail and in person, and showing films that endorsed woman suffrage.[32]

Printed propaganda in the form of pamphlets, leaflets, and flyers was a major component of the 1916 campaign in Iowa. The IESA took the warning from Nebraska's suffragists seriously, and beginning in July 1915 they published reams of literature that explicitly targeted farmers. When the fall harvest approached in late 1915, the IESA encouraged farmers to donate a bushel of corn from their yield to the campaign.

Other propaganda encouraged farm wives to support the cause, citing a host of reasons. One flyer noted that an estimated 16,000 farm women in the state owned land and paid taxes on it, but they had no say over their investments. Another article asserted that rural women held deep interests in issues related to agricultural production, like road maintenance, access to markets, and shipping costs. With the vote, women could reinforce their rights as farmers, property owners, and taxpayers. In this case, the IESA acknowledged that farm women's domestic identities were connected explicitly to agricultural production.[33]

Propaganda formed the backdrop for the activities of the Spencer Woman's Club, which followed the "Plan of Organization" to the letter. While they organized, distributed, and lectured as activists in an official way, they also brought woman suffrage into their everyday interactions. No aspect of their lives was off limits, and suffragists seamlessly integrated the cause into their social and religious networks. At the height of campaign efforts, suffrage leaders hosted numerous social gatherings, including bridge clubs, Philanthropic Educational Organization (P.E.O.) socials, and sewing circles. Three suffragists, Florence May Nichols, Lydia Chamberlain, and Martha Perine, each welcomed the members of the Improved Auction Bridge Club into their homes. Goldie Rice, a leader from the Second Ward, served an "elaborate luncheon" to the Dickens Embroidery Club. Attendees gushed at the lovely flower arrangements and pleasant accommodations. Although members did not elaborate about the content of their conversations, woman suffrage was undoubtedly a main topic. The members of the U-Go I-Go Club reported that they conducted "several informal talks" about the prospect of enfranchisement.[34]

Not only did social groups discuss woman suffrage, but many churches, particularly the Methodist, Baptist, Lutheran, and Congregational ones, also took up the matter. Many of Clay County's suffragists were members of these religious denominations, and they infused the cause into their regular programs. Advocates in the Baptist Church hosted a suffrage institute conducted by the Clay County WCTU and led by state organizer Laura Hale. The Congregational, Methodist, and Lutheran churches each held dinners at various points during the campaign to entice parishioners to vote for the amendment. While these activities gave churchgoers an opportunity to engage with woman suffrage, in other cases suffragists practically forced their religious communities to endorse it. In April 1916 five female congregants went before Spencer's Congregational Church asking for support for woman suffrage. After the women had presented their arguments, the male parishioners held a vote and confirmed, with a nearly unanimous verdict, their favorable stance. While the women's willingness to agitate for the suffragist cause in this context demonstrated that politics was central to their identities, the response of the community was also remarkable. No one questioned the women's displays of political activism. There was no boundary between politics, networks of sociability, and female religious activities.[35]

By April 1916 a massive grassroots campaign was in full swing in Clay County, and local suffragists found success by rooting their claims in terms of civic responsibility. They had targeted informal social and religious networks, exploiting these relationships to increase sentiment in favor of the cause, and had encountered little resistance. The interactions produced confidence, and some even anticipated a victory. But when Maria McMahon, one of the organizers from the MWSA, arrived in late April 1916, she had a different take on their campaign. While they had done well in Spencer, the county seat, they had left the rest of Clay County, especially its farmers, uninformed about woman suffrage. McMahon challenged local leaders to travel outside of Spencer, engaging with people they did not know. When the IESA issued plans for locals to participate in a statewide automobile tour in May 1916, McMahon encouraged the Spencer Woman's Club to arrange an automobile canvass of Clay County. At each stop, the activists planned to hold an open-air meeting and conduct a door-to-door survey.[36]

During the first three weeks of May 1916, suffragists across Iowa engaged in a massive automobile canvass, traveling to farms and villages and speaking with anyone willing to listen. McMahon and a group of local advocates visited almost every small town and village in Clay County. Hundreds of people gathered at each stop, and newspapers reported that rural residents gave "enthusiastic" responses to this "popular subject of the day." To celebrate their successful tour, suffragists held a mass meeting in Spencer, and observers reported that over 300 people attended. Speakers tore down "time-worn arguments about woman's place being in the home." According to the lecturers, the nineteenth-century assertions that woman suffrage provoked divorce and family upheaval were the ridiculous rants of cantankerous old men.

Twentieth-century Progressive reform had enhanced the public activism demonstrated for decades by women in the Midwest. The ballot for women was no longer a radical proposition. Instead, it ensured that women could uplift their homes and contribute to the civic development of their communities.[37]

While Clay County activists exulted in a vibrant campaign, they did not realize the extent to which developments outside that campaign would complicate the primary election. These developments incited controversy and dramatically increased interest in the election. Questions emerged among election officials who found the voter registration guidelines of the "special election bill" to be confusing. In response, George Cosson, Iowa's attorney general, issued a vague decision that required voters to register for the woman suffrage amendment but not for the rest of the primary election ballot. County officials scrambled to follow the ruling, but ambiguity continued to provoke contradictions. In Clay County the county auditor, Alonzo Chamberlain, whose wife, Lydia, was a founding member of the Spencer Woman's Club and held a leadership position on the Third Ward Committee of the campaign, sought further clarification from Cosson. After corresponding with Cosson's office, Chamberlain assured residents that only voters in the county seat, Spencer, had to register. Other auditors, confused just like Chamberlain, reached different conclusions, creating a haphazard system of registration that ultimately complicated the results of the primary. The quagmire subsequently led suffragists to level accusations of voter fraud because so many unregistered Iowans had voted.[38]

While officials attempted to sort out the voter registration guidelines, lingering discontent with temperance also influenced how people voted in the primary election. In 1915 the Iowa legislature had passed a controversial prohibition bill, and the state went dry in January 1916. Angst about prohibition consumed the governor's race. The distinguishing feature of each candidate's platform was his stance on temperance. When the leading Democratic candidate, William Meredith, pledged himself "dry," the Republican Party was plunged into chaos. Republicans usually aligned with temperance, so the party fell into disarray as delegates scrambled to elect a "wet" candidate to steal Democrats disillusioned with Meredith. George Cosson, the attorney general and a temperance advocate, went head-to-head with William Harding, the lieutenant governor and an anti-prohibitionist, in a race for the

Republican gubernatorial nomination. The temperance issue magnified the importance of the primary election, and election officials noted that many Democrats switched their party affiliation to vote in the Republican primary and secure Harding's nomination. Harding eventually won the Republican nomination.[39]

While prohibition spurred many anti-temperance voters to switch their party affiliation, others grew concerned about increased taxes. Reform cost money, and some constituencies felt the pinch more than others. In particular, farmers rallied against initiatives that they believed levied "extravagant" taxes, especially those that would pay for a program to pave roads. At the time, landowners shouldered the costs of road construction, and many farmers opposed paved roads, organizing Farmers Tax-Payers' Leagues in protest. Leading farm journals, including the *Iowa Homestead,* encouraged farmers to support Harding, the "wet" candidate for the Republican nomination, because he resisted "hard" roads. Sensing a golden opportunity, anti-suffragists pounced, targeting farmers who opposed higher taxes. In late May 1916, an unnamed group took out full-page advertisements in the most prominent farm journals, making explicit connections between woman suffrage and high taxes. One advertisement thundered, "Remember! *Woman Suffrage Means High Taxes.*" It warned that women, armed with the ballot, would enact "hysterical legislation . . . uncalled for bond issues," and higher taxes. The IESA refuted the negative publicity in a series of newspaper articles, hoping to prevent the tax issue from derailing the campaign, but it was too late.[40]

Iowans went to the polls on June 5, 1916, casting their ballots on woman suffrage for the first and only time. Weeks of intensive campaigning culminated in a single day, filled with anxiety and hope. In Clay County, suffragists cheered when they learned that the amendment had passed by 124 votes. Turnout was low there, however, with only 662 ballots cast for the measure. In contrast, almost 1,660 people voted in the gubernatorial election. Perhaps Chamberlain's interpretation of Cosson's voter registration guidelines was the reason for the disparity. In Iowa, the statewide electoral trend contrasted with that of Clay County, as 30,000 more people cast a ballot on the woman suffrage amendment than in the gubernatorial election. As returns trickled in across the state, the IESA learned that voters had defeated the amendment by a slim margin of just over 10,000 votes. Dunlap was heartbroken, writing to Catt that the results were "very bitter." Suffragists had conducted one of the most extensive grassroots campaigns in the state's history, and they had expected to win.

As suffragists analyzed the results, they followed a well-worn pattern that assigned blame to outsiders and unexpected forces. In their correspondence, they blamed the tax issue and anti-prohibition sentiment for stoking fears among Iowans. They leveled their most intense criticism at Germans, however, casting blame for the defeat in terms of ethnicity and religion. They claimed that four heavily German "wet" counties in eastern Iowa had effectively swung the election against woman suffrage. They also targeted Germans living in rural areas generally, especially German Catholics, arguing that they had failed to counteract the adverse vote of the four eastern counties. County chairpersons provided anecdotes in their reports that upheld this biased assessment, comparing Germans to other immigrant groups. Many locals noted that while enlightened Swedes and Norwegians had supported the amendment, ignorant Germans had almost always opposed it.[41]

Although Germans had voted more often against woman suffrage, they were not to blame for the defeat of the amendment. A month after the primary, Dunlap admitted that the campaign had not been as well organized as the IESA had envisioned. While advocates in some places, like Clay County, had conducted effective campaigns, more often local leaders had failed to live up to the IESA's plans. Dunlap confessed that the amendment had flopped because suffragists had not convinced a majority of Iowans, not just Germans, to support it. Dunlap's confession fell on deaf ears. The conversation shifted quickly away from her concession when the WCTU revealed the findings of an inquiry into the electoral results. Investigators discovered that 13,609 unregistered voters had cast ballots on the amendment. Another 2,289 votes did not correspond to any names listed in poll books. The WCTU did not mince words; they claimed that the election was a fraud. The language they used was telling. They cited a "total disregard or ignorance of the registration laws," with "flagrant" violations of electoral rules by "incompetent" voters. The defeat had not been the product of simple human error; it had been voter fraud perpetrated by Germans in order to deprive women of their rights. Accusing Germans of electoral espionage seemed drastic, but in the summer of 1916 it was a sure bet. As the United States inched closer to entering World War I, Americans were anxious. Nativism was increasing, which normalized anti-German rhetoric. For leaders in the IESA and NAWSA to claim that Germans had defeated the amendment was a brilliant strategy.[42]

Minnesota: A Convention in Pipestone

At the conclusion of Iowa's campaign, Maria McMahon and Rene Stevens returned to Minnesota, bruised by the loss but determined to change hearts toward woman suffrage. Stevens headed back to the southwestern section of the state and decided to hold a convention in August 1916 in Pipestone County, choosing that county because it shared a border with South Dakota. Since South Dakotans were in the process of considering yet another amendment in November of that year, Stevens hoped that highlighting the campaign efforts there could inspire Minnesotans to enact legislation for themselves. While she had planned to delegate the work to local supporters, she found that the people there were unreliable. After a week in Pipestone with little to show for it, Stevens offered a cynical example of one of the many conversations she'd had.

> "Do they want the vote? O yes, they were 'born suffragists.' Do they want the Convention? O, dear lady—why how could you I-I uncle John—When did you say? Yes—uh, thoughtfully, August, yes, August! Uncle John's coming in August and I'm going to the Lakes! And why I don't think you could get a soul to hear you!! Seems as tho' [*sic*] everybody's interested in something else more'n [*sic*] they are in suffrage.' (Little nervous laugh— Bracing up and with conviction) 'But it's coming! Oh it's coming—nothing can stop it!'"

Only after direct confrontations with leading business owners, newspaper editors, and government officials did Stevens find enough support to stage the Pipestone convention. She advertised widely for it, finally visiting Lyon County and placing announcements in both the *Marshall News Messenger* and the *Lyon County Reporter*. Both editors sheepishly admitted that they had avoided printing material on the suffragist cause, but they promised to promote the convention to their readers. While the *Lyon County Reporter* published a three-paragraph article a week before the gathering, the *Marshall News Messenger* missed the deadline completely, running a short missive a day late. Despite the obstacles, Stevens pulled off a remarkable convention. A few days before, a caravan of MWSA leaders had embarked from Minneapolis, stopping at small towns along their route. Clara Ueland remembered that it was a "triumphant tour." A number of women from Lyon County traveled to Pipestone County to hear Ueland, along with Senator O. A. Lende, speak in favor of woman suffrage. Before she could organize additional meetings, however, Stevens received word that suffragists in South Dakota had requested her help. By September Stevens was working in northern South Dakota, near Aberdeen. Maria McMahon, who had challenged suffragists in Clay County to campaign among rural voters, also traveled west, doing work in southeastern South Dakota and visiting Yankton County in October. Consigned to the back burner once again, woman suffrage in Minnesota had to wait.[43]

South Dakota Reconsiders Woman Suffrage in 1916

When yet another amendment passed the South Dakota legislature that aimed at enshrining woman suffrage in the state's constitution, suffragists braced for a grueling campaign. In 1914, the SDUFL had organized by districts composed of a few counties, but in 1916 the group decided to rely on county workers. By dividing the state into smaller units, SDUFL president Mamie Pyle theorized that suffragists could reach every resident easily. In practice, however, the plan did not account for counties in which no leader emerged. In Yankton County, previous leaders, mostly members of the Nineteenth Century Club, refused to reorganize the YUFL. Kathryn Schuppert, the architect of the 1914 campaign, had moved to Illinois when her husband took a job there, and so plans in the county languished. No one stepped up to orchestrate activities at the local level, so the SDUFL had no choice but to take charge.

The 1916 campaign in Yankton County was a far cry from the one in 1914. It consisted of two speakers, arriving two months apart, whose presence punctuated an otherwise dull campaign. The first lecturer, Leslie Benedict, arrived in August 1916. Her arguments magnified those articulated two years earlier. While she contended that the vote enhanced women's respected role as protector of the home, she also pointed out the significant influence women had on war matters, especially maintaining the food supply, promoting health and sanitation, and educating future democratic leaders. Benedict's solo act was effective but limited, and with no local activism, residents had little exposure to the cause. In October Maria McMahon traveled to Yankton County. She had spent nearly a year on the road, canvassing southwest Minnesota, northwest Iowa—including Clay County—and southeast South Dakota. The on-the-job-training had paid off, and McMahon had matured into a sophisticated organizer. At Mission Hill her speech inspired a petition drive, a township canvass, and public debate. At Volin, a large crowd demonstrated significant interest in the cause. Sentiment did not increase, however, after McMahon's departure. Like Benedict's visit, McMahon's trip failed to inspire widespread support among locals.[44]

While Yankton County residents responded to the 1916 campaign in South Dakota with apathy, at the state level, leaders in the SDUFL encountered outright hostility. Politics had shifted since the previous campaign, and prohibition and taxation provoked a backlash against woman suffrage. As in Iowa, anti-suffragists claimed that woman suffrage raised taxes, suggesting that women more often supported expensive programs and initiatives that cost taxpayers money. They also explicitly linked prohibition to woman suffrage. On the 1916 ballot were two amendments, one securing woman suffrage and one establishing statewide prohibition. Anti-prohibitionists pounced, arguing that suffragists were merely temperance reformers in disguise. Suffragists attempted to separate themselves from the WCTU, but it was difficult. Many suffragists, especially in rural areas, were also members of the WCTU. Suffragists comfortably touted female virtue without realizing that many voters believed prohibition was at the heart of morality politics. As the election neared, assaults, both rhetorical and physical, increased markedly. In Lincoln County, northwest of Yankton County, an unknown assailant attacked Leslie Benedict in her hotel room. Benedict escaped unharmed, but reports indicated that the man had mistakenly believed she was a prohibitionist, not a suffragist.[45]

Suffragists also faced antagonism during the 1916 campaign because they represented the strength of Progressive politics in South Dakota. A small number of people aggressively opposed that cause because it had gained tremendous support. They resorted to violence and intimidation because they recognized that public opinion had shifted and the Progressive impulse had overtaken the state. The 1916 election results revealed the extent to which Progressivism had infiltrated politics.

Progressives outnumbered Stalwarts in the Republican Party. The Republican Peter Norbeck won the governorship because of his platform of reform. The prohibition measure passed by almost 10,000 votes, effectively ending local option laws. Woman suffrage lost, but only by a slim margin of less than 5,000 votes.[46]

Although defeat in 1916 provided little consolation for the SDUFL, two related outcomes gave them hope for future campaigns. With prohibition secured, suffragists could quell any lingering discussions of the alleged connection between temperance and woman suffrage. By silencing liquor interests, voters had removed a major opponent of the cause. In addition, as the United States edged closer to entering the European conflict, suffrage advocates positioned German immigrants as a scapegoat on which to cast blame for the loss. Suffragists artfully crafted their argument. While they explicitly asserted that Germans more often opposed woman suffrage because they wrongly associated it with temperance, suffragists implicitly framed their claims within the growing anti-German sentiment stemming from increased concern over World War I. In 1914 suffragists like Anna Howard Shaw had warned of German immigrants who took out first papers in order to vote against democratic principles. In 1916 the SDUFL expanded its attack, suggesting that Germans were conspiring against woman suffrage in an elaborate plot designed to curb American values of liberty and freedom. The SDUFL offered only suspicions, but once the United States entered World War I in 1917, distrust fueled fear and provoked anti-German hysteria.[47]

Civic Responsibility, Loyalty, and World War I

While the campaigns in South Dakota and Iowa had admittedly ended in defeat, there had still been measurable success. Suffragists had claimed the ballot as an extension of established political identities rooted in civic responsibility. In the process, they had politicized the home and their civic duty toward it. These arguments had effectively persuaded more voters to support woman suffrage, albeit slowly. In Minnesota, sentiment in favor of the cause seemed to inch forward at a glacial pace, but leaders counted any degree of exposure to it as a success when the state lacked any referenda or official campaigns. In South Dakota, suffragists pointed out that the margins of defeat had narrowed between 1910 and 1916, which encouraged them to submit a seventh bill to the South Dakota legislature in the spring of 1917. In Iowa, the 1916 campaign had electrified advocates, and after an initial mourning period, suffragists recommitted themselves to the cause. Many women, like the members of the Spencer Woman's Club, devoted themselves wholeheartedly to political issues. After the 1916 election the group in Spencer discussed political matters, such as the "legal status of women" and the rights of "the woman citizen," at nearly every meeting. They sent resolutions endorsing woman suffrage to their respective senators and representatives. They recognized themselves as citizens entitled to full political rights, even if Iowa voters did not. At the state level, the IESA immediately reintroduced another bill to the Iowa legislature that would enfranchise women. They refused to accept the results of the 1916 campaign. At the national level, the leaders of NAWSA reconfigured their plans. One historian argues that it was the campaign in Iowa that "convinced Mrs. Catt that women faced insurmountable odds in most state referenda." Catt determined that NAWSA had to focus its efforts on a federal amendment while combining local, state, and national efforts into a cooperative "winning plan." When she presented the plan to the executive committee in September 1916, she reenergized NAWSA, steering the group toward a nationwide victory only four years later.[48]

America's entry into World War I in April 1917 dramatically reshaped the woman suffrage movement in the Midwest. While some suffrage advocates initially hesitated to take sides, as soon as the United States entered the conflict against Germany, most suffragists joined the war effort wholeheartedly. The decades of civic responsibility had prepared them well to participate in activities on the home front. In addition, Progressive reform had emphasized a close relationship with the government, and midwestern women had no trouble navigating the plethora of state and federal agencies and administrative councils created during wartime. Moreover, because women had redefined their political identities, placing the home at the center of their activism, they could engage in the war effort publicly without fear of disapproval or censure. In fact, midwesterners celebrated the patriotism demonstrated by rural women, so much so that women often set the standard of loyalty in the Midwest during World War I. The context of the war effort ultimately elevated loyalty as the true measure of citizenship. For suffragists, the connection between patriotism and citizenship was a gift. It gave them leverage on which to articulate political identities rooted in loyalty and informed by years of civic responsibility. It also allowed them to situate their plight as disenfranchised citizens against the threat of enfranchised foreigners, especially Germans. As anti-German hysteria grew to a fever pitch in the Midwest in 1917 and 1918, suffragists embraced nativism to achieve the right to vote.

Chapter 5

FIGHTING FOR DEMOCRACY: WOMAN SUFFRAGE, LOYALTY, AND WORLD WAR I

On September 30, 1918, President Woodrow Wilson startled leaders in the Senate when he arrived at their chambers to deliver an address in favor of woman suffrage. His personal presence there signaled the importance of his topic. Just nine months earlier, the House of Representatives had passed a woman suffrage amendment to the Constitution, and victory in the Senate meant that the measure would move to the states for ratification. Wilson's impassioned speech deemed woman suffrage a "war measure." He directly linked woman suffrage to World War I, arguing that female enfranchisement was "vital to the winning of the war." Wilson crafted his claims carefully. He asserted that women, as loyal citizens, had embraced the war effort wholeheartedly. They had sacrificed at home when their fathers, husbands, brothers, and sons left to fight overseas. Wilson demanded that the Senate reward their patriotism. Wilson also emphasized World War I as the "war to end all wars." He hoped that the end of hostilities in Europe could bring lasting peace across the globe. According to Wilson, the only way to ensure peace was for nations to adopt democracy. The European conflict was not only a military struggle, but also an ideological turning point in global political affairs, pitting democracy against autocracy. For Wilson, then, there was a fatal flaw in a political system that denied the ballot to women. How could Wilson "make the world safe for democracy" when half of its adult citizens could not vote? The United States government appeared hypocritical when it celebrated the rights of its citizens but continued to disenfranchise women. Woman suffrage promised to purify democracy at the exact moment that Wilson sought to position the United States as a global advocate of liberty and freedom.[1]

Despite Wilson's heartfelt plea, the Senate defeated the proposed constitutional amendment by a mere two votes. While Wilson did not persuade enough senators to endorse woman suffrage that day, his words resonated beyond Washington, DC. He delivered his address at the height of campaign efforts for a woman suffrage amendment to the state constitution in South Dakota—the seventh in the state since 1890—and residents there embraced his message enthusiastically. For over a week after Wilson delivered his speech, newspapers across South Dakota published articles that discussed the arguments he offered. In one article, entitled "Half a Democracy," the author encouraged people to read the speech and deliberate carefully on its contents. He justified his support by quoting two paragraphs from Wilson's address. Wilson argued that rejecting woman suffrage undermined the United States' claim that it was the "great, powerful, [and] famous democracy of the west" sent to save European nations from the tyranny of oppression and the destruction of war. How could the United States bring about a "new age" of peace when only half its population could exercise their constitutional rights? The author used Wilson's words to warn South Dakotans that if woman suffrage failed, warring countries would "cease to believe in us" and "cease to follow or to trust us," effectively threatening America's position as a champion of democracy. The connection between postwar peace and woman suffrage was clear and powerful. It cast the suffragist cause as a patriotic war measure. Across the Midwest, suffragists subtly shifted their rhetorical approach with the onset of American participation in World War I. They still emphasized women's civic responsibility, but now they imbued it with claims of patriotism and loyalty. They also infused nativism into their arguments when they pitted the wartime sacrifice of native-born women against the alleged treachery of foreign-born German immigrants.[2]

Prowar sentiment produced a wave of activity on the home front in support of soldiers fighting overseas, and across the Midwest, women participated energetically in these efforts. In many cases, they assumed pivotal leadership positions and garnered public acclaim for their roles. Decades of civic engagement, amplified by Progressivism, had given them credibility and experience in local politics and community building. War transformed their networks of activism, established through ladies' aid societies, federated women's clubs, and the WCTU, into patriotic organizations. Women were ubiquitous in wartime activities. They spearheaded Liberty Loan drives. They directed the American Red

Cross. They promoted food conservation and rationing. They joined local chapters of the Council of National Defense and the Committee of Public Information. The mobilization work they accomplished was highly public and visible, and it demonstrated their loyalty in unmistakable ways. Midwestern suffragists recognized that they could manipulate the patriotism displayed by rural women into unequivocal proof that women deserved the right to vote. They reconfigured their arguments again, claiming that women ought to be given the vote because of their patriotic service to the war effort. In doing so, they espoused the same vision of citizenship proffered by nativists across the region. Reputation, built on civic duty, proved an individual's fitness for citizenship.

As midwesterners joined the war effort, they reflected on the relationship between citizens and the nation. World War I mobilized people to serve their country in many ways besides military enlistment and despite qualities like gender, race, class, or age. As the editor of the *Press and Dakotan,* Yankton County's daily newspaper, remarked, "Until the war began the responsibility of citizenship seemed to consist chiefly of obeying the law," and most people, the author noted, did not take their own citizenship very seriously. The war tested that assumption in remarkable ways. When threatened by "an unscrupulous foe," citizenship became something "which cannot be evaded." The war issued an inescapable mandate to "give to the nation whatever it needs." The inclusive character of this unavoidable responsibility was profound. It extended not only to soldiers but also to those at home whose duty was to "buy Liberty Bonds, raise gardens, conserve wheat, [and] support the Red Cross . . . and relief agencies." It also included anyone who was a citizen of the United States, regardless of his or her status at birth. "Whether we were born, brought here, or came here, it is our duty, our responsibility to do everything that a loyal American citizen should do." The "seriousness of [this] task" made people "indignant at the slacker, who shirks all responsibility." World War I upended conventional ideas about citizenship at an important moment for midwestern suffragists. It turned citizenship into a measure of civic responsibility that pitted those who took their duty seriously against those who did not.[3]

World War I dramatically reshaped the context in which midwestern women advocated for the right to vote. State and national suffrage leaders argued that voting was a responsibility for those who took it seriously. They also welcomed new ideas about citizenship that downplayed gender distinctions. Moreover, they also pointed out the contradictory notions of citizenship, expressed most clearly in uneven assimilation expectations and inconsistencies within the naturalization process. Lax enforcement in local and state courts during the nineteenth century, along with contradictions like "alien suffrage," were problematic, claimed suffragists, especially as World War I increased Americans' fears of domestic conspiracies instigated by foreign-born spies. Paranoia grew against noncitizens, especially Germans, who could vote. A polarized political environment came to separate loyal citizens from deceitful foreigners. Across the country, people condemned "would-be Americans" and "hyphenated citizenship," lambasting the practice of emphasizing ethnic origin over national identity. Abstract notions of citizenship no longer sufficed. Instead, public demonstrations of loyalty and patriotism determined people's citizenship status. Cultural expressions of ethnicity, other than American ones, decreased dramatically, as public censures promoted homogeneity over ethnic diversity. Across the nation, Americans demanded assimilation in the form of actions, not words, to prove citizenship.[4]

Nativism sparked by World War I shattered the tolerance of ethnic diversity in the Midwest. During the nineteenth century, few people had questioned an individual's citizenship status. Many Germans chose to retain their ethnic traditions, and they celebrated their heritages openly through food, dress, and language. For decades, foreign born and native born lived together, establishing friendships but experiencing certain tensions by maintaining separate identities. Nativism weakened the ability to express these distinct cultural identities, enforcing conformity and curtailing separatist tendencies among immigrants. It also promoted nationalism, which called for an increased scrutiny of citizenship. Most midwesterners demanded absolute loyalty to the United States, a criterion largely determined by patriotic actions. Citizenship became a performance, not a status, and strict codes of behavior replaced ambiguity. Midwesterners also embraced loyalty because they had cherished it for decades. The earliest residents had privileged devotion to community, championing membership through civic engagement. While participation was an expectation, ethnic diversity had skewed the manner in which individuals contributed to society. For decades, belonging and civic duty had remained basically an impulse, contested by immigrants and contradicted by inequalities. World War I tipped the scales and changed the standards. It reemphasized the sense of community among midwesterners as they joined in a common purpose, and it encouraged them to conflate citizenship with an "American" identity. They embraced what Andrew Cayton called "generic" citizenship, stifling ethnic diversity out of fear, not by choice.[5]

Loyalty became the litmus test for citizenship, and midwesterners imposed a strict standard of behavior. They regulated ethnic expressions, such as dress, language, and food, by banning anything different as "un-American." In Iowa, Governor William Harding prohibited the use of any foreign language in public places. He included any conversations in churches or over the telephone. Officials in Ida County confiscated radios from German families, fearing the spread of secret messages. Marshall Bailey, a farmer from Clay County, remembered that "there was quite a bit of anti-German feeling." Bailey reported that leaders of the Liberty Loan campaigns feared disloyalty among German-Americans so much that they forced them to purchase more than the standard amount of bonds to prove their patriotism. State officials in South Dakota also ordered all ethnic Germans to speak English, including ministers. At the local level, many residents turned into amateur detectives, policing neighbors and friends whom they suspected as disloyal. They mainly targeted Germans and their second-generation children, who composed a significant portion of the population. Anyone who displayed unpatriotic actions risked a hefty penalty. Nativists relied on two pieces of legislation, the Espionage Act, passed in June 1917, and the Sedition Act, enacted in May 1918, to indict thousands of alleged German spies. The Espionage Act criminalized any action that impeded military activity, and made this punishable by a fine or even imprisonment. The Sedition Act extended the Espionage Act to cover a broad range of offenses, including speech and other expressions against the government or the war effort.[6]

As nativist tensions grew, rumors of German sabotage abounded across the Midwest. Authorities in Bon Homme County in South Dakota closed a mill operated by German Mennonites in response to baseless accusations that the proprietors were mixing ground glass with corn meal. In Hutchinson County, officers arrested thirty-one Germans who had signed a petition condemning the draft. Vigilantes even took the law into their own hands. In Yankton County, a group of masked men tarred and feathered a German druggist for openly criticizing the recklessness of anti-German paranoia. Newspapers stoked the public's fears by relentlessly publishing incendiary prowar and anti-German propaganda. Many editors reproduced information disseminated by the Committee on Public Information, a federal agency created to distribute prowar material, while others printed articles to incite terror in their readers. One article declared that "thousands, even millions, of enemies" were conspiring to "poison public opinion," "dynamite industries making munitions," and prolong the war to promote a "large loss of life." Local newspapers even published the names of "slackers," or men who avoided military service, to publicly shame them for their unpatriotic actions.[7]

Mobilizing for World War I

In counties across the Midwest, residents mobilized to defend the home front. Many people wanted to participate in the war even if they could not fight in Europe. Civilian mobilization was coordinated by the Council of National Defense, a federal organization created to promote the war effort by encouraging people to purchase Liberty Bonds, conserve food, and support the American Red Cross. By May 1917 individual states had begun to create their own councils, and soon counties formed local branches. While the legal authority of these councils was questionable, their members acted in an official manner, investigating reports of disloyalty with solemnity. Often the evidence was unfounded. In Scott County, Iowa, the council examined a case in which a German refused to applaud during a patriotic lecture. After a thorough scrutiny of the man's life, including inquiries about his friends, work, and citizenship status, the council dropped all charges. Despite the fragile legality of these councils, their members could enact draconian measures. Their power derived less from their capacity to enforce punishment and more from their ability to bully and intimidate. In Yankton County, South Dakota, the council ordered "all German enemies" to register with officials. Any non-naturalized man with ties to Germany had to furnish his fingerprints and four photographs for identification. On registration day, the *Press and Dakotan* gleefully reported that almost all those whom officials had expected to register had appeared in person with the proper paperwork. Immigrants apparently feared the perception of disloyalty more than the scrutiny of the council.[8]

In addition to the Council of National Defense, midwesterners eagerly joined the American Red Cross during World War I, which served as yet another way to propel patriots into the public spotlight. When the United States entered the war, the Red Cross moved to the center of civilian mobilization. In 1915 the Red Cross had only 22,000 members, but by the end of the war more than 20,000,000 adults had joined the organization. Its popularity skyrocketed in May 1917, when President Wilson tapped the Red Cross to serve as an auxiliary to the federal government, and through it about 8,000,000 women, along with children in the Junior Red Cross, produced 371,000,000 "relief articles," including hospital bandages, clothing, and other knitted items. The flexible schedule incentivized volunteerism, particularly among women who preferred the convenience of working from home, and people across the country flocked to the organization.[9]

Midwestern women most often chose to demonstrate their loyalty through the Red Cross. The decision to enroll was easy, since the tasks associated with the Red Cross fit neatly into established networks of female activism. Through their membership in federated women's clubs, ladies' aid societies, the WCTU, and other social groups, women knew how to mobilize around a cause. The work also required no training because much of it relied on female domestic skills. Almost all rural women knew how to sew or knit, many from an early age. Sewing skills also transcended class and ethnicity. Women who had little money to spare could always darn a pair of socks or stitch a bandage. Moreover, many immigrant women jumped at the opportunity to participate because it got their names into the local newspaper. Weekly reports in small-town publications celebrated the output of the Red Cross's members, often listing the names of the individuals alongside their contributions. Women in ethnic enclaves realized that contributing to the Red Cross could silence nativists. Not only did the Red Cross emphasize domestic work, but it also transformed ordinary household chores into public expressions of patriotism. Local communities highly valued it, and women enjoyed the publicity their efforts garnered.[10]

While midwesterners rooted out spies through the Council of National Defense and sewed clothing and bandages through the American Red Cross, they also raised tremendous sums of money for the war through Liberty Loan campaigns, with women often at the helm of these fund-raising activities. By the middle of 1917, officials in the federal government realized that the costs associated with the war were skyrocketing, and they grew desperate. A massive taxation plan was unpopular, so authorities decided to sell bonds. Between April 1917 and April 1919, the government instituted five bond drives, and Americans responded with passionate patriotism. As one historian noted, the results were "impressive." In total, Americans raised almost $20 billion, going "over the top," or pledging more than the quota, for each drive. Midwesterners were eager to prove their loyalty, and purchasing bonds served as a demonstrative measure of an individual's professions of national allegiance. As Liberty Loans became synonymous with patriotism during World War I, they also showcased women's activism. In the Midwest, women regularly directed Liberty Loan campaigns, orchestrating these massive patriotic fund-raisers as part of their established civic responsibilities. Bond drives mirrored previous political campaigns, particularly the ones for woman suffrage. Women worked at the county and township levels, conducting massive door-to-door canvasses of their respective neighborhoods. In addition, women in churches tapped into their experiences as fund-raisers. They held community-wide events, like dinners, socials, and bazaars, which they copied directly from the playbooks written by ladies' aid societies. As one newspaper reported, "loyal women" deserved all the credit for the success of the Liberty Loan campaigns.[11]

As the war effort intensified, federal officials turned to farmers in the Midwest to increase agricultural production, and women responded by turning their attention to food conservation. Through the Cooperative Extension Service, a federal agency created to apply scientific research to agriculture, midwesterners ramped up production. In Iowa, the number of hogs rose by 15 percent during the war while yields for crops like corn, wheat, and barley grew by 26 percent. While farmers grew more food, they also conserved more of it. The Cooperative Extension Service sent out home demonstration agents to encourage women to plant gardens, raise poultry, and conserve food by canning, preserving, and storing it. Midwestern women participated enthusiastically in "meatless" and "wheatless" days, believing that soldiers at war needed the calories more than those at home. In Yankton County, the Woman's Club—previously known as the Nineteenth Century Club—passed a series of resolutions and published them in the *Dakota Herald*. Among other things, the club's members encouraged their neighbors to cook the "simplest foods consistent with wholesomeness and health." Midwesterners recognized that women held huge power over food, and their decisions about what to serve at the dinner table mattered a great deal. In addition, canning became a patriotic act. Propaganda published in newspapers across the Midwest noted the simple, yet symbolic, work that canning meant to the war effort. According to one article, "Every bushel of potatoes properly stored, every pound of vegetables put by for future use, every jar of fruit preserved, adds that much to our insurance of victory." Food conservation further politicized the domestic work of rural women, and the message was clear. Loyal citizens not only enlisted to fight in Europe; they also canned vegetables, sold war bonds, and sewed bandages in their homes.[12]

Suffragists Join the War Effort

Just as loyalty prompted rural women in the Midwest to endorse the war, so too did it impel suffragists across the nation to participate in home-front activities and assert their patriotism. As historian Sara Evans notes, suffragists benefited greatly from "the highly visible support of women for this extremely popular war." Suffragists cited all of the home-front activities women engaged in, marshaling them as proof that women deserved the right to vote as devoted citizens. Initially, however, some suffragists balked at joining the conflict. For these women, like Carrie Chapman Catt, peace was their utmost concern, and they watched the situation unfolding in Europe with anxiety. As the United States became increasingly involved in the war, however, Catt and other peace advocates realized that they could not ignore it. Moreover, as the president of NAWSA, Catt sensed an opportune moment. She recognized that service to the war effort could give suffragists political leverage in favor of the cause by skillfully couching woman suffrage within Wilson's lofty "war aims." She argued that female enfranchisement confirmed the political values that Americans cherished, thereby upholding Wilson's plan to "make the world safe for democracy."[13]

Suffragists demonstrated their patriotism by taking leadership positions in organizations like the Council of National Defense, American Red Cross, and food conservation programs. In 1917, Wilson tapped the former NAWSA president Anna Howard Shaw to chair the Woman's Committee of the Council of National Defense. Wilson also appointed

Catt as an executive member of the Woman's Committee. Wilson's selection of Shaw and Catt was no accident; historians point out that it was a political move meant to signal the intimate connection between woman suffrage and the war. It also granted Shaw and Catt "insider status" in Washington, DC, which became crucial in 1918, when members of Congress introduced a federal woman suffrage amendment. In the Midwest, suffragists were ubiquitous in activities on the home front. Like Shaw and Catt, the presidents of state suffrage associations attained executive offices in state branches of the Council of National Defense. They also served on committees of food conservation programs and the American Red Cross. State suffrage advocates were easy choices for these positions. Their reputations as effective community organizers gave them an edge. They knew how to run campaigns and engage the public in a cause.[14]

As soon as the United States entered the war, suffrage leaders across the Midwest publicly pledged to transform suffrage work into war work. The immediacy of their patriotism led government officials to select suffragists for leadership positions. In April 1917 the governor of Minnesota, Joseph Burnquist, appointed Clara Ueland, president of the MWSA, to serve on the Food Production and Conservation Committee of the Minnesota Commission of Public Safety. The commission was a state agency that persecuted ethnic groups accused of radicalism and Americanized newcomers to the state. In South Dakota, Mamie Pyle, president of the SDUFL, served on the South Dakota Division of the Woman's Committee of the Council of National Defense. In Iowa, Anna Lawther, president of the IESA, threw herself wholeheartedly into war work. She served on the Iowa Division of the Woman's Committee of the Council of National Defense. She chaired the Women's Committee of the Iowa Food Administration. She led the Third Congressional District Committee of the Red Cross. She distributed circulars, explaining why the IESA championed the war. The IESA, she wrote, "stands for one ideal—service to the nation in both time of peace and in time of war." She summoned all suffragists to "co-operate with us in this new war service." Local activists responded enthusiastically, participating in every home-front activity and gaining public recognition for the items sewn, food canned, and bonds sold. With political identities honed by decades of civic engagement, these suffragists faced little public scrutiny as they navigated their new wartime roles.[15]

Americanization

Of all the activities on the home front, suffragists in the Midwest spent much of their time on Americanization efforts. Conditions in the region created a fear of foreigners, and suffragists eagerly jumped on the nativist bandwagon. A large immigrant population had flooded the region in the decades leading up to World War I. Many lived in isolated ethnic enclaves, speaking native languages and failing to assimilate. In addition, high percentages of Germans in midwestern states worried state and local political leaders. Concerned people at both levels introduced plans to educate immigrants and urge them to adopt American cultural values. They reasoned that if Germans discarded ethnic customs in favor of American ones, then they proved their loyalty. Americanization also offered suffrage advocates a chance to change minds in favor of the cause and ensure victory on future suffrage measures. Finally, suffragists crusaded against Germans because they harbored a grudge against them. They believed that opposition from German voters had crushed suffrage amendments, especially the two defeated in Iowa and South Dakota in 1916. In early 1917, suffragists began to hold Americanization classes across the Midwest in which they focused on domestic tasks, teaching female foreigners how to cook, clean, care for children, and sew during wartime. On the surface, their instructions about how to preserve food and sew Red Cross items seemed to stem from a sincere desire to help immigrants and promote the war effort. However, the lessons were not entirely benign. Canning and sewing became patriotic actions in the context of World War I nativism. Moreover, adopting American foods and wearing American fashions pressured ethnic groups to abandon their cultural distinctions.

Americanization also gave suffragists a golden opportunity to perform their citizenship by targeting family life among foreigners. Activists showcased their civic knowledge—and fitness for the ballot—by teaching foreigners about American politics. They did not have to stretch their political identities to do so. Decades of civic responsibility had prepared rural suffrage activists to educate immigrants. They understood loyalty and civic pride because they had demonstrated community activism for years. At the heart of the message suffragists delivered was the centrality of the home and family to the war effort.

They demanded a level of assimilation that surpassed simple political transformation, calling for a radical change in cultural identity. They targeted the family, believing that because people instilled cultural traditions in their homes, efforts aimed at the family could strike at the core of ethnic identity formation. In addition, the family remained a powerful ideal in American political life, and suffragists believed that the survival of democracy hinged on the values instilled in the home. To break the cycle of generational transference of ethnic traits, suffragists targeted foreign-born women. They exploited their gendered knowledge of the home—cooking, cleaning, sewing, and other domestic duties—in order to Americanize immigrant women, erasing cultural and political distinctions and encouraging homogeneity in the process. Like nativists across the country, midwestern suffragists praised conformity while admonishing ethnic difference, asserting their patriotism and, in the process, presenting their case for the ballot. Americanization was an effective, albeit insidious, way to standardize the ways midwesterners understood citizenship.

Iowa

Suffragists in Iowa passionately pursued Americanization. As Anna Lawther, president of the IESA, put it, "The Americanization of the alien is perhaps the most important question confronting us to-day in this country." The IESA lamented how easily immigrants could cling to their ethnic customs. Wartime demanded loyalty, and suffragists pressured immigrants to demonstrate their allegiance to the United States. In April 1917 Lawther began publishing "Suffrage Circulars" to advocates across the state. The IESA demanded that newspaper editors in every county publish propaganda that explained how to behave as an American. Members wrote to the editors of non-English newspapers, admonishing them for using the enemy's language. They distributed propaganda that promoted woman suffrage and discredited ethnic diversity at patriotic rallies, food preservation demonstrations, and other events. Lawther also endorsed the Americanization of the entire family, starting with second-generation children. She thought it hypocritical that the children of immigrants could enjoy American citizenship by birth and still continue to celebrate their ethnic heritages. She recognized that Americanization could succeed only when it interrupted the transmission of ethnic identities down the generations. If propaganda failed, Lawther encouraged suffragists to personally investigate the immigrants in their neighborhoods. She instructed activists to visit informally with non-native women in order to gauge their loyalty and report any suspicious people to the authorities.[16]

While the IESA did its best to incite fear of foreigners, local advocates struggled to condemn all immigrants. In Clay County, the Spencer Woman's Club regularly debated the "immigrant question" during World War I. While some members expressed sympathy for the foreigners' plight, others took a hard line, stating their suspicion of "enemies." They were careful to vilify all Germans, instead encouraging residents to engage in patriotic activities. The group revised its monthly meeting agendas to focus almost exclusively on war work, including sewing for the Red Cross and raising money to purchase Liberty Bonds.[17]

While suffragists in Iowa pursued Americanization, they also recommitted themselves to achieving the right to vote. They recalled the civic responsibility claim that had developed during the Progressive Era and linked it directly to the war effort, subtly modifying their arguments in the process. Before the war, the vote would have given women the power to purify politics, defend the home, and nurture the family. Wartime raised the stakes, making the ballot in the hands of women a safeguard for the nation and a protection for democracy. During a speech at the IESA's 1917 annual convention, Lawther echoed President Wilson's pleas. "Our war, our sacrifice," she proclaimed, "is made that the world may be made safe for Democracy." Woman suffrage became a war measure, designed to uplift democracy at the precise moment that it served as the political inspiration to the world. As Lawther connected woman suffrage to the war effort, the IESA submitted another amendment to Iowa's legislature. Lawther believed that she had loyalty on her side, and she grew convinced that Iowans were ready to give women the ballot. During the 1917 legislative session, both the House and Senate passed the measure without opposition, and the IESA was elated. The bill required a second approval during the next legislative session, however, which was scheduled for the following year. Victory seemed certain until the IESA learned that a clerk in the secretary of state's office had committed a procedural error that nullified any action on the amendment. The 1918 session closed with no vote on the bill, and the

IESA was outraged. A simple mistake had wasted two years of work for woman suffrage in Iowa.[18]

South Dakota

Just as it did in Iowa, the patriotic fervor inspired by World War I dramatically reshaped woman suffrage in South Dakota. Since 1890 South Dakota had had an ample record of activity for the suffragist cause, with six previous campaigns that had each ended in failure. During the late nineteenth century, close ties with the WCTU had fractured the state association, but since 1911 the South Dakota Universal Franchise League (SDUFL) had overseen the work. Under the presidency of Mamie Pyle, the SDUFL slowly won over South Dakotans, and the margin of defeat decreased with each subsequent campaign. By 1917, suffragists believed they could erase any remaining doubts by joining the war effort. Across the state, advocates sewed garments for the American Red Cross, joined the Council of National Defense, sold Liberty Bonds, and encouraged immigrants to Americanize. Their loyalty solidified their claims to the ballot so that, like Iowa's suffragists, South Dakota's advocates could argue convincingly that woman suffrage upheld democratic ideals.

In January 1917, the South Dakota legislature passed a bill to bring to voters a woman suffrage amendment at the 1918 general election. Suffragists considered the usual strategies, and Pyle planned for a typical campaign. As the United States inched closer to war, however, the legislature sprang into action. In March 1917, the Republican governor Peter Norbeck called a special session to pass emergency wartime legislation. Among the bills considered was the woman suffrage bill. Norbeck's concern was not female enfranchisement but foreigners who could vote on first papers. Anti-German hysteria had provoked fear that treasonous spies could malign democracy by sabotaging elections. To prevent a potential electoral disaster, Norbeck added a clause to the woman suffrage bill. The extra language lengthened the residency requirement for citizenship and confirmed that only naturalized citizens could vote, effectively eliminating the loophole that had allowed immigrants to vote on first papers. Suffragists in South Dakota were elated. With one swift action, Norbeck had created a Citizenship Amendment that explicitly linked participatory democracy with patriotism.[19]

When Norbeck tacked on a few additional lines to Amendment E, or the Citizenship Amendment, he simultaneously constricted and opened the boundaries of citizenship. The bill promised to enfranchise women while denying the same right to foreign-born men, many of whom had cast ballots for years on first papers. To most South Dakotans, the measure was neither contradictory nor hastily made. It reflected the paranoia provoked by the fear of ethnic outsiders that had taken hold of midwesterners since World War I had begun. It also confirmed that South Dakotans no longer understood citizenship as a status. The amendment erased the ambiguity that favored ethnic inclusion, adopting instead criteria that favored an "American" identity. The SDUFL saw no irony in prohibiting non-naturalized men from voting, even though they had done so legally. In fact, the amended bill delighted state leaders. Not only did it silence opponents who did not want to appear favorable to Germans, but it also made woman suffrage an actual, not just a theoretical, war measure.

The 1918 campaign in South Dakota was unlike any of the previous suffrage campaigns in that state. Whereas the campaigns in 1914 and 1916 had included attempts at direct grassroots organization by field workers, the 1918 campaign relied more on indirect strategies, especially propaganda in newspapers. For Pyle and other leaders of the SDUFL, war work was time-consuming, and woman suffrage often took a back seat to their other responsibilities. Pyle scaled back her plans for grassroots organizing, asking "only two or three women in every county" to serve on a central county committee. Coordinating these committees alongside Pyle were Maria McMahon and Rene Stevens, two veteran organizers who had worked in all three states only two years earlier. Another nationally trained woman, Elizabeth Pidgeon, assisted the SDUFL. McMahon arrived in South Dakota in mid-February, ready to orchestrate efforts on a broad scale. McMahon's major tasks were to schedule speakers and oversee work among the central campaign committees in each county.[20]

Local advocates and state leaders in South Dakota easily combined war work with campaigning for woman suffrage. Pyle split her time between the SDUFL and her position as head of the South Dakota Division of the Woman's Committee of the Council of National Defense, but there was considerable overlap. In early 1918, the Woman's Committee conducted a statewide canvass to register women aged sixteen and older for war work. At the same time, the SDUFL implemented a petition drive, gathering signatures in support of woman suffrage. It was difficult to tell where one effort ended and the other began. Canvassing had been a central tactic in previous woman suffrage campaigns spearheaded by the SDUFL, and Pyle tapped many suffragists living in local communities to lead both the war work registration drive and the petition campaign. In fact, in most counties in South Dakota, the head of the Red Cross or Woman's Committee was also the chair of the central campaign committee. In Yankton County, McMahon noted how busy the members of the central campaign committee were with the Red Cross and Woman's Committee work. Unlike previous campaigns in which lecturers spoke in churches or at city hall, McMahon gave her speeches at Red Cross and Woman's Committee meetings. As Pyle received field reports from McMahon, it did not take her long to recognize that the 1918 campaign held promise. "War conditions" and the work suffragists were doing on the home front made the connection between woman suffrage and patriotism obvious to just about everyone.[21]

In Yankton County local advocates organized a subtle grassroots campaign, preferring to agitate through printed propaganda more than through direct campaigning. At the helm was Harriet Bennett, the wife of Mark Bennett who edited the *Dakota Herald,* one of two local newspapers in Yankton County. In June 1918 Bennett printed the last issue of the *Dakota Herald,* probably because he had taken full-time work as postmaster. McMahon reported Mark to be an "ardent suffragist," while Harriet was a well-known civic leader and president of the federated Woman's Club. Serving alongside Harriet Bennett were Jennie Thompson and Electa Danforth, whose husband, Fred, was a banker. Thompson was single and a seamstress who lived with her elderly parents. Bennett, Thompson, and Danforth were Yankee civic leaders with experience in "managing organization work" and who also had "influence . . . energy, and wisdom." To McMahon, it was the perfect combination.[22]

The SDUFL worried less about forming suffrage clubs and more about stoking anti-German sentiment while celebrating the patriotism of midwestern women. Mamie Pyle, the president of the SDUFL, secretly hoped for the war to last through November 8, 1918, the date of the election, because the propaganda only worked in the context of wartime. Newspapers published a barrage of articles that verified this rhetoric. Headlines read, "Suffragists in War Work," "Woman Suffrage a War Measure," and "Amendment E Patriotic Act." Advertisements asked voters, "Are you 100% American?" and encouraged them to "Vote X Yes for Amendment E." (See figure 9.) The SDUFL repeated the same theme, pitting the "alien enemy" against patriotic women "sacrificing so deeply for the world struggle." They even blamed Germans for the loss of the 1916 woman suffrage amendment, publishing a map that showed the counties in which voters had defeated woman suffrage, with their percentage of German population. Without stating it explicitly, the SDUFL's map issued a clear warning to South Dakotans. German spies

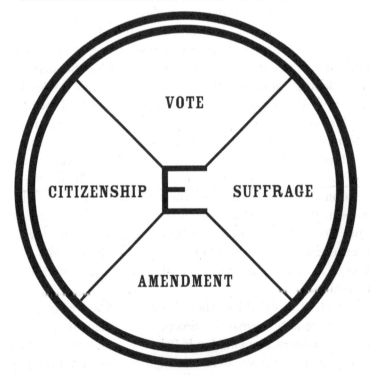

VOTE FOR AMENDMENT E – AMERICANISM AND SUFFRAGE

VOTE

CITIZENSHIP   SUFFRAGE

AMENDMENT

FIGURE 9. Newspaper propaganda from the 1918 South Dakota campaign. "Vote for Amendment E—Americanism and Suffrage," *Volin Advance,* Oct. 10, 1918.

had successfully plotted the defeat of the 1916 amendment, a measure that promoted democratic principles. If they had already ruined one election, then they could do it again.[23]

As the campaign approached the November 8 deadline, the SDUFL intensified its efforts to convince South Dakotans to vote in favor of the Citizenship Amendment. Throughout the month of October, they continued to disseminate propaganda that juxtaposed patriotic women with allegedly traitorous Germans, calling on all "loyal citizens" to support Amendment E. The measure was "essential to the welfare and progress of the state" for it uplifted democracy to its truest form. Building on arguments that highlighted women's civic responsibility, this material endorsed "100 percent Americanism" and anti-German rhetoric. In Yankton County, the editor of the *Press and Dakotan* echoed the message, daring his readers to stand "by our idealism, by our generosity, by our willingness to support our beliefs with our lives" and stop living as "half a democracy."[24]

By the fall of 1918, with pro-suffrage sentiment increasing, the SDUFL mounted a face-to-face campaign, distributing petitions and organizing speaking tours for trained lecturers. According to historian Patricia Easton, 95 percent of South Dakota women signed a petition, which she argues indicated their readiness to vote. In addition to a petition drive, the SDUFL also organized a lecture circuit for Carrie Chapman Catt, the president of NAWSA. Advocates in Yankton County were thrilled to learn of her coming lecture there, scheduled for October 14, and they advertised it prominently in the local newspapers. When Catt contracted influenza, however, Pyle regretfully canceled her engagements. As disappointing as Catt's absence was, it did not harm the outcome of the campaign. In fact, the patriotic fervor inspired by World War I was promoting the cause more than any other factor. According to reports, the election had everything to do with "100-percent American voters" defeating alien enemies.[25]

When officials tallied the election results on November 9, they noted that the 1918 election—"one of the most intense" in the state's history—had inspired a large voter turnout. The Citizenship Amendment passed with a whopping 64 percent of the total ballots cast and a margin of almost 20,000 votes. The timing of the election was fortuitous. Only three days after the election, on November 11, Germany agreed to an armistice with the Allies, thus ending hostilities. Mamie Pyle had gotten her wish for the war to outlast the campaign. The results also revealed how deeply South Dakotans embraced nativism. It sharply influenced their conceptions of citizenship, constricting it to those who were deemed loyal. Measuring loyalty was difficult, but in the context of World War I, it came down to patriotic demonstrations in support of the war effort. Rural women excelled at this test, serving publicly in the American Red Cross, the Council of National Defense, and Liberty Loan campaigns. Moreover, they benefited from prolonged anti-German paranoia, the same fear that had added the stricter naturalization requirements to the Citizenship Amendment in the first place. With most Americans caught up in the wartime fervor, woman suffrage in South Dakota emerged victorious.[26]

Minnesota

Across the border, suffragists in Minnesota also reconfigured their plans when the United States entered World War I. A large immigrant population, including many Germans, initially balked at demands to support the war effort. As nativism grew, however, antiwar outbursts decreased and most Minnesotans caught the patriotic spirit. Sensing an opportunity to link woman suffrage to World War I, Clara Ueland, the president of the Minnesota Woman Suffrage Association (MWSA), encouraged suffragists to do their part for the war. Advocates stitched items for the Red Cross, endorsed the activities of the Council of National Defense, sold bonds during Liberty Loan campaigns, and participated wholeheartedly in food conservation initiatives. As a result, Minnesotans slowly warmed to the suffragist cause. After decades of limited activity, the MWSA was ready to bring its message to Minnesotans across the state. In a series of "Dear Suffragist" letters, Ueland proclaimed that woman suffrage promised to make the United States a "democracy in fact as well as in name." Like Lawther in Iowa, Ueland argued that democracy in its purest form required universal suffrage regardless of gender. Unfortunately, practical roadblocks remained. Amending Minnesota's constitution was almost impossible, so Carrie Chapman Catt and the MWSA sought a more viable strategy. As part of her "winning plan," Catt instructed the state association to agitate for presidential suffrage by legislative action.

In January 1917, four months before the United States entered World War I, the MWSA regrouped. Under the direction of Ueland, state workers created a directory of all district and county suffragists. With these names, the MWSA hoped to organize the state by selecting local leaders, but as they compiled their lists, they found a haphazard assortment of advocates. Many counties lacked even one identified suffragist, including Lyon County. Ueland recognized the difficulty in grassroots mobilization, but she deemed it necessary in order to convince members of the state legislature to endorse presidential suffrage. The MWSA planned to send a barrage of evidence, including petitions, resolutions, and letters, to representatives to prove that their constituents supported the cause. As early as the summer of 1917, the MWSA delivered petitions to each local leader, designating a specific quota of signatures for each county. Once suffragists had collected enough signatures, they sent them back to the MWSA for distribution. In addition, the state association sought endorsements from organizations across the state. The size or prominence of the group did not matter; instead, the MWSA wanted to impress each representative with an overwhelming number of resolutions from the counties in his district. Finally, Ueland instructed individuals to correspond with their state leaders by sending candid letters expressing their desire to vote. Some local suffragists even arranged personal meetings, to the delight of the MWSA.[27]

As the MWSA carried out these initiatives, conflicts arose among factions of suffragists in Minnesota. Some advocates believed that the MWSA pursued tepid strategies with weak results. It was time to be provocative and use drastic tactics. In January 1917 the Minnesota Equal Franchise League (MEFL), a group that had remained an auxiliary to the MWSA since 1914, persuaded a member of the state House to introduce a woman suffrage amendment to the state's constitution. The MEFL had rejected Catt's mandate to secure presidential suffrage by legislative action, believing that voters in Minnesota were ready to embrace an immense grassroots campaign to enfranchise women. Ueland and the rest of the MWSA were horrified. Minnesota's constitution required that an amendment earn the majority of all votes cast in the election, not just on the measure itself. Woman suffrage thus faced impossible odds, and the MWSA knew it. Ueland swiftly intervened, contacting members of the Minnesota legislature who understood the MWSA's stance. When the Senate voted to indefinitely postpone the bill, the MWSA breathed a sigh of relief, but the respite was short-lived.[28]

By the fall of 1917, tensions among suffragists in Minnesota were brewing again, this time over the MWSA's relationship with Alice Paul and the National Woman's Party (NWP). In 1913, when Paul had taken the helm of the Congressional Union, she impressed Ueland and other leaders of the MWSA. The Congressional Union's visible tactics were welcome in a state where woman suffrage agitation had stagnated. Parades, open-air meetings, and other demonstrations had broken the silence in Minnesota, and Ueland appreciated their effectiveness out of practicality, not radicalism. During the 1916 elections, however, Paul had intensified the militancy of the Congressional Union, openly campaigning against the Democrats, the party in national power, for failing to pass a federal woman suffrage amendment. Aghast, Catt and NAWSA tried to rein in the Congressional Union, seeking to avoid partisanship, but Paul rejected Catt's pleas. In June 1916 Paul left NAWSA and merged the Congressional Union with the NWP, which actively campaigned against Wilson and the Democrats through the November 1916 elections. By January 1917 the NWP, frustrated at Wilson's stubborn refusal to endorse the suffragist cause, had begun picketing the White House.[29]

The militancy of the NWP placed Ueland and the MWSA in a precarious situation. While Ueland respected Paul's electrifying campaign strategies, she also grew worried as the NWP's protests aroused intense criticism, especially after the United States had declared war on Germany. Ueland eventually sided with Catt and NAWSA. It was too risky— and patriotism too important to their claims to the ballot—to associate publicly with the NWP. Ueland's decision riled her critics. In the fall of 1917, a pro-NWP faction attempted to replace the entire MWSA leadership corps, including Ueland, at the MWSA's annual convention, but Ueland gathered her supporters and secured the presidency for another term. She stood firm in her commitment of the MWSA to do its part in Catt's "winning plan."[30]

While Ueland deftly handled her critics, she still faced skepticism from Minnesotans about woman suffrage. Decades of inaction had hampered grassroots mobilization, and in many counties it took more than a year for the campaign for presidential suffrage to materialize. Gaining favor among residents was difficult, and translating that support into affirmative votes in the state legislature was a huge task. For months petitions remained unsigned, endorsements unprinted, and letters unwritten while Minnesotans wrestled with their stance on the suffragist cause, many for the first time. Reluctance initially marked their attitudes, and only with encouragement from the MWSA did people endorse woman suffrage publicly. Once Minnesotans proclaimed their support, however, the floodgates opened. Why did sentiments shift so rapidly? Although there was little direct interaction with the suffragist movement, interest had percolated for years. As women built communities and established records of civic responsibility, they challenged the perceived radicalism associated with female political activism. Public service alone, however, could not secure woman suffrage. For decades, Minnesota's unbending constitution had troubled the MWSA, and this aimlessness had led to paralysis. World War I, along with Catt's mandate for presidential suffrage by legislative action, resurrected the group. When woman suffrage finally entered into public discourse, it incited a wave of activity, both from ordinary Minnesotans and state suffrage leaders.

The MWSA pressed forward its campaign to gain favor for woman suffrage, ramping up its organization in local communities and cajoling state legislators to support the cause. While as many as six field workers canvassed Minnesota, Ueland directly lobbied members of the House and Senate. Despite her hard work, the legislature rejected presidential suffrage in 1917. Undeterred, Ueland had sympathizers reintroduce another bill. The timing was impeccable. World War I had engulfed Minnesota, and rural women heartily endorsed the war effort, joining the Red Cross, Liberty Loan drives, and Americanization efforts. Ueland explicitly linked woman suffrage to patriotism. At the MWSA's 1917 annual convention she proclaimed, "American suffragists can stand by their country and at the same time give allegiance to the cause of suffrage." While Ueland's statement seemed defensive, it actually revealed the significance that patriotic loyalty held for gendered constructions of citizenship. Loyalty demanded that rural women sacrifice on the home front during World War I, and that same impulse drove their claims to enfranchisement. The vote was as much a demonstration of loyalty as any other war service was. Minnesotans embraced the connection between the war and the ballot. By the summer of 1918 locals had rallied around the cause, signing petitions, writing their representatives, and endorsing presidential suffrage.[31]

Lyon County exemplified the drastic transformation in attitudes toward woman suffrage that occurred among Minnesotans at this time. After decades of inaction, residents finally engaged with the cause, and their indifference turned into support. There is little evidence to determine how exactly they changed their minds, but World War I, along with encouragement from the MWSA, undoubtedly influenced their stance. In June 1918 the MWSA sent letters to three legislators, John Gislason, K. Knudson, and Fred Norwood, who represented Lyon County. The correspondence inquired about their position on woman suffrage and especially their vote to ratify a potential federal amendment. All three men answered the question "May we expect your support?" with a resounding "Yes." Norwood even included a short note, writing, "I most surly [*sic*] stand for the ratification of the suffrage amendment, first, last, and all the time," and signing it "Yours for victory." Ueland may have thought the intensity of Norwood's endorsement strange or unexpected, but he merely reflected the speed with which people in Lyon County took up the suffragist cause. Shortly after receiving word from the three legislators, the MWSA sent Grace Randall, a young field organizer, to Lyon County. Randall met with prominent women in Marshall, the county seat, and Minneota, another small town.[32]

Although she said little about her time in Lyon County, Randall must have touched a nerve. By August 1918 two pairs of women, Laura Lowe and Minnie Matthews in Marshall, the county seat, and Harriet Sanderson and Tillie Deen in Minneota, had agreed to direct a petition campaign. The four were recognized community leaders, with reputations established through the Red Cross, ladies' aid societies, and a number of woman's clubs, including the Current News Club. Although they belonged to a variety of organizations, these women worked independently of these groups. The MWSA set quotas at a majority of the number of voters at the last election for both men and women. For Lowe and Matthews in Marshall, the target was 313. Sanderson and Deen sought 124 names in Minneota. As the women gathered signatures, they encountered ignorance and opposition, which probably did not surprise them much. In October 1918 Lowe sought help, writing to state headquarters and requesting "literature" and "plans for conducting the campaign." She claimed that she had written twice before but had received no reply. Clara Heckrich, the corresponding secretary of the MWSA, apologized, explaining that their records regarding Lyon

County were "somewhat mixed." She promptly sent instructions, pamphlets, and other ephemera.[33]

The quartet labored doggedly for another month, combating anti-suffrage sentiment and struggling to counter unforeseen obstacles. An outbreak of influenza swept across the Midwest in the fall of 1918, and communities like Marshall and Minneota imposed strict quarantines. In Marshall, Lowe and Matthews reported that the epidemic prevented them from visiting a number of homes, and influenza eventually cut the petition drive short when Lowe contracted it. The epidemic also halted efforts in Minneota, especially when at least a dozen people died during the canvass. In addition to illness, the draft hurt the petition drive there. Deen claimed that at least fifty men could not sign the petition because they were serving overseas. Despite the hardships of illness and war, the four suffragists amassed an impressive amount of signatures. Lowe and Matthews collected the names of 130 men and 311 women, while Sanderson and Deen gathered 79 signatures from men. In November 1918 Clara Ueland sent a personal response to the suffragists in Lyon County, thanking them for their determination. "We think you have done very well indeed."[34]

While signed petitions served as direct evidence of increasing support for woman suffrage among residents in Minnesota, state suffrage leaders also sought endorsements from respected organizations. The opinions of these groups, which were recognized as the collective authorities in their respective fields, mattered a great deal because they could influence public attitudes. Suffragists also reasoned that a resolution, vetted and approved by a majority of various organizations' members, could help to sway legislators, many of whom were either members themselves or aspired to be. In 1917 a host of reputable organizations endorsed woman suffrage, including the State Dairyman's Association, the State Local Option Association, the State Editorial Association, the Good Roads Conference, the State Letter Carriers' Association, the State Federation of Women's Clubs, the Minnesota Educational Association, the Minnesota Christian Endeavor Union, and the Farmers' Grain Dealers Association. The sheer diversity of groups that supported the cause testified to the de-radicalization of woman suffrage in Minnesota. By 1918 it seemed almost fashionable to pass a pro-suffrage resolution, and organizations from local communities joined the growing chorus of statewide approvals. In Lyon County nine women's groups had endorsed the cause by January 1919, including five social clubs, three Red Cross auxiliaries, and one ladies' aid society. It was an astounding number for a county that had almost no record of previous activity in support of the suffragist cause. The MWSA gathered a plethora of endorsements like these during World War I as woman suffrage shed its radical image and gained popular support as a war measure.[35]

Minnesotans responded enthusiastically to the petition drives and endorsement campaigns on behalf of woman suffrage, and eventually the legislature took up the cause. In January 1919, legislators overwhelmingly supported a resolution that called on the United States Senate to pass a suffrage amendment at the federal level. It was a lopsided victory, 100 to 28 votes, and suffragists rejoiced. In fact, "so much enthusiasm and strength developed" that one representative, influenced by a mysterious group called the Minnesota Equal Suffrage Constitutional Amendment League, snuck in an amendment to the state's constitution. To the MWSA's dismay, the measure passed by a large majority. While Ueland and other state suffrage leaders were flattered that the legislature had finally endorsed woman suffrage, they did not want a state amendment. The MWSA had neither the time nor the resources to conduct an intense amendment campaign. Moreover, Carrie Chapman Catt had given Ueland explicit instructions to pursue presidential suffrage as part of her "winning plan." Suffragists also recognized the impossibility of amending Minnesota's constitution given the requirement that an amendment win a majority of all votes cast at an election. For two months, members of the MWSA carefully explained to legislators why presidential suffrage by legislative action was preferable to an amendment. Ueland spent countless hours at the capitol building, laying out her case. Finally, on February 28, the Senate indefinitely postponed the amendment. No longer distracted by other options, the Minnesota legislature passed presidential suffrage, the House voting 103 to 24 and Senate coming in at 49 to 11. Historian Barbara Stuhler remarks that the widespread support for presidential suffrage testified to the "deft strategies of the MWSA." Grassroots organization, including petition drives, endorsement campaigns, and the mobilization of voters across Minnesota, had galvanized members of the legislature to support woman suffrage. In addition, the MWSA benefited from the patriotic response of rural women to World War I. Ueland expertly linked civic responsibility to wartime civilian mobilization. On March 24, 1919,

Governor Joseph Burnquist signed the law, and women in Minnesota won the right to vote in presidential elections.[36]

Ratification

By 1919 suffragists in the Midwest had achieved remarkable victories, considering that only a few years earlier the cause had been generally unpopular. In Minnesota, women could vote in presidential elections, while in South Dakota, women enjoyed full enfranchisement with the passage of the Citizenship Amendment. In Iowa, suffragists rebounded from the clerical error that had stalled woman suffrage in the legislature, submitting another bill for statewide woman suffrage that year. While midwesterners signaled their support of the cause, activity at the federal level flourished. In May 1919 President Wilson called Congress into a special session to assess postwar issues. On the agenda was a federal amendment granting women the right to vote, which the House passed in May and the Senate in June. While suffragists across the United States celebrated, they also lamented the timing of the decision. Many state legislatures met only in spring, and sometimes every other year, which meant that the ratification process could drag on for months. Suffragists determined that in order for women to vote in the 1920 election, they had to persuade governors to call special sessions of their state legislatures to meet outside of the standard schedule. Arranging these sessions was difficult, but since the measure required approval from thirty-six states, suffragists realized that a delay in only a handful of states could foil ratification nationwide. Momentum was key, and suffragists wasted no time.

In June 1919 Congress submitted the Nineteenth Amendment to the states, and suffragists in the Midwest immediately coordinated intensive ratification efforts in their respective states. The response was swift and overwhelmingly supportive. On July 2, 1919, the Iowa General Assembly called a special session to ratify the Nineteenth Amendment. The House voted 96 to 5 in favor while the Senate passed it unanimously, 45 to 0. Iowa became the tenth state to ratify the measure. Three months later, the governor of Minnesota, Joseph Burnquist, called a special session. On September 8, 1919, the House approved the measure 126 to 6 while the Senate followed shortly after with a margin of 60 to 5. As historian Barbara Stuhler notes, the entire process took less than thirty minutes. Minnesota was the fifteenth state to ratify the Nineteenth Amendment. In fact, half of the first fifteen states to ratify the measure were located in the Midwest. On December 4, 1919, South Dakota joined the ratification effort when Governor Peter Norbeck called members of the legislature into a special session to approve the Nineteenth Amendment. South Dakota became the twenty-first state to ratify it. Finally, in August 1920, Tennessee ratified the measure, and the Nineteenth Amendment became law. Women in the United States had earned the right to vote, with just under three months to spare before the 1920 election.[37]

With its history of opposition to woman suffrage, the Midwest seemed an unlikely source for immediate and unfettered support of the Nineteenth Amendment. Special sessions were rare and often unpopular, but in states across the region, governors and members of the legislature expressed few qualms about calling them to ratify this measure. In addition, deliberations at these sessions were astoundingly brief, and the outcomes produced nearly unanimous support for the cause. The abrupt reversal of opinion among midwesterners deserves a second look. Why did hostility turn to endorsement of woman suffrage in such a short period of time? How did suffragists change minds to favor the cause? The answers are complicated, but they reveal the power of World War I to influence public opinion about the meanings of citizenship.

For decades suffragists had clamored for inclusion, relying on an argument that shifted from equality as individuals in a democratic political system to equality as citizens whose civic responsibility demonstrated their ability to participate in matters of the state. Progressivism amplified those claims, allowing suffragists to assure voters that politics would not degrade the sanctity of the home. They argued that the ballot promised to protect the home and uplift its inhabitants, an assertion that softened attitudes toward female enfranchisement. When World War I broke out, suffragists built on their contentions as political actors, positioning themselves as patriotic citizens whose participation in the war effort confirmed their fitness for the ballot. It also did not hurt their case when they compared their loyalty against the alleged treachery of German-born immigrants. Citizenship became a performance of loyalty, and most women in the region readily starred in the principal roles. Midwesterners reacted positively to the Nineteenth Amendment because they had committed themselves to a narrow vision of citizenship. Opposing the suffragist cause now seemed absurd. How could they deny the vote to midwestern women when their loyalty confirmed them as citizens? Before the war, woman suffrage had faced ambiguity and confusion. When World War I clarified the requirements for citizenship to include loyalty as the primary measure, it removed any lingering doubts about woman suffrage.

Conclusion

REMEMBERING WOMAN SUFFRAGE: GENDER AND MIDWESTERN IDENTITY

In 1978, a team of oral history interviewers traveled across Iowa to speak with elderly farmers about living in Iowa during the late nineteenth and early twentieth centuries. The researchers inquired about a variety of topics, from inheritance practices to disease control. They asked about the arrival of the first veterinarians, the farmers' purchase of their first tractors, and the hardships of the Great Depression. Most respondents gave detailed answers to these types of questions, in some cases offering exact measurements, detailed chronologies, and complete genealogical records. While the interviews varied to match the interests of the subjects, the interviewers usually asked a series of questions about life in early Iowa. Many farmers recalled the vibrant social relationships forged on the prairies and fostered in churches and schools. Dances, pie socials, suppers, picnics, and other events filled the calendars of most Iowans, and community flourished when neighbors congregated to raise a barn, build a local schoolhouse, or furnish a library. The interviews confirmed that women were ubiquitous in these activities, part of an inclusive political and social culture that blurred gender distinctions.

While these retired farmers spoke in great detail about these topics, only a few offered scattered recollections when the interviewers asked about woman suffrage. That the researchers thought to include a question about the movement was unexpected but prescient. While the interviewees gave little insight into what they thought about the cause, the interviews confirmed that Iowans knew about it. They remembered suffrage campaigns, like the one in 1916. They had considered the issue carefully, albeit temporarily, out of collectively held ideas about gender and politics. They recalled that enfranchising women was contentious at first, a prospect proposed by radical suffragists living outside the state. Despite their patchy memories, a remarkable pattern emerged out of their responses. Even fifty years later, elderly Iowans, especially women, recalled the movement fondly.

Ruby Howorth, who farmed with her husband, James, in Crawford County, spoke about how residents there responded to the ratification of the Nineteenth Amendment. Ruby claimed French, Danish, and German heritage while James was English. Ruby was active in the local Methodist church. For four years, from 1925 to 1929, she taught in a one-room country school before her marriage to James. During the 1920s and 1930s she continued to teach in Crawford City while James farmed. After a series of questions about bootlegging and anti-prohibition sentiment in Crawford County, the interviewer asked Ruby if she remembered woman suffrage. While she was only thirteen years old in 1920, she offered a brief recollection. "Well, I think you have, it took a few years before the women went and voted, you know what I mean. They didn't just all crowd in. It just wasn't that important to them." While Ruby offered no justification for why women were slow to go to the polls, the interviewer asked Ruby if she had voted in every election in which she was eligible. "Um-hm," she replied, matter-of-factly. While Ruby's interview reveals some initial hesitancy, it also showcases how midwestern women ultimately embraced the right to vote.[1]

In another interview, Mary Renze, who farmed with her husband, Edward, in Carroll County, offered positive comments about the suffragist cause. When asked what she remembered, she replied, "Well I thought it was just great . . . we could go along and vote, sure." Edward, whose father was a German immigrant, added that they went together to vote "every time," meaning in every election. The interviewer also asked how Mary had heard about the cause, to which she replied, "Well, in papers." With her answer, Mary confirmed that disseminating propaganda through newspapers had been critical in gaining support among midwesterners like the Renzes who lived far from town. In addition, like Ruby, Mary held positive memories of woman suffrage. Suffragists, from local advocates to national leaders, had accomplished an impressive feat by the early twentieth century when they de-radicalized the movement and attracted diverse support as a result.[2]

Margaret Weberg of Crawford County gave the most vivid recollection of woman suffrage. In Denison, the county seat, the WCTU was active in promoting the ballot for women even though "people were not so much against suffrage work as they were against prohibition." According to Weberg, despite how the residents of Crawford County felt about prohibition, they were able to separate it from woman suffrage, a feat NAWSA had believed impossible for most voters. It was not the WCTU that threatened the prospects for female enfranchisement in Crawford County. Instead, as Weberg explained, men had no "bad feelings" against the cause, but they "felt that the women didn't know enough to vote." Traditional views on domesticity dictated that "women should stay in the home," and at that time, most women did not work outside it. By the early twentieth century, however, gendered work patterns were changing, and some young women became employed as "stenographers, store clerks, teachers, and [in] maid service." These subtle shifts in female employment were part of bigger changes in gender norms taking place at the time that softened attitudes toward woman suffrage. Weberg vividly recalled the 1916 campaign. She had just turned eighteen, and although she did not participate, her mother, a teacher whose grandfather had immigrated to the United States from England, did. "When it came to be voted upon, the men folk became vocal—then the women had to deliver electioneering and campaigning." Even though the 1916 amendment failed, "there wasn't a feeling against it. The women were, though less educated, more accepted as equals. A partnership was needed to get by."[3]

Weberg's memories confirmed how midwesterners understood gender, politics, and citizenship during the late nineteenth and early twentieth centuries. Settling the region required intense community-building efforts, which fostered gender inclusivity and encouraged mutuality. Decades of community development, especially among Yankee women, forged a deep sense of communal belonging and civic responsibility. They artfully transformed civic activism into claims for woman suffrage. Midwestern Yankee suffragists toiled for decades in failed late-nineteenth-century campaigns, reeling time and time again as defeat temporarily stymied them. But tenacity and conviction always refocused their efforts. In the twentieth century, Yankee suffragists began to downplay a message of individual equality as liberal citizens, arguing that civic responsibility made them into contributing citizens fit for the ballot. Progressive reform amplified their already established civic activism. When the United States entered World War I, most midwestern women mobilized, transforming their civic responsibility into war work. Yankee women became leaders in Liberty Loan campaigns, the American Red Cross, and the Council of National Defense. Citizenship became a performance of loyalty, and women excelled at it.

Women in the Midwest did not achieve the ballot simply because they proved their loyalty. Yankee suffragists cleverly pitted native-born women against foreign-born men, questioning the latter's fitness for citizenship by criticizing their national identities. Among the immigrants from Europe who settled the Midwest, Germans were suspect. They often chose to live in isolated enclaves, and in some cases they preferred not to assimilate. Ethnic diversity was a hallmark of life in the Midwest during these decades, and it flourished as much as it provoked tension. Anxiety built as war broke out in Europe, and Yankee suffragists manipulated long-standing ethnic wariness into outright discrimination. They attacked Germans and German Americans whose lifestyles they believed were "un-American." They praised those native-born women who demonstrated patriotism while admonishing Germans whom they felt resisted participation in the war effort. Hyper-loyalty during World War I forced foreigners to Americanize and confirmed female enfranchisement in the three states studied here.

Investigating woman suffrage in the Midwest reveals how the meanings of citizenship changed in the region from 1870 to 1920. Settlement encouraged residents to contribute to community development, emphasizing civic duty and blurring gendered and ethnic boundaries. Midwestern political culture was inclusive, especially regarding gender, which gave Yankee suffragists an unparalleled opportunity to clamor for the right to vote on the basis of their civic activism. They belonged to communities by demonstrating civic duty. It was obligation that made them citizens, selfless and virtuous, just as Jefferson, Franklin, and other founders had envisioned. In this way, midwestern suffragists capitalized on the ambiguity created by abstract notions of civic virtue by demanding specificity, arguing that only "good" citizens—white, Anglo-Saxon, and Protestant—who contributed to the community should vote. While early-twentieth-century conceptions about citizenship crystallized around these ideas across the nation, in the Midwest, the shift was stark. Because ethnic plurality was vibrant in the late nineteenth century, the move to conformity in the early twentieth century was especially jarring.

Studying woman suffrage in the Midwest unveils a host of new ideas about the suffragist movement in the United States. Locality played a profound role in the ways people experienced the suffrage issue. In the Midwest, settlement patterns created diverse religious, political, and cultural contexts, making community the prism through which people understood and interacted with the cause. It was community that made people citizens, just as it was the community that shaped the outcomes of woman suffrage. In addition to the importance of locality, investigating midwestern suffrage activism reveals just how much suffragists, both local advocates and state and national leaders, embraced nativism. Although they expressed some initial hesitation, especially during the late-nineteenth-century campaigns in South Dakota, suffragists eventually turned into some of the first outspoken nativists. Long before the federal government enacted nativist policies during World War I, suffragists offered suspicions about ethnic Germans and their refusal to assimilate. They were not afraid to condemn what they believed to be "un-American" behavior even before the term came into widespread use. Like their national counterparts, midwestern Yankee suffragists transformed their region's political culture by adopting nativist rhetoric even before World War I made it fashionable. They were instrumental in making conformity, not diversity, a major hallmark of midwestern identity.

Notes

List of Abbreviations

The following abbreviations are used in citations of archives, manuscript and document collections, and other institutional resources in the notes.

CCHC   Clay County Heritage Center, Spencer, Iowa
IESA   Iowa Equal Suffrage Association
IFWC   Iowa Federation of Women's Clubs Collection
ISMC   Iowa Suffrage Memorial Commission Collection
IWA   Iowa Women's Archives, University of Iowa, Iowa City, Iowa
IWSR   Iowa Woman Suffrage Records
LFFP   La Follette Family Papers
LOC   Library of Congress
MHS   Minnesota Historical Society, St. Paul, Minnesota
MPP   Mamie Pyle Papers
MWSA   Minnesota Woman Suffrage Association Collection
PFP   Pickler Family Papers
SDSHS   South Dakota State Historical Society, Pierre, South Dakota
SHSIDM State Historical Society of Iowa, Des Moines, Iowa
SHSIIC   State Historical Society of Iowa, Iowa City, Iowa
SMHC   Southwest Minnesota History Center, Marshall, Minnesota
SWCC   Spencer Woman's Club Collection
USD   University of South Dakota, Vermillion, South Dakota
WCTU   Women's Christian Temperance Union Collection
WHS   Washington Historical Society, Tacoma, Washington

Introduction

1. "Universal Franchise," *Dakota Herald*, Sept. 25, 1914; "Yankton Universal Franchise League," *Press and Dakotan*, Oct. 2, 1914; "Yankton Universal Franchise League," *Press and Dakotan*, Oct. 31, 1914; "Universal Franchise," *Dakota Herald*, Sept. 29, 1914; "Yankton Universal Franchise League,"

Press and Dakotan, Oct. 2, 1914; "Yankton Universal Franchise League," *Press and Dakotan,* Oct. 9, 1914; "'Vote No' Was Popular," *Volin Advance,* Nov. 12, 1914. Ruth Lister lays out the two positions on which conceptions of citizenship are made. According to her, citizenship definitions stem from the balance between rights and obligations, or participation and status (active or passive). When Fitch declared that women were half citizens, then, she invoked Lister's conception that women had fulfilled their obligations (the passive status argument) but did not enjoy the rights that went with citizenship (the active participation argument). See Ruth Lister, *Citizenship: Feminist Perspectives* (New York: New York University Press, 1997), 13.

  2. Andrew R. L. Cayton and Susan E. Gray, "The Story of the Midwest: An Introduction," in *The Identity of the American Midwest: Essays on Regional History,* ed. Andrew R. L. Cayton and Susan E. Gray (Bloomington: Indiana University Press, 2001), 1, 9–10.

  3. Susan Gray, *The Yankee West: Community Life on the Michigan Frontier* (Chapel Hill: University of North Carolina Press, 1996), 2–6.

  4. Rogers Smith, *Civic Ideals: Conflicting Visions of Citizenship in U.S. History* (New Haven, CT: Yale University Press, 1999), 2.

  5. T. H. Marshall, *Citizenship and Social Class* (Cambridge: Cambridge University Press, 1950), 10–11; Smith, *Civic Ideals,* 2; Nancy Fraser and Linda Gordon, "Contract vs. Charity: Why Is There No Social Citizenship in the United States?" *Socialist Review* 22 (1992): 45–68; Bryan S. Turner, ed., *Citizenship and Social Theory* (London: Sage, 1993), 20–24; Sylvia Walby, "Is Citizenship Gendered?" *Sociology* 28 (May 1994): 379–84.

  6. Andrew R. L. Cayton, "The Anti-Region: Place and Identity in the History of the American Midwest," in *The Identity of the American Midwest,* 150–55; Smith, *Civic Ideals,* 2–15; Walby, "Is Citizenship Gendered?" 379–90.

  7. Smith, *Civic Ideals,* 2–15; Carroll Smith-Rosenberg, *This Violent Empire: The Birth of an American National Identity* (Chapel Hill: University of North Carolina Press, 2010), ix–xii.

  8. David Gerber, *American Immigration: A Very Short Introduction* (New York: Oxford University Press, 2011), 19; Dorothee Schneider, "Naturalization and United States Citizenship in Two Periods of Mass Migration: 1894–1930, 1965–2000," *Journal of American Ethnic History* 21 (Fall 2001): 52; Claire Prechtel-Kluskens, "The Location of Naturalization Records," *The Record* 3 (Nov. 1996): 21–22; Marian L. Smith, "Women and Naturalization, ca. 1802–1940," *Prologue: Quarterly of the National Archives* 30 (Summer 1998): 146–53.

  9. Kif Augustine-Adams, "With Notice of the Consequences: Liberal Political Theory, Marriage, and Women's Citizenship in the United States," *Citizenship Studies* 6 (2002): 5–20; Ann Marie Nicolosi, "'We Do Not Want Our Girls to Marry Foreigners': Gender, Race, and American Citizenship,"

NWSA Journal 13 (Autumn 2001): 5; Irene Bloemraad, "Citizenship Lessons from the Past: The Contours of Immigrant Naturalization in the Early 20th Century," *Social Science Quarterly* 87 (Dec. 2006): 942; Jamin Raskin, "Legal Aliens, Local Citizens: The Historical, Constitutional and Theoretical Meanings of Alien Suffrage," *University of Pennsylvania Law Review* 141 (April 1993): 1397–98.

10. Donald Morrison, "Aristotle's Definition of Citizenship: A Problem and Some Solutions," *History of Philosophy Quarterly* 16 (April 1999): 143–65; Curtis Johnson, "Who Is Aristotle's Citizen?" *Phronesis* 29 (1984): 73–90; Aristotle, *Politics*, III; Glenna Matthews, *The Rise of Public Woman: Woman's Power and Woman's Place in the United States, 1630–1970* (New York: Oxford University Press, 1992), 52–70; Alfred De Grazia, *Public and Private: Political Representation in America* (New York: Alfred A. Knopf, 1951), 3–12; Louis Masur, ed., *The Autobiography of Benjamin Franklin with Related Documents* (Boston: Bedford/St. Martin's, 2003); Stephen G. Salkever, *Finding the Mean: Theory and Practice in Aristotelian Political Philosophy* (Princeton, NJ: Princeton University Press, 1990), 233–36; Jean M. Yarbrough, *American Virtues: Thomas Jefferson on the Character of a Free People* (Lawrence: University of Kansas Press, 1998); Michael Schudson, *The Good Citizen: A History of American Civic Life* (New York: Free, 1998), 170–74.

11. Thomas Bender, *Community and Social Change in America* (New Brunswick, NJ: Rutgers University Press, 1978), 5–7; Kenneth P. Wilkinson, *The Community in Rural America* (New York: Greenwood, 1991), 2; Orville Vernon Burton, "Reaping What We Sow: Community and Rural History," *Agricultural History* 76 (Autumn 2002): 645.

12. Nancy Cott, *The Bonds of Womanhood: "Woman's Sphere" in New England, 1780–1835* (New Haven, CT: Yale University Press, 1997), xii–xxii, 1–9, 64–98; Paula Baker, "The Domestication of Politics: Women and American Political Society, 1780–1920," *American Historical Review* 89 (June 1984): 620–29; Linda Kerber, *No Constitutional Right to Be Ladies: Women and the Obligations of Citizenship* (New York: Hill and Wang, 1998), 10; Monique Lanoix, "The Citizen in Question," *Hypatia* 22 (Fall 2007): 122–26.

13. Lanoix, "The Citizen in Question," 122–26; Smith, *Civic Ideals*, 22; Aileen Kraditor, *The Ideas of the Woman Suffrage Movement, 1890–1920* (New York: W. W. Norton, 1981), 5–10, 44–45.

14. Kraditor, *The Ideas of the Woman Suffrage Movement*, 44–55; Baker, "The Domestication of Politics," 632–38; Sara Hunter Graham, *Woman Suffrage and the New Democracy* (New Haven, CT: Yale University Press, 1996), 30; Nancy Hardesty, *Women Called to Witness: Evangelical Feminism in the Nineteenth Century* (Knoxville: University of Tennessee Press, 1999), 129–33.

15. Sara Evans and Anne Firor Scott argue that through women's clubs, temperance unions, ladies' aid societies, and other female organizations, women reenvisioned the ways they could behave as "active" citizens. Evans chides historians for failing to confront the meanings of citizenship and accepting standard definitions that politics were inherently male. Scott asserts that women's clubs served as foundations for public and political participation. Through their volunteer activities, club women constructed themselves as active American citizens. Anne Firor Scott, *Natural Allies: Women's Associations in American History* (Urbana: University of Illinois Press, 1991), 1–4; Sara Evans, *Born for Liberty: A History of Women in America* (New York: Free, 1989), 4–5, 154; Maureen Flanagan, *America Reformed: Progressives and Progressivisms, 1890s–1920s* (New York: Oxford University Press, 2007), 42–46; Matthews, *The Rise of Public Woman,* 52–55, 177.

16. Baker, "The Domestication of Politics," 638–41; Flanagan, *America Reformed,* vi–viii; 33–46; Schudson, *The Good Citizen,* 168–80.

17. Kraditor, *The Ideas of the Woman Suffrage Movement,* 55–65; Graham, *Woman Suffrage and the New Democracy,* xiv–xvii, 11–33; Louise Newman, *White Women's Rights: The Racial Origins of Feminism in the United States* (New York: Oxford University Press, 1999), 14–18, 56–57.

18. Allison Sneider, *Suffragists in an Imperial Age: U. S. Expansion and the Woman Question, 1870–1929* (New York: Oxford University Press, 2008), 5–6, 15–17, 31; Graham, *Woman Suffrage and the New Democracy,* 22–30; Newman, *White Women's Rights,* 14–18, 56–57.

19. Elisabeth S. Clemens, "Organizational Repertoires and Institutional Change: Women's Groups and the Transformation of U.S. Politics, 1890–1920," *The American Journal of Sociology* 98 (Jan. 1993): 757–60; Teena Gabrielson, "Avenues to Virtue: Gender, Nature, and Citizenship at the Turn of the Century," paper presented at the annual meeting of the American Political Science Association, August 2003, 1–4; Baker, "The Domestication of Politics," 621; Susan Marshall, *Splintered Sisterhood: Gender and Class in the Campaign against Woman Suffrage* (Madison: University of Wisconsin Press, 1997), 12–14; "Universal Franchise," *Dakota Herald,* Sept. 25, 1914; Nickie Charles and Helen Hintjens, *Gender, Ethnicity, and Political Ideologies* (New York: Routledge, 1998), 16–21; Kimberly Jensen, *Mobilizing Minerva: American Women in the First World War* (Urbana: University of Illinois Press, 2008), 11–17.

20. I avoid adding a modifier to "feminism." Some scholars use "social," "radical," or "domestic" to delineate the term. The women in this study did not view their activism as a gradation or type of feminism, so I do not. Katherine Jellison, *Entitled to Power: Farm Women and Technology, 1913–1963* (Chapel Hill: University of North Carolina Press, 1993), 180; Mark Friedberger, "Women Advocates in the Iowa Farm Crisis of the 1980s," in

American Rural and Farm Women in Historical Perspective, ed. Joan M. Jensen and Nancy Grey Osterud (Washington, DC: Agricultural History Society, University of California Press, 1994), 224–34; William C. Pratt, "Using History to Make History? Progressive Farm Organizing during the Farm Revolt of the 1980s," *Annals of Iowa* 55 (Winter 1996): 40–42; Deborah Fink, *Agrarian Women: Wives and Mothers in Rural Nebraska, 1880–1940* (Chapel Hill: University of North Carolina Press, 1992), xiv–xv; Cayton and Gray, "The Story of the Midwest," 13; Virginia Scharff, "The Case for Domestic Feminism: Woman Suffrage in Wyoming," in *History of Women in the United States: Historical Articles on Women's Lives and Activities,* ed. Nancy Cott, vol. 19 (Munich: K. G. Saur Verlag, 1994), 36; Mary Neth, *Preserving the Family Farm: Women, Community, and the Foundations of Agribusiness in the Midwest, 1900–1940* (Baltimore: Johns Hopkins University Press, 1995); Joan Jensen, *Loosening the Bonds: Mid-Atlantic Farm Women, 1750–1850* (New Haven, CT: Yale University Press, 1986); Nancy Grey Osterud, *Bonds of Community: The Lives of Farm Women in Nineteenth-Century New York* (Ithaca, NY: Cornell University Press, 1991).

21. Jon Lauck, "'The Silent Artillery of Time': Understanding Social Change in the Rural Midwest," *Great Plains Quarterly* 19 (1999): 246–52.

22. "County-Level Results for 1870," Historical Census Browser, University of Virginia Library, http://mapserver.lib.virginia.edu/php/county .php; "County-Level Results for 1880," Historical Census Browser, University of Virginia Library, http://mapserver.lib.virginia.edu/php/county.php; "County-Level Results for 1890," Historical Census Browser, University of Virginia Library, http://mapserver.lib.virginia.edu/php/county.php.

23. Cayton, "The Anti-Region," 150–51; Cayton and Gray, "The Story of the Midwest," 3–4; Smith, *Civic Ideals,* 2–15, 347–55; Frederick Luebke, "Ethnic Group Settlement on the Great Plains," *The Western Historical Quarterly* 8 (Oct. 1977): 405–25; Robert P. Swierenga, "The Settlement of the Old Northwest: Ethnic Pluralism in a Featureless Plain," *Journal of the Early Republic* 9 (Spring 1989): 79; Schudson, *The Good Citizen,* 182–84.

Chapter 1

1. Andrew A. Meek, "Farm Life on the Prairie," *Lyon County Reporter,* Nov. 16, 1894.

2. Meek, "Farm Life on the Prairie."

3. Bender, *Community and Social Change in America,* 5–7.

4. Smith, *Civic Ideals,* 2; Cayton and Onuf, *The Midwest and the Nation,* 49.

5. Cayton and Onuf, *The Midwest and the Nation,* 55–56, 85.

6. Cayton and Onuf, *The Midwest and the Nation,* 68–75.

7. Samuel Gillespie and James E. Steel, *History of Clay County, Iowa from Its Earliest Settlements to 1909, Also Biographical Sketches of Many Prominent Citizens of the County as Well as Its Illustrious Dead* (Chicago: S. J. Clarke, 1909), 46–48; *History of Southeastern Dakota, Its Settlement and Growth, Geological and Physical Features—Counties, Cities, Towns, and Villages—Incidents of Pioneer Life—Biographical Sketches of the Pioneers and Business Men, with a Brief Outline History of the Territory in General* (Sioux City, Iowa: Western, 1881), 15–16, 18, 230–33; Donald Dean Parker, *History of Our County and State: Yankton County* (Brookings: South Dakota State College, 1959), 6, 12, 21; Jon Lauck, *Prairie Republic: The Political Culture of Dakota Territory, 1879–1889* (Norman: University of Oklahoma Press, 2010), 3–7. During the first years of settlement, farmers across the county dug many artesian wells, with depths from 300 to 500 feet. Yankton County became well known for its extensive system of artesian wells, many of which still flow today.

8. Gillespie and Steele, *History of Clay County*, 147–49; *History of Southeastern Dakota*, 15–16; Dorothy Schwieder, *Iowa: The Middle Land* (Iowa City: University of Iowa Press, 1996), 18–19; Gillespie and Steele, *History of Clay County*, 147–49; John Radzilowski, *Prairie Town: A History of Marshall, Minnesota* (Marshall, MN: Lyon County Historical Society, 1997), 6; C. F. Case, *History and Description of Lyon County, Minnesota, Including a Farm and Business Directory* (Marshall, MN: Messenger Printing House, 1884), 11–12. For more on the Dakota War, see Kenneth Carley, *The Sioux Uprising of 1862* (St. Paul, MN: Minnesota Historical Society, 1976); Jerry Keenan, *The Great Sioux Uprising: Rebellion on the Plains, August–September, 1862* (Cambridge, MA: Da Capo, 2003).

9. Gillespie and Steele, *History of Clay County*, 46–47, 66, 92, 158; Radzilowski, *Prairie Town*, 26; Case, *History and Description of Lyon County, Minnesota*, 16, 22; Arthur Rose, *An Illustrated History of Lyon County, Minnesota* (Marshall, MN: Northern History, 1912), 105; Torgny Anderson, *The Centennial History of Lyon County, Minnesota* (Marshall, MN: Henle, 1970), 38.

10. Lauck, *Prairie Republic*, 7; John Hudson, "Migration to an American Frontier," *Annals of the Association of American Geographers* 66 (June 1976): 242–65; Gillespie and Steele, *History of Clay County*, 79; "Census Report," *Lyon County Reporter*, Sept. 24, 1890; Parker, *History of Our County and State*, 52; Robert Karolevitz, *Yankton—The Way It Was!: Being a Collection of Historical Columns* (Yankton, SD: Yankton Daily Press and Dakotan, 1998), 80; Case, *History and Description of Lyon County*, 15; Lyon County, Minnesota, "County-Level Results for 1890," Historical Census Browser, University of Virginia Library, http://mapserver.lib.virginia.edu/php/county.php; Yankton County, South Dakota, "County-Level Results for 1890," Historical Census Browser, University of Virginia

Library, http://mapserver.lib.virginia.edu/php/county.php; Clay County, Iowa, "County-Level Results for 1890," Historical Census Browser, University of Virginia Library, http://mapserver.lib.virginia.edu/php/county.php.

11. Parker, *History of Our County and State*, 3–5, 22–23, 27, 39, 50; *History of Southeastern Dakota*, 32, 230–33; "Briefly Told," *Press and Dakotan*, May 28, 1890; Karolevitz, *Yankton—The Way It Was*, 80, 127.

12. "How to Make a Town," *Lyon County Reporter*, April 26, 1895; Radzilowski, *Prairie Town*, ix.

13. Michael Goldberg, *An Army of Women: Gender and Politics in Gilded Age Kansas* (Baltimore: Johns Hopkins University Press, 1997), 32–37; Cayton and Onuf, *The Midwest and the Nation*, 68–75.

14. Goldberg, *An Army of Women*, 32–37; "When the Farmer Comes to Town," *Spencer Herald*, July 2, 1915.

15. Karolevitz, *Yankton—The Way It Was*, 84; Lauck, *Prairie Republic*, 8–9; Hudson, "Migration to an American Frontier," 246; Gillespie and Steele, *History of Clay County*, 62, 66–67; Gray, *The Yankee West*, 12; Leonard and Iva Rensink Oral History Interview, page 5, folder 11, box 1, Oral History Project 4, State Historical Society of Iowa, Iowa City, Iowa [hereafter SHSIIC].

16. Swierenga, "The Settlement of the Old Northwest," 76–79; Cayton and Gray, "The Story of the Midwest," 15; Luebke, "Ethnic Group Settlement on the Great Plains," 412, 417, 427–28; Cayton and Onuf, *The Midwest and the Nation*, 27; Hudson, "Migration to an American Frontier," 258.

17. Radzilowski, *Prairie Town*, 93; Annette Atkins, *Creating Minnesota: A History from the Inside Out* (St. Paul, MN: Minnesota Historical Society Press, 2007), 72–81; Luebke, "Ethnic Group Settlement," 412; Cayton and Onuf, *The Midwest and the Nation*, 114–16.

18. Karolevitz, *Yankton—The Way It Was*, 84; Luebke, "Ethnic Group Settlement," 412.

19. Cayton and Gray, "The Story of the Midwest," 3; In Minnesota, Belgians and French-Canadians were known for their tense relationship, while Polish and Icelandic immigrants clashed as well. Radzilowski, *Prairie Town*, 116–17.

20. Brownie MacVey Oral History Interview, page 1, folder 6, box 1, Oral History Project 4, SHSIIC.

21. Parker, *History of Our County and State*, 26; Gillespie and Steele, *History of Clay County*, 174, 177; Karolevitz, *Yankton—The Way It Was*, 87–88; Lauck, *Prairie Republic*, 52, 71; Radzilowski, *Prairie Town*, 107–8.

22. Paul Fox Oral History Interview, page 11–12, folder 1, box 1, Oral History Project 4, 1978, SHSIIC; "Florence Flashes," *Lyon County Reporter*, March 30, 1893; "Florence Flashes," *Lyon County Reporter*, Feb. 2, 1894; "Florence Flashes," *Lyon County Reporter*, April 26, 1895. News of debating societies populated the pages of the local newspapers in the counties in this study. Yankton County had the Willow Dale Literary Society. See "[Local News]," *Dakota Herald*, Jan. 12, 1904.

23. Case, *History and Description of Lyon County*, 19; Gillespie and Steele, *History of Clay County*, 163; Donald Marti, *Women of the Grange: Mutuality and Sisterhood in Rural America, 1866–1920* (New York: Greenwood, 1991), 1–12, 27–31.

24. Gillespie and Steele, *History of Clay County*, 142–45; "Farmers' Institute," Jan. 28, 1897, *Clay County News*; "Farmers' Institute," Feb. 4, 1897, *Clay County News*; "Farmers in Session," Feb. 18, 1897, *Clay County News*; "Canning," Feb. 25, 1897, *Clay County News*; "Domestic Economy," March 11, 1897, *Clay County News*.

25. Parker County Historical Society, *History of Clay County*, 19–20; "County Improvement Association," *Spencer Herald*, Sept. 17, 1913; "Picnic Great Success," *Spencer Herald*, Oct. 1, 1913; "Clay County Picnic," *Spencer News*, Sept. 30, 1913; Gillespie and Steele, *History of Clay County*, 142; Paul Swaim, *Webb, Iowa 1976* (N.p: n.p., 1976), 68, Clay County Heritage Center, Spencer, Iowa [hereafter CCHC].

26. Lauck, *Prairie Republic*, 60; Karl Raitz, "Ethnic Maps of North America," *Geographical Review* 68 (July 1978): 346; Robert Swierenga, "The Little White Church: Religion in Rural America," *Agricultural History* 71 (Autumn 1997): 417; Cayton and Onuf, *The Midwest and the Nation*, 49.

27. Gillespie and Steele, *History of Clay County*, 51, 64.

28. Robert C. Ostergren, "Prairie Bound: Migration Patterns to a Swedish Settlement on the Dakota Frontier," in *Ethnicity on the Great Plains*, ed. Frederick Luebke (Lincoln: University of Nebraska Press, 1980), 88; Case, *History and Description of Lyon County*, 51; Lauck, *Prairie Republic*, 17.

29. Gillespie and Steele, *History of Clay County*, 93–94, 124; *Centennial History of Bethany Lutheran Church*, Church History Collection, CCHC; Yankton County Historical Society, *History of Yankton County, South Dakota* (Dallas: Curtis Media, 1987), 131.

30. Anderson, *The Centennial History of Lyon County*, 45–47; Charles Vandersluis, *Ninety Years at St. Paul's* (Marshall, MN: Ousman Printing, 1977), 10; Yankton County Historical Society, *History of Yankton County*, 140, 142; Gillespie and Steele, *History of Clay County*, 156.

31. Cayton and Gray, "The Story of the Midwest," 19; "Lively City Election," *Spencer Herald*, March 18, 1914; "Democracy Wins," *Press and Dakotan*, April 7, 1890; "Cottonwood Chips," *Lyon County Reporter*, Oct. 13, 1892; "The Women Know," *Lyon County Reporter*, Oct. 27, 1892.

32. Lauck, *Prairie Republic*, 5, 49; Case, *History and Description of Lyon County*, 16–17; Cayton and Onuf, *The Midwest and the Nation*, 109–16.

33. Kathleen Neils Conzen, "Pi-ing the Type: Jane Gray Swisshelm and the Contest of Midwestern Regionality," in *The Identity of the American Midwest*, 93; Cayton and Onuf, *The Midwest and the Nation*, 109–18.

34. Case, *History and Description of Lyon County*, 16–17, 20; Nancy Vargas, "Election Patterns of Lyon County: Comparison between Ethnicity and Voting," senior seminar paper, 1988, Southwest Minnesota State University, Southwest Minnesota History Center, Marshall, Minnesota [hereafter SMHC]; Luebke, "Ethnic Settlement on the Great Plains," 428–29.

35. Herbert Schell, *History of South Dakota* (Pierre, SD: South Dakota State Historical Press, 2004), 225–34; Heather Cox Richardson, *Wounded Knee: Party Politics and the Road to an American Massacre* (New York: Basic Books, 2010), 145–52; "The Alliance Picnic," *Press and Dakotan*, June 13, 1890; "From Vallers," *Lyon County Reporter*, Oct. 15, 1890; Rose, *An Illustrated History of Lyon County*, 121; "Republican Victories," *Lyon County Reporter*, Nov. 9, 1894.

36. Flanagan, *America Reformed*, vi–viii, 8–10, 33–34; Atkins, *Creating Minnesota*, 113.

37. Eileen L. McDonagh and H. Douglas Price, "Woman Suffrage in the Progressive Era: Patterns of Opposition and Support in Referenda Voting, 1910–1918," *The American Political Science Review* 79 (June 1985): 415–35; Gillespie and Steele, *History of Clay County*, 95; "Ballot Right System," *Spencer Herald*, March 13, 1912; Cayton and Onuf, *The Midwest and the Nation*, 61, 88.

38. Karolevitz, *Yankton—The Way it Was*, 127.

39. Karolevitz, *Yankton—The Way it Was*, 127.

40. Radzilowski, *Prairie Town*, 72, 125–30; "Cottonwood Chips," *Lyon County Reporter*, June 16, 1892; "Cottonwood Currants," *Lyon County Reporter*, March 15, 1895; "Temperance Topics," *Lyon County Reporter*, April 5, 1895. The first temperance meetings held in Cottonwood were in 1892, but by 1895 the sentiment among residents was strong enough for at least a temporary ban on alcohol.

Chapter 2

1. "Around Home," *Lyon County Reporter*, Nov. 2, 1894.

2. Lister, *Citizenship*, 1–10; Kerber, *No Constitutional Right to Be Ladies*, 36–42.

3. Cott, *The Bonds of Womanhood*, xii–xxii, 1–9, 64–98; Baker, "The Domestication of Politics," 620–29; Kerber, *No Constitutional Right to Be Ladies*, 10.

4. Kerber, *No Constitutional Right to Be Ladies*, xx–xxiv, 8–10, 26–41.

5. Scott, *Natural Allies*, 1–4; Evans, *Born for Liberty*, 4–5; Goldberg, *An Army of Women*, 3–5.

6. Brownie MacVey Oral History Interview, page 18, folder 6, box 1, Oral History Project 4, SHSIIC; Neth, *Preserving the Family Farm*, 40–42;

The quotation comes from a settler in Beadle County, Dakota Territory, in Lauck, *Prairie Republic*, 51.

7. Helen Swanson, *Logan Township: A Little History, A Lot of Memories* (N.p.: Helen Swanson, 2010), 52–53; "In Social Circles," *Spencer News,* April 5, 1916; [Peterson Historical Committee], *Peterson Iowa 1856–1980,* 94, CCHC; [Greenville Historical Committee], *Greenville, Iowa, USA,* V6, CCHC; Neth, *Preserving the Family Farm,* 70.

8. Neth, *Preserving the Family Farm,* 110.

9. Patricia Bizzell, "Frances Willard, Phoebe Palmer, and the Ethos of the Methodist Woman Preacher," *Rhetoric Society Quarterly* 36 (Autumn 2006): 377–84; Judith Meyer, "Ethnicity, Theology, and Immigrant Church Expansion," *Geographical Review* 65 (April 1975): 180–92.

10. Mrs. C. H. Austin, "Women's Work for the Church," in "Lynd United Methodist Church Circuit Records and History 1867–1951," SMHC. According to historian Louise Noun, suffragist Elizabeth Cady Stanton was aware of the financial influence of ladies' aid societies. According to Noun, Stanton "thought women should secure equal rights in administering church affairs before they spent their time and energy in raising money for these institutions." See Louise Noun, *Strong-Minded Women: The Emergence of the Woman-Suffrage Movement in Iowa* (Ames: Iowa State University Press, 1969), 121.

11. "Briefly Told," *Press and Dakotan,* April 10, 1890; Karolevitz, *Yankton—The Way It Was,* 50.

12. "Briefly Told," *Press and Dakotan,* April 10, 1890.

13. "Another Equal Suffrage Speaker," *Press and Dakotan,* April 10, 1890; "The Equal Suffrage Lectures," *Press and Dakotan,* April 10, 1890; "Briefly Told," *Press and Dakotan,* April 11, 1890.

14. "First Congregational Church Spencer, Iowa," folder 5, box 1, Church History Collection, CCHC; Gillespie and Steele, *History of Clay County,* 196.

15. "Suffragette Here Sunday," *Spencer News-Herald,* April 12, 1916; "Clay County Women Organize Suff Club," *Spencer News-Herald,* April 19, 1916; Gillespie and Steele, *History of Clay County,* 196.

16. "Langdon," *Spencer Herald,* Aug. 6, 1915; [Langdon Centennial Committee], *Langdon: Celebrating 100 Years, 1899–1999: The Langdon Legacy* (N.p: n.p., 1999). The Clay County Heritage Society in Spencer, Iowa, owns a copy of the centennial booklet created to mark the 100th anniversary of the town of Langdon. "Langdon," *Spencer News-Herald,* May 31, 1916.

17. Yankton County Historical Society, *History of Yankton County,* 138.

18. Vandersluis, *Ninety Years at St. Paul's,* 10–11, 29–36, 38.

19. Anderson, *The Centennial History of Lyon County Minnesota,* 49, 52–53; Karolevitz, *Yankton—The Way It Was,* 59, 61, 82. For more on the origins of Sacred Heart Hospital, see Robert F. Karolevitz, *A Commitment* *to Care: The First 100 Years of Sacred Heart Hospital, 1897–1997* (Freeman, SD: Pine Hill, 1997); Paul Theobald, "Country School Curriculum and Governance: The One-Room School Experience in the Nineteenth-Century Midwest," *American Journal of Education* 101 (Feb. 1993): 116–26.

20. *Centennial First Baptist Church, August 10, 1867–1967* (N.p.: n.p., 1967), 12–16, Church Histories Collection, CCHC; "Spencer Baptist Church Nearly 100 Years Old," *Sunday Times*, July 19, 1966.

21. Radzilowski, *Prairie Town*, 31, 105–8; Karolevitz, *Yankton—The Way It Was*, 88. The Order of the Eastern Star, the counterpart to the Masons, organized in 1881. The Women's Relief Corps, connected to the Grand Army of the Republic, opened in 1890. The Rebekah Lodge, partnered with the Odd Fellows, began in 1895. The Minpah Lodge, auxiliary to the Modern Woodmen of America, formed in 1896. Willis Goudy, "Population in Iowa's Incorporated Places: 1850–1986," Iowa State University Extension, State Library of Iowa, State Data Center Program, March 1988, http://www.iowa datacenter.org/archive/2011/02/citypop.pdf.

22. Holly Berkley Fletcher, *Gender and the American Temperance Movement in the Nineteenth Century* (New York: Routledge, 2008), 107; *History of Southeastern Dakota*, 239–40; Karolevitz, *Yankton—The Way It Was*, 81.

23. Data for the 1880 Census for South Dakota is unavailable. Yankton County, South Dakota, "County-Level Results for 1890," Historical Census Browser, University of Virginia Library, http://mapserver.lib.virginia.edu /php/county.php; Karolevitz, *Yankton—The Way It Was*, 127; "W. C. T. U.," *Press and Dakotan*, April 5, 1890.

24. Lyon County, Minnesota, "County-Level Results for 1890," Historical Census Browser, University of Virginia Library, http://mapserver.lib .virginia.edu/php/county.php; "Cottonwood Chips," *Lyon County Reporter*, June 16, 1892; "Cottonwood Currants," *Lyon County Reporter*, March 15, 1895; "Temperance Topics," *Lyon County Reporter*, April 5, 1895; "Around Home," *Lyon County Reporter*, Feb. 4, 1892; "Balaton Briefs," *Lyon County Reporter*, Jan. 12, 1894; Radzilowski, *Prairie Town*, 72, 124–30.

25. "W. C. T. U. Resolutions," *Lyon County Reporter*, Aug. 20, 1891; "W. C. T. U. Resolutions," *Lyon County Reporter*, July 15, 1891.

26. "Our Duty," *Lyon County Reporter*, Nov. 30, 1894; "Around Home," *Lyon County Reporter*, June 8, 1892.

27. "Is Woman's Ballot Necessary?" *Clay County News*, June 19, 1884; ["The following is a report . . ."], *Clay County News*, April 17, 1884; "Minutes of the Second Annual Convention of the Clay County Women's Christian Temperance Union," *Clay County News*, June 5, 1884; "County Convention," *Clay County News*, June 12, 1884; ["The W. C. T. U. will meet . . ."], *Clay County News*, Jan. 18, 1884; "W. C. T. U. in Riverton," *Clay County News*, March 20, 1884; Gillespie and Steele, *History of Clay County*, 95; "Ballot Right System," *Spencer Herald*, March 13, 1912; Clay County, South

Dakota, "County-Level Results for 1890," Historical Census Browser, University of Virginia Library, http://mapserver.lib.virginia.edu/php/county .php.

28. Evans, *Born for Liberty,* 139–40.

29. ["Local News"], *Dakota Herald,* Jan. 8, 1904; ["Local News"], *Dakota Herald,* Jan. 8, 1904; ["Local News"], *Dakota Herald,* Jan. 15, 1904; ["Local News"], *Dakota Herald,* Jan. 22, 1904. The members of the Nineteenth Century Club changed its name to the Woman's Club sometime between February and April 1916. See "Nineteenth Century Club Meeting," *Dakota Herald,* Feb. 1, 1916; "Woman's Club Gives Banquet," *Dakota Herald,* April 21, 1916.

30. Constitution and Bylaws, Current News Club Collection, SMHC; Radzilowski, *Prairie Town,* 72, 168; "Noble Work of Women," *Marshall News Messenger,* Feb. 4, 1916; "Current News Club," *Marshall News Messenger,* Jan. 7, 1916; "Prevent Death Increase," *Marshall News Messenger,* Feb. 18, 1916; "The Knitting Record," *Marshall News Messenger,* Aug. 2, 1918.

31. "History of Spencer Federated Woman's Club," loose paper in Spencer Woman's Club Minute Book, 1894–1901, Spencer Woman's Club Collection [hereafter SWCC], CCHC; Spencer Woman's Club Minute Book, 1894–1901, pages 10, 79, SWCC, CCHC; Spencer Woman's Club Scrapbook, page 2, SWCC, CCHC; Gillespie and Steele, *History of Clay County,* 175.

32. Spencer Woman's Club Minute Book, 1894–1901, pages 33, 142–44, 177, 188, SWCC, CCHC; Spencer Woman's Club Minute Book, 1901–1911, page 178, SWCC, CCHC; Spencer Woman's Club Scrapbook, page 3, SWCC, CCHS; Gillespie and Steele, *History of Clay County,* 176. See Everly Centennial Committee, *Through the Years,* 117, CCHC; "Clay County Women Tell of Work Done," *Spencer News-Herald,* May 24, 1916.

Chapter 3

1. Susan B. Anthony and Ida Husted Harper, eds., *The History of Woman Suffrage,* vol. 4 (Indianapolis, IN: Hollenbeck, 1902), 557–58. According to the fourth volume of *The History of Woman Suffrage,* the "figures show unmistakably that the falling off in the size of the vote was almost wholly among the opponents."

2. Linda Lumsden, *Rampant Women: Suffragists and the Right of Assembly* (Knoxville: University of Tennessee Press, 1997), xii–xxv.

3. William E. Lass, *Minnesota: A History* (New York: W. W. Norton, 2000), 215.

4. Nineteenth Amendment Celebration Committee, "Minnesota Woman Suffrage Chronology," folder 7, box 7, Barbara Stuhler Papers, Manuscripts Collection, Minnesota Historical Society, St. Paul, Minnesota [hereafter MHS]; Barbara Stuhler, *Gentle Warriors: Clara Ueland and the Minnesota Struggle for Woman Suffrage* (St. Paul, MN: Minnesota Historical Society, 1995), 20–22; Ethel Hurd, *Woman Suffrage in Minnesota: A Record of Activities in Its Behalf since 1847* (Minneapolis, MN: Inland, 1916), 31; Barbara Stuhler, "Organizing for the Vote: The Minnesota's Woman Suffrage Movement," in *The North Star State: A Minnesota History Reader,* ed. Anne J. Aby (St. Paul, MN: Minnesota Historical Society, 2002), 226–30. Stearns persuaded legislators to use affirmative wording for the bill, "For the amendment of Article VII relating to electors—Yes." Historian William Folwell believes that the amendment passed by almost 5,000 votes—24,340 in favor to 19,468 opposed—because it forced men to go to the trouble of crossing out the "yes" and writing "no" in its place.

5. William Anderson and Albert James Lobb, *A History of the Constitution of Minnesota: With the First Verified Text* (Minneapolis: University of Minnesota Press, 1921), 145–47. According to Anderson and Lobb, the proposition that changed the amending process did not even pass its own standards. Anthony and Harper, *History of Woman Suffrage,* 4:772–73, 778–79.

6. "Should We Ask for the Suffrage?" *Lyon County Reporter,* Oct. 12, 1895. The *Lyon County Reporter* printed articles, all of the same title, in the October 19, October 26, November 2, November 9, and November 16 editions of the newspaper. Van Rensselaer was an art and architecture critic who commented most often on landscapes and gardens. As an elite, she supported enfranchisement but also subscribed to the "separate spheres" dichotomy in which women and men each had their proper place. She wrote the "Should We Ask for the Suffrage?" series for the *World* publication. See Judith K. Major, *Mariana Griswold Van Rensselaer: A Landscape Critic in the Gilded Age* (Charlottesville: University of Virginia Press, 2013).

7. "One Drawback to the Woman Suffrage Cause," *Lyon County Reporter,* Nov. 2, 1895; "Woman Suffrage," *Lyon County Reporter,* April 19, 1895.

8. "Women," *Lyon County Reporter,* Oct. 17, 1895. Countless articles published from 1891 to 1898 in the *Lyon County Reporter* discussed the status of women. Some of the articles were reprints, but many were new, written by reporters or editors, mostly unnamed.

9. In 1894 the General Assembly granted women suffrage on municipal and school bonds, but pro-suffrage sentiment did not grow afterward. Noun, *Strong-Minded Women,* 1, 121; L. W. Meyers to Joseph Dugdale, April 21, 1870, D879, Joseph Dugdale Papers, State Historical Society of Iowa, Des Moines, Iowa [hereafter SHSIDM]; Anthony and Harper, *The History of Woman Suffrage,* 4: xxi, 628, 634–36; "To the Honorable Senate and House of Representatives of the State of Iowa," Legislative Petition, 1878, folder 20, box 6, Iowa Woman Suffrage Records [hereafter IWSR], SHSIDM.

10. "The Banner Club of Iowa," *Woman's Column*, 1892, box 21, IWSR, SHSIDM; Independence Political Equality Club Minutes, pages 13, 16–17, 31, 40–42, 49, folder 9, box 6, IWSR, SHSIDM. Secretary's Book, Charles City Political Equality Club Minutes, Jan. 2, 1892, Jan. 16, 1892, Feb. 22, 1893, SHSIIC; Secretary's Book, Charles City Political Equality Club Minutes, Feb. 13, 1892, SHSIIC. On March 7, 1890, members of the Independence Political Equality Club debated the issue of citizenship. Women sought answers in sources ranging from *Webster's Dictionary* to the Fourteenth Amendment. The group decided that a woman "is a citizen and the courts have said so time and time again."

11. Mary Simmerson Cunningham Logan and John A. Logan, *The Part Taken by Women in American History* (Wilmington, DE: Perry-Nalle, 1912), 736; Frances Willard and Mary Livermore, eds., *A Woman of the Century: Fourteen Hundred-Seventy Biographical Sketches Accompanied by Portraits of Leading American Women in All Walks of Life* (Chicago: Charles Wells Moulton, 1893), 417; 1870 U.S. Census, Cass, Clayton Co., Iowa, population schedule, Gap Township, p. 3 [penned], p. 167 [stamped], digital image, Ancestry.com, citing NARA microfilm publication M593, roll 383; Gillespie and Steele, *History of Clay County*, 95. The county history book notes that "for over a quarter of a century there have been no saloons in the city of Spencer. The sentiment today [1909] is very decided against the saloon. In 1898 the last big fight on the question of saloon or no saloon was decided and the saloon element was badly defeated."

12. Marriage of Eva Sober to Malcolm M. Gilchrist, Film Number 141034, Ancestry.com; Iowa, Select Marriages Index, 1758–1996 [database online]; Provo, Utah: Ancestry.com Operations, 2014; 1880 U. S. Census, Butler Co., Iowa, population schedule, Pittsford Twn., p. 6 [penned], digital image, Ancestry.com, NARA microfilm publication T9, roll 330; 1880 U. S. Census, Clay Co., Iowa, population schedule, Spencer, p. 14 [penned], digital image, Ancestry.com, NARA microfilm publication T9, roll 333.

13. "The Ladies of Spencer," *Clay County News*, Jan. 11, 1884.

14. Anthony and Harper, *History of Woman Suffrage*, 4:628–30.

15. "Woman Suffrage," *Clay County News*, May 8, 1884; "Minutes of the Second Annual Convention of the Clay County Woman's Christian Temperance Union," *Clay County News*, June 5, 1884.

16. "Minutes of the Second Annual Convention of the Clay County Woman's Christian Temperance Union," *Clay County News*, June 5, 1884; "Equal Suffrage," *Clay County News*, May 15, 1884; "Equal Suffrage," *Clay County News*, May 22, 1884; Willard, *A Woman of the Century*, 417.

17. "Equal Suffrage," *Clay County News*, May 22, 1884; "Equal Suffrage," *Clay County News*, June 17, 1884.

18. "A Negative Speaks," *Clay County News*, May 29, 1884; Nancy Cott, "Marriage and Women's Citizenship in the United States, 1830–1934,"

American Historical Review 103 (Dec. 1998): 1440–74; Nicolosi, "We Do Not Want Our Girls to Marry Foreigners," 5.

19. "Communicated," *Clay County News*, July 3, 1884.

20. "Woman's Sphere from a Biblical Standpoint," *Clay County News*, July 31, 1884; Anthony and Harper, *History of Woman Suffrage*, 4: xxii.

21. "Woman Suffrage," *Clay County News*, Aug. 7, 1884.

22. "Strange Logic," *Clay County News*, Oct. 30, 1884; "Woman Suffrage," *Clay County News*, Nov. 6, 1884.

23. "Rejoinder," *Clay County News*, Nov. 13, 1884; "Rejoinder," *Clay County News*, Nov. 20, 1884; "Woman Suffrage," *Clay County News*, Nov. 27, 1884; "Woman Suffrage," *Clay County News*, Dec. 11, 1884; "Brooke's Rejoinder," *Clay County News*, Jan. 8, 1885; "Woman Suffrage," *Clay County News*, Jan. 22, 1885; "Brooke's Rejoinder," *Clay County News*, Feb. 5, 1885.

24. Anthony and Harper, *History of Woman Suffrage*, 4:628–33; "Call for Suffrage Conventions," *Clay County News*, May 20, 1897.

25. "Equal Suffrage," *Clay County News*, June 3, 1897.

26. Anthony and Harper, *History of Woman Suffrage*, 4:628–33; "News of the Week," *Clay County News*, Sept. 16, 1897; "Suffrage Convention," *Clay County News*, Sept. 23, 1897; "County Woman Suffrage Conference," *Clay County News*, May 26, 1898; "Equal Suffragists at Ida Grove," *Clay County News*, April 21, 1898.

27. Anthony and Harper, *History of Woman Suffrage*, 4:555; Schell, *History of South Dakota*, 214–38.

28. "South Dakota: Equal Suffrage Work," *The Union Signal*, Nov. 7, 1889, Scrapbook 1880 to 1890, box 10, Emma Smith DeVoe Papers, Washington Historical Society, Tacoma, Washington [hereafter WHS]; Karolevitz, *Yankton—The Way It Was*, 81; Anthony and Harper, *History of Woman Suffrage*, 4:554; Ida Hustad Harper, *The Life and Work of Susan B. Anthony: Including Public Addresses, Her Own Letters, and Many from Her Contemporaries during Fifty Years*, vol. 2 (Indianapolis, IN: Bowen-Merrill, 1898), 679–84.

29. "The President of the South Dakota," *Press and Dakotan*, March 18, 1890; "Mrs. Bones Talks," *Press and Dakotan*, March 22, 1890. The *Press and Dakotan* had a field day publishing the attacks on Anthony in its paper. See "Mrs. Bones, of South Dakota," *Press and Dakotan*, February 24, 1890; "Susan B. and Marietta," February 24, 1890; "An Equal Suffrage Meeting," February 26, 1890; "Charges against Susan," *Press and Dakotan*, April 21, 1890.

30. "The Equal Suffrage Campaign," *Press and Dakotan*, March 23, 1890; "Susan B. Says So," *Press and Dakotan*, April 4, 1890.

31. "Call for a Convention, Opposed to Equal Suffrage," Scrapbook 1880 to 1890, box 10, Emma Smith DeVoe Papers, WHS.

32. Anthony and Harper, *History of Woman Suffrage*, 4:555–56; Harper, *Life and Work of Susan B. Anthony*, 2:683.

33. "The Equal Suffrage Campaign," *Press and Dakotan*, March 23, 1890; "Acknowledgements from South Dakota," *The Woman's Journal*, Feb. 22, 1890, Scrapbook 1880 to 1890, box 10, Emma Smith DeVoe Papers, WHS; "In the Field," *The Dakota Ruralist*, June 28, 1890, Scrapbook 1880 to 1890, box 10, Emma Smith DeVoe Papers, WHS.

34. "In the Field," *The Dakota Ruralist*, June 28, 1890, Scrapbook 1880 to 1890, box 10, Emma Smith DeVoe Papers, WHS; "A Coming Lecture," *Press and Dakotan*, April 4, 1890; "Briefly Told," *Press and Dakotan*, April 5, 1890; "Miss Hindman's Lecture," *Press and Dakotan*, April 9, 1890; "Last Night's Suffrage Lecture," *Press and Dakotan*, April 29, 1890; "Briefly Told," *Press and Dakotan*, April 10, 1890; "Another Equal Suffrage Speaker," *Press and Dakotan*, April 10, 1890; "The Equal Suffrage Lectures," *Press and Dakotan*, April 10, 1890; "Briefly Told," *Press and Dakotan*, April 11, 1890; "A County Convention," *Press and Dakotan*, May 31, 1890. At the district WCTU meeting in early April, local leaders heard addresses in support of woman suffrage. "W. C. T. U.," *Press and Dakotan*, April 5, 1890; "Briefly Told," *Press and Dakotan*, June 2, 1890.

35. "Latest from the Field," *The Woman's Tribune*, June 7, 1890, Scrapbook 1880 to 1890, box 10, Emma Smith DeVoe Papers, WHS; Harper, *Life and Work of Susan B. Anthony*, 2:684.

36. In Yankton County, delegates to the Independent convention were a mix of Yankees and foreign-born men, but most were farmers or engaged in agriculture. "Independent Convention," *Press and Dakotan*, July 5, 1890; Anthony and Harper, *History of Woman Suffrage*, 4:556; Dorinda Riessen Reed, *The Woman Suffrage Movement in South Dakota* (Vermillion: University of South Dakota Press, 1958), 29; Schell, *History of South Dakota*, 223–30; Susan B. Anthony to Alice Pickler, June 14, 1890, folder 37, box 6674, Pickler Family Papers [hereafter PFP], South Dakota State Historical Society, Pierre, South Dakota [hereafter SDSHS]. In its platform drafted in June 1890, the Farmers' Alliance declared itself in favor of woman suffrage and Prohibition, as it had in December 1889. A month later, the Alliance excluded both reforms from its revised platform.

37. "A State Equal Suffrage Mass Convention," *Press and Dakotan*, July 3, 1890; "Equal Suffrage Meeting," *Press and Dakotan*, July 9, 1890; "Equal Suffragists," *Press and Dakotan*, July 10, 1890. "The Independent, Prohibition, and Woman's Suffrage," *Press and Dakotan*, Sept. 8, 1890; "An All Around Talk about South Dakota," *Press and Dakotan*, July 31, 1890; "The Convention," *The Dakota Ruralist*, July 19, 1890, Scrapbook 1880 to 1890, box 10, Emma Smith DeVoe Papers, WHS.

38. Schell, *History of South Dakota*, 223–41; Harper, *Life and Work of Susan B. Anthony*, 686–87; "The State Convention," *Press and Dakotan*, Aug. 27, 1890; "From Mitchell," *Press and Dakotan*, Aug. 27, 1890; "The

Convention," *Press and Dakotan*, Aug. 29, 1890; "Equal Suffrage," *Press and Dakotan*, Aug. 30, 1890; Anthony to Pickler, June 14, 1890, folder 37, box 6674, PFP, SDSHS.

39. "The Convention," *Press and Dakotan*, Aug. 29, 1890; "Equal Suffrage Convention," *The [Mitchell] Daily Gazette*, Aug. 26, 1890, Scrapbook 1880 to 1890, box 10, Emma Smith DeVoe Papers, WHS; "Subject and Sovereign," Speech, 1892 [dated 1888 or 1893 in archives, but this is incorrect because Catt states that "two years ago there was a woman suffrage amendment campaign in that state" on page 38], folder 3, box 4, Carrie Chapman Catt Papers, New York Public Library, Stephen A. Schwartzman Building, New York, New York.

40. "Headquarters Equal Suffrage Association of South Dakota," July 16, 1890, folder 42, box 6674, PFP, SDSHS. While Anthony never explicitly stated it, she probably targeted farmers with these directions. She believed that farmers were dissatisfied with Republican and Democratic "bosses" and "machines" that ignored their interests. If farmers, whether or not they were members of the Independent Party or Farmers' Alliance, could abandon Republicans and Democrats, Anthony probably hoped they would be more open to woman suffrage. Local groups, like those in Yankton County, still showed interest.

41. Nettie C. Hall to Elizabeth Wardall, Aug. 20, 1890, folder 8, box 6674, PFP, SDSHS; Nettie C. Hall to Susan B. Anthony, Aug. 29, 1890, folder 8, box 6674, PFP, SDSHS; Nettie C. Hall to Elizabeth Wardall, Aug. 30, 1890, folder 8, box 6674, PFP, SDSHS.

42. "Briefly Told," *Press and Dakotan*, Sept. 5, 1890; "Briefly Told," *Press and Dakotan*, Sept. 6, 1890; Julia B. King to William Bailey, Aug. 19, 1890, folder 8, box 6674, PFP, SDSHS; "W. C. T. U.," *Press and Dakotan*, Sept. 20, 1890.

43. Carrie Chapman Catt to State Office, Sept. 17, 1890, folder 13, box 6674, PFP, SDSHS; McDonagh and Price, "Woman Suffrage in the Progressive Era," 576–78; Mr. Nichols to William Bailey, Sept. 26, 1890, folder 4, box 6674, PFP, SDSHS; Julia B. Nelson to William Bailey, Oct. 3, 1890, folder 3, box 6674, PFP, SDSHS; Julia B. Nelson to William Bailey, Oct. 13, 1890, folder 4, box 6674, PFP, SDSHS; J. M. King to William Bailey, Oct. 20, 1890, folder 3, box 6674, PFP, SDSHS.

44. "Equal Suffrage," *The Hecla Citizen*, June 27, 1890, Scrapbook 1880 to 1890, box 10, Emma Smith DeVoe Papers, WHS; Mrs. J. M. Way to William Bailey, Oct. 20, 1890, folder 5, box 6674, PFP, SDSHS; "Briefly Told," *Press and Dakotan*, Oct. 15, 1890; "Briefly Told," *Press and Dakotan*, Oct. 17, 1890; "Briefly Told," *Press and Dakotan*, Oct. 20, 1890.

45. The official results were 45,862 against and 22,072 in favor, with a majority opposed of 23,790. "The Election," *Press and Dakotan*, Nov. 4, 1890; "Briefly Told," *Press and Dakotan*, Nov. 5, 1890; "Independent Day," *Press and Dakotan*, Sept. 27, 1890; "The Issue," *Press and Dakotan*, Oct. 1,

1890; "Independent Ring Rule," *Press and Dakotan,* Oct. 9, 1890; "A Woful [*sic*] Blunder," *Press and Dakotan,* Oct. 13, 1890; "An Independent Meeting," *Press and Dakotan,* Oct. 22, 1890; Anthony and Harper, *History of Woman Suffrage,* 4:556–57; "To Voters," *Press and Dakotan,* Oct. 27, 1890; "The Election," *Press and Dakotan,* Nov. 4, 1890.

46. "Letter from South Dakota," *The Woman's Tribune,* June 20, 1891, Scrapbook 1880 to 1890, Box 10, Emma Smith DeVoe, WHS; Harper, *Life and Work of Susan B. Anthony,* 2:689–94; Anthony and Harper, *History of Woman Suffrage,* 4:556. Anthony called the formation of the Independent Party the "greatest disappointment of the campaign." Eleanor Flexner called the 1890 campaign in South Dakota "murderous" and a "fiasco." Catt caught typhoid fever after the campaign and nearly died. Eleanor Flexner, *Century of Struggle: The Woman's Rights Movement in the United States* (Cambridge, MA: Harvard University Press, 1996), 214, 230; Wanda Hendricks, *Gender, Race, and Politics in the Midwest: Black Club Women in Illinois* (Bloomington: Indiana University Press, 1998), 76–78.

47. Anthony and Harper, *History of Woman Suffrage,* 4:555–61.

48. Anna Howard Shaw to Clara Williams, Oct. 17, 1898, folder 22, box 6676, PFP, SDSHS; Carrie Chapman Catt to Jane Rooker Breeden, Jan. 12, 1898, folder 1, box 1, Jane Rooker Breeden Papers, SDSHS; Anna Howard Shaw to Clara Williams, Oct. 17, 1898, folder 22, box 6676, PFP, SDSHS. Eventually, the NAWSA gave a paltry one hundred dollars' worth of literature, a drop in the bucket, to the campaign. State suffragists raised a total of $1,500. In a sympathetic turn, NAWSA paid to send Laura Gregg back to the state on a month-long lecture tour. The SDESA admitted, however, that poor local organization limited her effectiveness, as sometimes she went days without a speaking engagement. See Anthony and Harper, *History of Woman Suffrage,* 4:557; Emma Cranmer to Clare Williams, Aug. 30, 1898, folder 20, box 6676, PFP, SDSHS; Carrie Chapman Catt to Clare Williams, Oct. 24, 1898, folder 20, box 6676, PFP, SDSHS.

49. Schell, *History of South Dakota,* 229–41.

50. "Directions to Officers of the Local Clubs Auxiliary to the South Dakota Equal Suffrage Association," folder 24, box 6676, PFP, SDSHS.

51. "Equal Suffrage," *Press and Dakotan,* Sept. 20, 1898; Carrie Chapman Catt to Clare Williams, July 26, 1898, folder 22, box 6676, PFP, SDSHS; Carrie Chapman Catt to Clare Williams, Aug. 29, 1898, folder 23, box 6676, PFP, SDSHS.

52. Doane Robinson, *History of South Dakota,* vol. 1 (Indianapolis, IN: B. F. Bowen, 1904), 910–13; *Twelfth Census of the United States, 1900* (Washington, DC: National Archives and Records Administration, 1900); *Thirteenth Census of the United States, 1910,* NARA microfilm publication, Records of the Bureau of the Census, Record Group 29, National Archives, Washington, DC; Matilda Vanderhule to Clare Williams, Aug. 11, 1898, folder 9, box 6676, PFP, SDSHS. Matilda especially targeted Scandinavian farmers in the area, noting "four or five places where the Scandinavian women could do work." Matilda Vanderhule to Clare Williams, Aug. 5, 1898, folder 8, box 6676, PFP, SDSHS; Carrie Chapman Catt to Anna Simmons, undated, folder 20, box 6676, PFP, SDSHS.

53. Matilda Vanderhule to Clare Williams, Sept. 10, 1898, folder 10, box 6676, PFP, SDSHS. Matilda Vanderhule to Clare Williams, Oct. 4, 1898, folder 17, box 6676, PFP, SDSHS; "Around Home," *Press and Dakotan*, Aug. 28, 1898. Emma Cranmer to Clare Williams, Aug. 30, 1898, folder 20, box 6676, PFP, SDSHS.

54. Matilda Vanderhule to Clare Williams, Aug. 22, 1898, folder 6, box 6676, PFP, SDSHS; "Cranmer Ends Clay Co. Tues. Aug. 16," folder 8, box 6676, PFP, SDSHS; Matilda Vanderhule to Clare Williams, Aug. 5, 1898, folder 8, box 6676, PFP, SDSHS; Matilda Vanderhule to Clare Williams, Aug. 5, 1898, folder 8, box 6676, PFP, SDSHS; Matilda Vanderhule to Clare Williams, Aug. 9, 1898, folder 9, box 6676, PFP, SDSHS; Matilda Vanderhule to Clare Williams, Aug. 11, 1898, folder 9, box 6676, PFP, SDSHS; Fred L. Richter to Clare Williams, Sept. 10, 1898, folder 10, box 6676, PFP, SDSHS; Emma A. Cranmer to Clare Williams, Aug. 30, 1898, folder 20, box 6676, PFP, SDSHS.

55. Adena Vanderhule to Clare Williams, Aug. 22, 1898, folder 6, box 6676, PFP, SDSHS; Carrie Chapman Catt to Clare Williams, July 26, 1898, folder 22, box 6676, PFP, SDSHS; Adena Vanderhule to Clare Williams, Oct. 4, 1898, folder 17, box 6676, PFP, SDSHS.

56. Adena Vanderhule to Clare Williams, Oct. 4, 1898, folder 17, box 6676, PFP, SDSHS; Adena Vanderhule to Clare Williams, Oct. 17, 1898, folder 16, box 6676, PFP, SDSHS.

57. Anthony and Harper, *History of Woman Suffrage*, 4:555–61; Carrie Chapman Catt to Jane Rooker Breeden, Jan. 12, 1898, folder 1, box 1, Jane Rooker Breeden Papers, SDSHS; Anna Howard Shaw to Clara Williams, Oct. 17, 1898, folder 22, box 6676, PFP, SDSHS; Carrie Chapman Catt to Clare Williams, Oct. 24, 1898, folder 20, box 6676, PFP, SDSHS; Julia Sterling to Clare Williams, Sept. 5, 1898, folder 11, box 6676, SDSHS; Julia Sterling to Clare Williams, Sept. 13, 1898, folder 11, box 6676, PFP, SDSHS. Sterling reported that "we were getting ready for thrashers (If you have ever lived on a farm you know what that means) and I forgot all about writing as I had intended to do." Della King to Henry Brooks, Aug. 11, 1898, folder 9, box 6676, PFP, SDSHS. Ida Hazlett to Clare Williams, Aug. 20, 1898, folder 21, box 6676, PFP, SDSHS.

58. Carrie Chapman Catt to Clare Williams, Oct. 24, 1898, folder 20, box 6676, PFP, SDSHS; Carrie Chapman Catt to Clare Williams, Nov. 7, 1898, folder 20, box 6676, PFP, SDSHS.

59. "Overview of Work during the Nineteenth Century," folder 30, box

6679, PFP, SDSHS; Philena Everett Johnson to Alice Pickler, July 22, 1909, folder 19, box 6677, PFP, SDSHS.

60. Matilda Vanderhule to Carrie Chapman Catt, Dec. 30, 1898, folder 24, box 6676, PFP, SDSHS; Philena Everett Johnson to Alice Pickler, July 22, 1909, folder 19, box 6677, PFP, SDSHS.

61. Flexner, *Century of Struggle*, 214, 221–30; Corrine McConnaughy, *The Woman Suffrage Movement in America: A Reassessment* (New York: Cambridge University Press, 2013).

62. Anthony and Harper, *History of Woman Suffrage*, 4:316–18.

63. Carrie Chapman Catt to Clare Williams, Nov. 7, 1898, folder 20, box 6676, PFP, SDSHS.

Chapter 4

1. "Clay County Women Tell of Work Done," *Spencer News-Herald*, May 24, 1916.

2. Lumsden, *Rampant Women*, xxv.

3. Jo Freeman, *A Room at a Time: How Women Entered Party Politics* (Lanham, MD: Rowman and Littlefield, 2000), 47–50; Baker, "The Domestication of Politics," 638–41.

4. Flexner, *Century of Struggle*, 221–29; Baker, "The Domestication of Politics"; Freeman, *A Room at a Time*, 20–25; Jensen, *Mobilizing Minerva*, x.

5. Schneider, "Naturalization and United States Citizenship in Two Periods of Mass Migration," 55–58.

6. Flexner, *Century of Struggle*, 230–32, 241–68.

7. Graham, *Woman Suffrage and the New Democracy*, 33–72.

8. Genevieve McBride, *On Wisconsin Women: Working for Their Rights from Settlement to Suffrage* (Madison: University of Wisconsin Press, 1993), 195–99; "Iowa Federation of Women's Clubs Yearbook 1916–1917," page 21, folder 3, box 5, Iowa Federation of Women's Clubs Collection [hereafter IFWC], Iowa Women's Archives, University of Iowa, Iowa City, Iowa [hereafter IWA]; *Forty-Second Annual Convention of the W. C. T. U. of Iowa*, page 23, box 11, WCTU, IWA; *Forty-Third Annual Report of the W. C. T. U.*, pages 44–46, box 11, WCTU, IWA; Mamie Pyle to Mrs. G. A. Purley, Feb. 6, 1918, folder 4, box 1, Mamie Pyle Papers [hereafter MPP], University of South Dakota, Vermillion, South Dakota [hereafter USD]; Graham, *Woman Suffrage and the New Democracy*, 61–73.

9. Flexner, *Century of Struggle*, 230–32, 241–68.

10. Carrie Chapman Catt to Alice Pickler, Sept. 3, 1902, folder 18, box 6677, PFP, SDSHS; Philena Everett Johnson to Alice Pickler, July 22, 1909, folder 19, box 6677, PFP, SDSHS; Ella S. Stewart to Philena Johnson, May

19, 1909, folder 19, box 6677, PFP, SDSHS; Reed, *The Woman Suffrage Movement in South Dakota*, 55–56.

11. Schell, *History of South Dakota*, 258–69.

12. Philena Johnson to Emma Smith DeVoe, Dec. 13, 1910, box 5, Emma Smith DeVoe Papers, WHS; Ida Hustad Harper, ed., *History of Woman Suffrage*, vol. 6 (New York: J. J. Little and Ives, 1922), 586–88; "Suffragists Uneasy," *Dakota Herald*, Sept. 20, 1910; "For Woman Suffrage," *Dakota Herald*, Nov. 1, 1910; "Suffrage Meeting," *Dakota Herald*, Nov. 8, 1910; William John McMurty, *Yankton College: A Historical Sketch* (Yankton, SD: n.p., 1907), 134–42; "Favors Woman Suffrage," *Dakota Herald*, Nov. 5, 1910; "Women and the Ballot," *Dakota Herald*, Nov. 1, 1910; "Fullerville Floaters," *Dakota Herald*, Nov. 4, 1910; "Fullerville Floaters," *Dakota Herald*, Nov. 11, 1910.

13. Patricia O'Keefe Easton, "Woman Suffrage in South Dakota: The Final Decade, 1911–1920," *South Dakota History* 13 (1983): 208.

14. Easton, "Woman Suffrage in South Dakota," 208–10.

15. Rena Bowers to Jean Wilkinson, Feb. 28, 1914, folder 20, box 6677, PFP, SDSHS; "Rena E. Bowers Dates," folder 20, box 6677, PFP, SDSHS; Mrs. O. A. Anderson to Mrs. Rice, March 16, 1914, folder 20, box 6677, PFP, SDSHS; Anna Steadman to Mrs. Rice, March 23, 1914, folder 20, box 6677, PFP, SDSHS; Jean Wilkinson to Anna Steadman, March 28, 1914, PFP, SDSHS; Anna Steadman to Anna Simmons, April 4, 1914, folder 20, box 6677, PFP, SDSHS; WCTU to Rena Bowers, April 6, 1914, folder 20, box 6677, PFP, SDSHS; Harry E. Rice to Jean Wilkinson, April 9, 1914, folder 20, box 6677, PFP, SDSHS; Anna Simmons to R. L. Fitch, April 10, 1914, folder 20, box 6677, PFP, SDSHS; Rena Bowers to Anna Simmons, April 1, 1914, folder 20, box 6677, PFP, SDSHS; Jean Wilkinson to Rena Bowers, April 1, 1914, folder 20, box 6677, PFP, SDSHS; Rena Bowers to Jean Wilkinson, April 9, 1914, folder 20, box 6677, PFP, SDSHS; Rena Bowers to Jean Wilkinson, April 20, 1914, folder 20, box 6677, PFP, SDSHS; "Mission Hill Items," *Press and Dakotan*, Oct. 30, 1914; "That Equal Suffrage Doesn't Work," *Volin Advance*, April 23, 1914.

16. "Yankton College Notes," *South Dakota Educator* 30 (Nov. 1916): 30–31; "Suffs. Getting Active in the State," *Dakota Herald*, June 19, 1914; "Meeting of Franchise League," *Dakota Herald*, July 3, 1914; David P. Thelen, *Robert M. La Follette and the Insurgent Spirit* (Madison: University of Wisconsin Press, 1976).

17. Kathryn Schuppert to Jean Wilkinson, July 11, 1914, folder 22, box 6677, PFP, SDSHS; "Miss Fola La Follette," *Dakota Herald*, July 3, 1914; "Yankton Chautauqua at Garfield Park," *Dakota Herald*, July 3, 1914; Flora La Follette to George Middleton, July 10, 1914, folder 7, box 1, A11, La Follette Family Papers [hereafter LFFP], Library of Congress [hereafter LOC]; Flora La Follette to Belle Case La Follette, July 11, 1914, folder 7, box 1, A11, LFFP, LOC; Flora La Follette to Robert La Follette, July 11, 1914, folder 7, box 1, A11, LFFP, LOC; Flora La Follette to George Middleton, July 11, 1914, folder 7, box 1, A11, LFFP, LOC; Flora La Follette to George Middleton, July 15, 1914, folder 7, box 1, A11 LFFP, LOC; Flora La Follette, "The World of Busy Women: Suffragetting on the Chautauqua Circuit," folder 10, box 1, E151, LFFP, LOC; "Comments on Chautauqua Work," *Press and Dakotan,* newspaper clipping, folder 9, box 1, E151, LFFP, LOC; "Suffrage Day a Big Success," *Dakota Herald,* July 17, 1914.

18. For war coverage in Yankton County's local newspapers, see "France Declares War on Austria," *Dakota Herald,* Aug. 11, 1914; "Austria-Hungry Declares War," *Dakota Herald,* Aug. 14, 1914; "Belgian Check German Advance," *Dakota Herald,* Aug. 14, 1914; "Germans Marching on Brussels," *Dakota Herald,* Aug. 21, 1914. Shaw's visit received publicity, albeit less comprehensive than the war, in both the *Dakota Herald* and *Press and Dakotan.* "Local and Personal," *Press and Dakotan,* Sept. 1, 1914; "Rev. Anna Shaw Speaks Sept. 2," *Dakota Herald,* Aug. 28, 1914; "Dr. Anna Shaw Speaks," *Press and Dakotan,* Sept. 3, 1914; "Dr. Anna Shaw Delivers Address," *Dakota Herald,* Sept. 4, 1914; Easton, "Woman Suffrage in South Dakota," 634–35.

19. "Yankton Universal Franchise League," *Press and Dakotan,* Sept. 26, 1914; "Universal Franchise," *Dakota Herald,* Sept. 25, 1914; "Universal Franchise," *Dakota Herald,* Oct. 16, 1914; "Yankton Universal Franchise League," *Press and Dakotan,* Oct. 17, 1914; "Universal Franchise," *Dakota Herald,* Oct. 20, 1914; "Yankton Universal Franchise League," *Press and Dakotan,* Oct. 24, 1914; "Yankton Universal Franchise League," *Press and Dakotan,* Oct. 31, 1914.

20. "Yankton Universal Franchise League," *Press and Dakotan,* Oct. 31, 1914; "Those Who Are Fighting," *Dakota Herald,* Oct. 13, 1914; "Prohibition Is an Issue," *Dakota Herald,* Oct. 16, 1914; "Those Referred Laws and Amendments," *Dakota Herald,* Oct. 23, 1914; "So the People May Know," *Press and Dakotan,* Nov. 2, 1914; "'Vote No' Was Popular," *Volin Advance,* Nov. 12, 1914; "Suffrage Welcome to New States," *Dakota Herald,* Nov. 17, 1914. The vote in Yankton County was 1,705 against and 810 in favor of woman suffrage.

21. Catherine McCullough to Clara Ueland, Feb. 15, 1915, 1:250–51, microfilm, Minnesota Woman Suffrage Association Collection [hereafter MWSA], MHS; Clara Ueland to [no recipient], Dec. 27, 1916, 2:334, MWSA, MHS; Nineteenth Amendment Celebration Committee, "Minnesota Woman Suffrage Chronology," folder 7, box 7, Barbara Stuhler Papers, MHS; Maud Stockman to Miss Savage, Jan. 31, 1915, 1:240, 242, MWSA, MHS; Clara Ueland to Mary Sumner Boyd, Jan. 17, 1916, 1:413–14, MWSA, MHS. Stockman had "grave doubts" about the presidential suffrage bill in 1915, explaining that although suffragists had gained support in the Senate, the measure lacked a majority in the House. Stockman's prediction became reality when the House failed to pass the bill with the required two-thirds majority. In 1917 a measure to grant women presidential suffrage failed by four votes in the Senate.

22. "List of Clubs Paid" [1912], 9:432, MWSA, MHS.

23. Stuhler, *Gentle Warriors*, 775–91; Clara Ueland to "Suffragist," Aug. 5, 1915, 1:291–92, MWSA, MHS; Clara Ueland to "Suffragist," Nov. 23, 1915, 1:371–72, MWSA, MHS; "Plan for Work for Suffrage District Association" [1916], 10:3, MWSA, MHS; "President's Address, 1916," 8:95–100, MWSA, MHS.

24. Clara Ueland to "Suffragist," Aug. 5, 1915, 1:291–92, MWSA, MHS; Clara Ueland to "Suffragist," Nov. 23, 1915, 1:371–72, MWSA, MHS; "Plan for Work for Suffrage District Association" [1916], 10:3, MWSA, MHS; "President's Address, 1916," 8:95–100, MWSA, MHS. Barbara Stuhler correctly pointed out that the MWSA had struggled to align rural people to the cause. The problem was as much the MWSA as it was the realities of rural life. The "practical hurdles of farm chores and distances from towns" made it difficult to enlist rural people in suffrage work. Stuhler, *Gentle Warriors,* 108; Leone Erie to [MWSA], May 24, 1916, 1:672, MWSA, MHS; "Excerpts from Mrs. Stevens' Letters from Worthington for Minnesota Board Mtg.," March 19, 1916, 1:472–74, MWSA, MHS; Rene Stevens to Ethel Briggs, March 25, 1916, 1:483–85, MWSA, MHS; Ethel Briggs to Rene Stevens, March 28, 1916, 1:489, MWSA, MHS; Rene Stevens to Ethel Briggs, April 5, 1916, 1:516–20, MWSA, MHS; Rene Stevens to Ethel Briggs, April 7, 1916, 1:530–31, MWSA, MHS; [MWSA] to Mrs. G. L. Jacquot, May 19, 1916, 1:646–47, MWSA, MHS. There was also a "Norwegian congregation" in Lincoln County that Stevens identified as a potential place for a speech and organizational efforts, but the correspondence revealed that Stevens never visited that church.

25. Schwieder, *Iowa: The Middle Land,* 211–29.

26. "Flora Dunlap," folder 23, box 7, IWSR, SHSIDM; "Suffrage, 1915 Yearbook pg 147," unpublished document, folder 25, box 1, Iowa Suffrage Memorial Commission Collection [hereafter ISMC], IWA; *Forty-Second Annual Report of the W. C. T. U. of Iowa, Iowa City, Iowa, Sept. 28–Oct. 1, 1915, Proceedings of the W. C. T. U. of Iowa,* pages 25, 148, box 11, Women's Christian Temperance Union Collection [hereafter WCTU], IWA; Annual Convention Meeting Minutes, 1915, Minutes of the Iowa Equal Suffrage Association, folder 5, box 9, IWSR, SHSIDM.

27. "Suffragists Elated over the First Victory," *Des Moines Tribune,* July 1912, Suffrage Scrapbook, folder 1, box 2, IWSR, SHSIDM; "Opinion Is Divided on Suffrage Deal," newspaper clipping, 1912, Suffrage Scrapbook, folder 1, box 2, IWSR, SHSIDM; "Woman Suffrage Notes," *Spencer Herald,* Aug. 14, 1912; Noun, *Strong-Minded Women,* 253; Iowa Equal Suffrage

Association [hereafter IESA], "A Plan of Organization and Work for the Woman's Suffrage Campaign in Iowa," folder 16, box 1, ISMC, IWA.

28. Spencer Woman's Club, Minute Book 1910–1915, SWCC, CCHC; "Free Exhibition," *Spencer Herald*, Jan. 24, 1912; "Farmers' Institute," *Spencer Herald*, Feb. 7, 1912; Spencer Woman's Club, Scrapbook, SWCC, CCHC; "Garbage," *Spencer Herald*, July 8, 1914; "City Council Passes Garbage Ordinance," *Spencer News-Herald*, March 22, 1916; "What About Your Garbage?" *Spencer News-Herald*, May 3, 1916; "Birth Registration," *Spencer News*, March 24, 1914.

29. Spencer Woman's Club, 1911–1912 Program, SWCC, CCHC; Spencer Woman's Club, 1912–1913 Program, SWCC, CCHC; Spencer Woman's Club, Minute Book 1910–1915, SWCC, CCHC; "Woman's Club Hold Suffrage Meeting Tuesday Afternoon," *Spencer Herald*, Oct. 16, 1912.

30. "Woman's Suffrage Lecture," *Spencer Herald*, Nov. 4, 1914.

31. Spencer Woman's Club, Minute Book 1915–1925, SWCC, CCHC; "Spencer Club for Suffrage," *Spencer News*, Jan. 14, 1916; Spencer Woman's Club, 1915–1916 Program, SWCC, CCHC.

32. "Shall the Women Vote," *Spencer Herald*, July 9, 1915; "Suffrage Association," *Spencer Herald*, Aug. 13, 1915; "Equal Suffrage Column," *Spencer News*, Aug. 17, 1915; "Clay County Women Tell of Work Done," *Spencer News-Herald*, May 24, 1916; "Getting Ready for the June 5 Battle," *Spencer News-Herald*, April 26, 1916; "Women Loyal Workers," *Spencer News-Herald*, May 17, 1916; "Ballot a Home Safeguard," *Spencer News-Herald*, May 17, 1916; "Suffragette Here Sunday," *Spencer News-Herald*, April 12, 1916; "Clay County Women Organize Suff Club," *Spencer News-Herald*, April 19, 1916.

33. "Farm Women Need the Ballot," *Spencer News*, Feb. 8, 1916; "Twenty Interesting Facts about Woman Suffrage," *Spencer News*, Feb. 15, 1916; "Women Big Taxpayers," *Spencer News-Herald*, May 17, 1916.

34. "Entertained Today," *Spencer News-Herald*, April 26, 1916; "Entertains at Bridge," *Spencer News-Herald*, May 10, 1916; "Club Meets at Perine's," *Spencer News-Herald*, May 10, 1916; "In Social Circles," *Spencer News-Herald*, May 3, 1916; "U-Go I-Go Meet," *Spencer News-Herald*, April 26, 1916.

35. "Let Th'wimin Do Th'work," *Spencer News-Herald*, May 3, 1916; "Getting Ready for the June 5 Battle," *Spencer News-Herald*, April 26, 1916; "In Social Circles," *Spencer News-Herald*, May 24, 1916; "Clay County Women Tell of Work Done," *Spencer News-Herald*, May 24, 1916; "W. C. T. U's Meet Today," *Spencer News Herald*, May 3, 1916; "Langdon," *Spencer News-Herald*, May 31, 1916.

36. "Local News Notes," *Spencer News-Herald*, April 26, 1916; "Suffs Now Hard at It," *Spencer News-Herald*, May 10, 1916; "Elaborate Preparations for Automobile Campaign," folder 6, box 10, IWSR, SHSIDM.

37. "Local News Notes," *Spencer News-Herald,* April 26, 1916; "Suffs Now Hard at It," *Spencer News-Herald,* May 10, 1916; "Two Speakers Here during Week," *Spencer News-Herald,* May 24, 1916; "Suff Worker Here Soon," *Spencer News-Herald,* May 17, 1916; "Getting Ready for the June 5 Battle," *Spencer News-Herald,* April 26, 1916; "Local News Notes," *Spencer News-Herald,* June 14, 1916.

38. "Spencer Voters to Register for June?" *Spencer News-Herald,* April 19, 1916; "Demos Name Ticket for County Offices," *Spencer News-Herald,* April 26, 1916; "To Register Next Week," *Spencer News-Herald,* May 17, 1916; "Three Elections to Be Held Monday," *Spencer News-Herald,* May 31, 1916; "An Open Letter," *Spencer News-Herald,* May 24, 1916.

39. "Liquor Is a Big Primary Issue," *Spencer News-Herald,* May 17, 1916; Carrie Chapman Catt and Nettie Rogers Shuler, *Woman Suffrage and Politics: The Inner Story of the Suffrage Movement* (New York: Charles Scribner's Sons, 1926), 218.

40. "Good Roads Special Draws a Fair Crowd," *Spencer News-Herald,* April 19, 1916; "To the Iowa Farmer!" *The Iowa Homestead,* May 25, 1916, page 25, box 24, IWSR, SHSIDM; Noun, *Strong-Minded Women,* 258; Flora Dunlap, "A Final Word to the Voters of Iowa," folder 2, box 11, IWSR, SHSIDM; Flora Dunlap to Carrie Chapman Catt, June 12, 1916, folder 2, box 11, IWSR, SHSIDM.

41. Flora Dunlap to Carrie Chapman Catt, June 12, 1916, folder 2, box 11, IWSR, SHSIDM; Flora Dunlap to Carrie Chapman Catt, July 1, 1916, folder 2, box 11, IWSR, SHSIDM; Rose Geyer to Carrie Chapman Catt, Aug. 2, 1916, folder 2, box 11, IWSR, SHSIDM.

42. Harding defeated Cosson in the Republican primary, and in November 1916 Harding defeated Meredith, the Democratic candidate. Schwieder, *Iowa: The Middle Land,* 221–29; Effie Jones to Carrie Chapman Catt, June 30, 1916, folder 2, box 11, IWSR, SHSIDM; "Equal Suffrage Badly Defeated," *Dakota Herald,* June 9, 1916; "Suffrage Amendment Thought Lost," *Spencer News-Herald,* June 7, 1916; "Report of Twelve Counties Worked by Mrs. McMahon," 1:387–89, MWSA, MHS; "How They Voted in Clay County," *Spencer News-Herald,* June 7, 1916; Noun, *Strong-Minded Women,* 254–56; Flora Dunlap to Carrie Chapman Catt, June 12, 1916, folder 2, box 11, IWSR, SHSIDM; IESA, "Notes on Equal Suffrage in Iowa for 1916–1917," folder 16, box 1, ISMC, IWA; Catt and Shuler, *Woman Suffrage and Politics,* 217–18; Thomas Ryan, "Male Opponents and Supporters of Woman Suffrage: Iowa in 1916," *Annals of Iowa* 45 (Winter 1981): 538–50; Carrie Chapman Catt to Flora Dunlap, Feb. 26, 1916, folder 2, box 11, IWSR, SHSIDM; Flora Dunlap to Carrie Chapman Catt, Feb. 28, 1916, folder 2, box 11, IWSR, SHSIDM; "Annual Address," in *Forty-Second Annual Convention of the W. C. T. U. of Iowa,* page 27, WCTU, IWA; Flora Dunlap to Carrie Chapman Catt, July 1, 1916, folder 2, box 11, IWSR, SHSIDM; Rose Geyer to Carrie

Chapman Catt, Aug. 2, 1916, folder 2, box 11, IWSR, SHSIDM; "Donations for Suffrage Work," in *Forty-Third Annual Report of the W. C. T. U. of Iowa*, page 66, box 11, WCTU, IWA; Spencer Woman's Club, Minute Book 1915–1925, SWCC, CCHS; "Alleged Irregularities of Vote on the Woman's Suffrage Amendment in Iowa June 5, 1916," folder 16, box 1, ISMC, IWA.

43. Rene Stevens to Ethel Briggs, June 26, 1916, 1:800–802, MWSA, MHS; Rene Stevens to Ethel Briggs, July 3, 1916, 2:3–7, MWSA, MHS; Rene Stevens to Ethel Briggs, July 20, 1916, 2:79–81, MWSA, MHS; "On to Pipestone," 8:154, MWSA, MHS; "President's Address, 1916," 8:95–100, MWSA, MHS; "Suffragets Will Meet on Next Thurs. and Fri.," *Lyon County Reporter*, July 26, 1916; "Suffrage at Pipestone," *Marshall News Messenger*, Aug. 4, 1916; Ethel Briggs to Stevens, Aug. 10, 1916, 2:182, MWSA, MHS; Rene Stevens to Ethel Briggs, Aug. 21, 1916, 2:190–93, 196–97, MWSA, MHS; Clara Ueland to Rene Stevens, Aug. 26, 1916, 2:200, MWSA, MHS. A short time after Stevens arrived in South Dakota, she received word from leaders in New York that they wanted her assistance there.

44. Easton, "Woman Suffrage in South Dakota," 216; "Leslie Benedict Lectures to Voters," *Dakota Herald*, Aug. 1, 1916; "Suffrage Activity at Mission Hill," *Dakota Herald*, Oct. 26, 1916; "News Items," *Dakota Herald*, Oct. 19, 1916; "Local News," *Volin Advance*, Nov. 2, 1916; "Local News," *Volin Advance*, Sept. 14, 1916; "The Rival Wooers," *Volin Advance*, Sept. 14, 1916.

45. "More Men and Better Votes," *Dakota Herald*, Oct. 19, 1916; "Woman Suffrage Means Higher Taxes," *Dakota Herald*, Nov. 2, 1916; "Suffragist Benedict Attacked," *Dakota Herald*, Oct. 26, 1916.

46. Schell, *History of South Dakota*, 266–69; Easton, "Woman Suffrage in South Dakota," 215–19.

47. Schell, *History of South Dakota*, 266; Easton, "Woman Suffrage in South Dakota," 215–19.

48. Spencer Woman's Club, Program 1916–1917, SWCC, CCHC; Spencer Woman's Club Minute Book 1915–1925, SWCC, CCHC; Spencer Woman's Club, Program 1919–1920, SWCC, CCHC; Noun, *Strong-Minded Women*, 257.

Chapter 5

1. "Woman Suffrage a War Measure," *Press and Dakotan*, Sept. 30, 1918; Robert P. Saldin, *War, the American State, and Politics since 1898* (New York: Cambridge University Press, 2011), 80–83; Flexner, *Century of Struggle*, 300–304.

2. "Half a Democracy," *Press and Dakotan*, Oct. 5, 1918.

3. "Responsibility," *Press and Dakotan*, April 20, 1918; "Christian Citizenship," *Press and Dakotan*, May 18, 1918.

4. "Damn the Hyphen," *Dakota Herald,* Aug. 1, 1916; "Repression Approved," *Lesterville Ledger,* Sept. 14, 1917; "The Socialist Movement," *Lesterville Ledger,* Sept. 21, 1917; "Pacifists and Kaiserites," *Lesterville Ledger,* Oct. 5, 1917; Lumsden, *Rampant Women,* 33.

5. Gary Okihiro, *Common Ground: Reimagining American History* (Princeton, NJ: Princeton University Press, 2001), 4–15; Nancy Derr, "Iowans during World War I: Study of Changes under Stress" (PhD diss., George Washington University, 1979), 560–66; Schwieder, *Iowa: The Middle Land,* 163; Cayton, "The Anti-Region," *The Identity of the American Midwest,* 150–51.

6. Schwieder, *Iowa: The Middle Land,* 187–88; Marshall Bailey Oral History Interview, pages 8–9, folder 15, box 1, Oral History Project 4, SHSIIC; Erik Kirschbaum, *Burning Beethoven: The Eradication of German Culture in the United States* (New York: Berlinica Publishing, 2015); Frederick Luebke, *Bonds of Loyalty: German-Americans and World War I* (DeKalb: Northern Illinois University Press, 1974); Cayton and Onuf, *The Midwest and the Nation,* 118.

7. "Twelve Held on Slacker Charge," *Lesterville Ledger,* Aug. 17, 1917; "Germans Rounded Up," *Lesterville Ledger,* Aug. 31, 1917; "In Re Hutchinson County," *Volin Advance,* Sept. 13, 1917; "Repression Approved," *Lesterville Ledger,* Sept. 14, 1917; "The Socialist Movement," *Lesterville Ledger,* Sept. 21, 1917; "Pacifists and Kaiserites," *Lesterville Ledger,* Oct. 5, 1917; "Serve Kaiser or America," *Press and Dakotan,* Jan. 12, 1918; "Secret Enemies at Home," *Dakota Herald,* March 28, 1918; "Details on Attack of O. H. Carlson at Lesterville," *Press and Dakotan,* April 12, 1918; "Why Should They?" *Lesterville Ledger,* April 26, 1918; "Mennonite Mill Said to Be Closed Today," *Press and Dakotan,* Feb. 18, 1918; "Are Politics Dead?" *Lesterville Ledger,* Nov. 30, 1917; "Should Learn English Tongue," *Press and Dakotan,* June 7, 1918; "List of Slackers for Yankton County," *Press and Dakotan,* Jan. 7, 1918.

8. Schwieder, *Iowa: The Middle Land,* 187; "All German Enemies Required to Register," *Volin Advance,* Jan. 24, 1918; "Registration Day Big Success in Yankton County," *Press and Dakotan,* Jan. 28, 1918; "All German Alien Enemies Required to Register," *Lesterville Ledger,* Feb. 1, 1918; "Lesterville People Register Freely," *Lesterville Ledger,* Feb. 1, 1918; William Breen, *Uncle Sam at Home: Civilian Mobilization, Wartime Federalism, and the Council of National Defense, 1917–1919* (Westport, CT: Greenwood, 1984).

9. Marian Moser Jones, *The American Red Cross from Clara Barton to the New Deal* (Baltimore: Johns Hopkins University Press, 2013), 157.

10. Jones, *The American Red Cross from Clara Barton to the New Deal,* 157; "Red Cross Does Patriotic Work," *Lesterville Ledger,* Feb. 22, 1918; "Busy Year for the Red Cross," *Press and Dakotan,* Oct. 25, 1918. The *Press* *and Dakotan* reported that women in Yankton County produced 16,627 articles in a year.

11. Robert Zieger, *America's Great War: World War I and the American Experience* (Lanham, MD: Rowman and Littlefield, 2001), 75–77; "Women Doing their 'Best,'" *Press and Dakotan,* April 12, 1918; "Women's Fourth Liberty Loan Report for Yankton County," *Press and Dakotan,* Nov. 2, 1918.

12. Schwieder, *Iowa: The Middle Land,* 148–49; "Women's Club Passes Resolutions," *Dakota Herald,* April 26, 1917; "Women Told to Can," *Volin Advance,* Aug. 2, 1917; "What Can the Women Do," *Lesterville Ledger,* May 11, 1917; "Women's Work in War Time," *Press and Dakotan,* Jan. 7, 1918.

13. Flexner, *Century of Struggle,* 275–77; Evans, *Born for Liberty,* 169; Trisha Franzen, *Anna Howard Shaw: The Work of Woman Suffrage* (Urbana: University of Illinois Press, 2014), 170–75.

14. Flexner, *Century of Struggle,* 275–77; Franzen, *Anna Howard Shaw,* 170–80.

15. Catt to Executive Council, Feb. 5, 1917, 2:4–17–18, MWSA, MHS; Ueland to "Suffragist," April 27, 1917, 2:479, MWSA, MHS; Stuhler, *Gentle Warriors,* 145–54; Anna B. Lawther, Suffrage Circular, April 23, 1917, IWSR, SHSIDM.

16. Spencer Woman's Club, Minute Book, 1915–1925, SWCC, CCHC; Anna Lawther, Suffrage Circular, April 21, 1917, folder 1, box 22, IWSR, SHSIDM; Anna Lawther, Suffrage Circular, March 1, 1917, folder 1, box 22, IWSR, SHSIDM; Anna Lawther, Suffrage Circular, Oct. 4, 1917, folder 1, box 22, IWSR, SHSIDM.

17. Spencer Woman's Club, Minute Book, 1915–1925, SWCC, CCHS; Anna Lawther, Suffrage Circular, April 21, 1917, folder 1, box 22, IWSR, SHSIDM; Anna Lawther, Suffrage Circular, March 1, 1917, folder 1, box 22, IWSR, SHSIDM; Anna Lawther, Suffrage Circular, Oct. 4, 1917, folder 1, box 22, IWSR, SHSIDM.

18. Anna Lawther, Minutes of the Iowa Equal Suffrage Association, 1908–1919, page 182, folder 3, box 9, IWSR, SHSIDM; Noun, *Strong-Minded Women,* 257–61.

19. "Suffrage Amendment Again," *Dakota Herald,* Jan. 18, 1917; "Suffrage Up Again," *Volin Advance,* Feb. 1, 1917; "Dakota Suffs Are Hopeful," *Dakota Herald,* May 16, 1918; Easton, "Woman Suffrage in South Dakota," 634–35.

20. Mia Campbell to "Madam Chairman," Dec. 29, 1917, folder 3, box 1, MPP, USD; Mamie Pyle to Ann Webb, Feb. 7, 1918, folder 4, box 1, MPP, USD; Mamie Pyle to E. M. Barkley, Feb. 8, 1918, folder 4, box 1, MPP, USD; Mamie Pyle to Mrs. E. R. Geiger, Feb. 16, 1918, MPP, USD.

21. Gina Smith Campbell to "Madam Chairman," Dec. 29, 1917, folder 3, box 1, MPP, USD; Mamie Pyle to Ann Webb, Feb. 7, 1918, folder 4, box 1, MPP, USD; Maria McMahon to Mamie Pyle, folder 6, box 1, MPP, USD.

22. Maria McMahon to Mamie Pyle, Feb. 27, 1918, folder 6, box 1, MPP, USD; U.S. Census Bureau, *Thirteenth Census of the United States* (Washington, DC: National Archives, 1910).

23. "Suffrage Flag Has Sixteen Stars," *Press and Dakotan*, May 1, 1918; "Suffragists in War Work," *Press and Dakotan*, May 25, 1918; "Woman Suffrage a War Measure," *Press and Dakotan*, Sept. 30, 1918; "Amendment E Patriotic Act," *Press and Dakotan*, Sept. 30, 1918; "President Wilson to Mrs. Potter," *Volin Advance*, May 2, 1918; "The Soldiers on Suffrage," *Press and Dakotan*, Sept. 30, 1918; "Are You 100% American?" *Volin Advance*, Sept. 26, 1918; "How South Dakota Voted on Suffrage Amendment in 1916," *Press and Dakotan*, Sept. 30, 1918; Easton, "Woman Suffrage in South Dakota," 633–36.

24. "Election Only a Week Away," *Press and Dakotan*, Oct. 28, 1918; "Noted Men of South Dakota for Suffrage," *Press and Dakotan*, Nov. 4, 1918; "How Campaign Looks at Close," *Press and Dakotan*, Nov. 4, 1918; "Half a Democracy," *Press and Dakotan*, Oct. 5, 1918.

25. "Famous Suffrage Woman Coming to Yankton," *Press and Dakotan*, Oct. 7, 1918; "Mrs. Carrie Chapman Catt," *Press and Dakotan*, Oct. 8, 1918; "Carrie Chapman Catt Opera House Meeting Postponed!" *Press and Dakotan*, Oct. 9, 1918; "Election Only a Week Away," *Press and Dakotan*, Oct. 28, 1918; "Noted Men of South Dakota for Suffrage," *Press and Dakotan*, Nov. 4, 1918; "How Campaign Looks at Close," *Press and Dakotan*, Nov. 4, 1918; "Half a Democracy," *Press and Dakotan*, Oct. 5, 1918; Easton, "Woman Suffrage in South Dakota," 635–37.

26. "1918 South Dakota," 00017, South Dakota Correspondence, LOC; Easton, "Woman Suffrage in South Dakota," 636–37; "Politics Are Adjourned since the Election," *Lesterville Ledger*, Nov. 8, 1918; "Mission Hill Department," *Press and Dakotan*, Nov. 7, 1918; "1918 South Dakota," 00017, South Dakota Correspondence, LOC.

27. Clara Ueland to Winifred Bartlett, Oct. 11, 1917, 2:786, MWSA, MHS; Clara Heckrich to Mary Sumner Boyd, April 5, 1917, 2:470, MWSA, MHS; Carrie Chapman Catt to "Presidents and Congressional Chairmen," May 18, 1917, 2:558–60, MWSA, MHS; "Passed by the Non-Partisan League," April 10, 1918, 9:258, MWSA, MHS; Clara Ueland to "Dear Suffragist," June 20, 1917, 2:610; MWSA, MHS; Ueland to M. Eleanor Wilson, July 30, 1917, 2:684, MWSA, MHS; Bertha C. Moller to Clara Ueland, July 16, 1917, 2:651, MWSA, MHS; Stuhler, *Gentle Warriors*, 150–59.

28. Ethel Briggs to Rene Stevens, Jan. 15, 1917, 2:390, MWSA, MHS; Clara Ueland to A. H. Peterson, Jan. 18, 1917, 2:396, MWSA, MHS; "State Convention," Nov. 16–17, 1917, 3:56–59, MWSA, MHS; Stuhler, *Gentle Warriors*, 129–43.

29. Stuhler, *Gentle Warriors*, 129–43.

30. "State Convention," Nov. 16–17, 1917, 3:56–59, MWSA, MHS; Stuhler, *Gentle Warriors*, 129–43.

31. Clara Ueland, address [Nov. 16, 1917], 8:102, MWSA, MHS; MWSA convention, Nov. 1917 minutes, 14:738, MWSA, MHS.

32. Clara Ueland to John B. Gislason, June 1, 1918, 3:399, MWSA, MHS; Clara Ueland to K. Knudson, June 1, 1918, 3:401, MWSA, MHS; Clara Ueland to F. F. Norwood, June 1, 1918, 3:396, MWSA, MHS; Minder to Clara Ueland, Oct. 16, 1918, 3:832–33, MWSA, MHS; "Yellow Medicine and Lyon Co. Senators," 1918, 9:139, MWSA, MHS; Clara Heckrich to Grace Randall, July 11, 1918, 3:568, MWSA, MHS; Grace Randall to Clara Heckrich, July 12, 1918, 3:569, MWSA, MHS; Grace Randall to Clara Heckrich, July 20, 1918, 3:572, MWSA, MHS. Norwood was a member of the Nonpartisan League.

33. Names of People Sent Petitions by the MWSA, Aug. 1918, 3:587, MWSA, MHS; Clara Ueland to unnamed, Aug. 18, 1918, 3:585, MWSA, MHS; Laura Lowe to Clara Ueland, Oct. 14, 1918, 3:808, MWSA, MHS; "Presented to Congregational Ladies' Aid by Laura W. Lowe, Chairman," July 24, 1918, 9:319, MWSA, MHS; Clara Heckrich to Laura Lowe, Oct. 15, 1918, 3:818, MWSA, MHS; Laura Lowe to Clara Heckrich, Nov. 12, 1918, 4:131, MWSA, MHS; Clara Ueland to Laura Lowe, Nov. 19, 1918, 4:243, MWSA, MHS; Rene Stevens to Laura Lowe, Jan. 21, 1919, 5:225, MWSA, MHS; Rene Stevens to Stella Cook, Jan. 21, 1919, 5:218, MWSA, Stella Cook to Rene Stevens, Jan. 26, 1919, 5:319–20, MWSA, MHS; Rene Stevens to Stella Cook, Jan. 30, 1919, 5:391, MWSA, MHS; Tille Deen to Clara Ueland, Jan. 16, 1919, 5:155–57, MWSA, MHS; Clara Ueland to Tille Deen, Jan. 22, 1919, 5:255, MWSA, MHS; Tille Deen to Clara Ueland, Feb. 2, 1919, 5:438–39, MWSA, MHS; Clara Ueland to Tille Deen, Feb. 5, 1919, 5:459, MWSA, MHS.

34. Laura Lowe to Clara Heckrich, Nov. 12, 1918, 4:131, MWSA, MHS; Clara Ueland to Laura Lowe, Nov. 19, 1918, 4:243, MWSA, MHS; Rene Stevens to Laura Lowe, Jan. 21, 1919, 5:225, MWSA, MHS; Rene Stevens to Stella Cook, Jan. 21, 1919, 5:218, MWSA, Stella Cook to Rene Stevens, Jan. 26, 1919, 5:319–20, MWSA, MHS; Rene Stevens to Stella Cook, Jan. 30, 1919, 5:391, MWSA, MHS; Tille Deen to Clara Ueland, Jan. 16, 1919, 5:155–57, MWSA, MHS; Clara Ueland to Tille Deen, Jan. 22, 1919, 5:255, MWSA, MHS; Tille Deen to Clara Ueland, Feb. 2, 1919, 5:438–39, MWSA, MHS; Clara Ueland to Tille Deen, Feb. 5, 1919, 5:459, MWSA, MHS.

35. Clara Heckrich to Mary Sumner Boyd, April 5, 1917, 2:470, MWSA, MHS; Carrie Chapman Catt to "Presidents and Congressional Chairmen," May 18, 1917, 2:558–60, MWSA, MHS; "Passed by the Non-Partisan League," April 1918, 9:258, MWSA, MHS; "Endorsements," Nov. 1918, 9:320–21, MWSA, MHS; Harriet Sanderson to Grace Randall, Nov. 23, 1918, 4:324–35, MWSA, MHS; Clara Heckrich to Harriet Sanderson, Nov. 26, 1918, 4:360, MWSA, MHS; Harriet Sanderson to Grace Randall, Jan. 21, 1919, 5:235–36, MWSA, MHS; Rene Stevens to Harriet Sanderson,

Feb. 7, 1919, 5:515, MWSA, MHS; "List (Incomplete) of Resolutions, 1919," 9:353–54, MWSA, MHS; Tillie Deen to Clara Ueland, Jan. 16, 1919, 5:155–57, MWSA, MHS; Clara Ueland to Tillie Deen, Jan. 22, 1919, 5:255, MWSA, MHS; Tillie Deen to Clara Ueland, Feb. 2, 1919, 5:438–39, MWSA, MHS; Clara Ueland to Tillie Deen, Feb. 5, 1919, 5:459, MWSA, MHS. The groups that endorsed woman suffrage from Lyon County were the Lyon County Auxiliary of the American Red Cross, the Marshall Congregational Ladies' Aid Society, the Minneota News and Art Club, the Fortnightly Club, the Get-To-Gether Club, the Fordland Auxiliary of the American Red Cross, the Friday Exchange Club, the Eidsvold Auxiliary of the American Red Cross, and the Alpha Camp Chapter of the Royal Neighbors of America.

36. Clara Ueland to Carrie Chapman Catt, Jan. 23, 1919, 5:282–83, MWSA, MHS; Nettie Shuler to Clara Ueland, March 4, 1919, 5:641, MWSA, MHS; Stuhler, *Gentle Warriors*, 168–70.

37. Flexner, *Century of Struggle*, 300–317; Stuhler, *Gentle Warriors*, 170–80.

Conclusion

1. James and Ruby Howorth Oral History Interview, page 15, folder 18, box 1, Oral History Project 4, SHSIIC.

2. Edward and Mary Renze Oral History Interview, page 40, folder 61, box 2, Oral History Project 4, SHSIIC.

3. Bryan and Margaret Weberg Oral History Interview, page 20, folder 5, box 1, Oral History Project 4, SHSIIC.

Supply Chains. Washington, DC: US Department of Agriculture Economic Research Service.

Kloppenburg, Jack Jr., John Hendrickson, and G. W. Stevenson. 1996. "Coming in to the Foodshed." *Agriculture and Human Values* 13 (3): 33–42.

Koc, Mustafa, Rod MacRae, Ellen Desjardins, and Wayne Roberts. 2008. "Getting Civil about Food: The Interactions between Civil Society and the State to Advance Sustainable Food Systems in Canada." *Journal of Hunger and Environmental Nutrition*, 3 (2–3): 122–44.

Korzenny, Felipe, and Betty Ann Korzenny. 2005. *Hispanic Marketing: A Cultural Perspective*. New York: Routledge.

Krome, Margaret, and George Reistad. 2014. *Building Sustainable Farms, Ranches, and Communities: A Guide to Federal Programs for Sustainable Agriculture, Forestry, Entrepreneurship, Conservation, Food Systems, and Community Development*. National Center for Appropriate Technology, https://attra.ncat.org/attra-pub/summaries/summary.php?pub=279.

Kumanyika, Shiriki Kinika, and Sonya Grier. 2006. "Targeting Interventions for Ethnic Minority and Low-Income Populations." *Future of Children* 16 (1): 187–207.

Kures, Matt. 2013. *Foundational Research for the Transform Milwaukee Initiative*. Madison: University of Wisconsin Extention.

Lawson, Laura. 2005. *City Bountiful: A Century of Community Gardening in America*. Berkeley: University of California Press.

Leib, Emily Broad. 2012a. *Good Laws, Good Food: Putting Local Food Policy to Work for Our Communities*. Jamaica Plain, MA: Harvard Law School Food Law and Policy Clinic. http://blogs.law.harvard.edu/foodpolicyinitiative/files/2011/09/FINAL-LOCAL-TOOLKIT2.pdf.

———. 2012b. *Good Laws, Good Food: Putting State Food Policy to Work for Our Communities*. Jamaica Plain, MA: Harvard Law School Food Law and Policy Clinic.

Lengnick Laura, Michelle Miller, and Gerald G. Marten. 2015. Metropolitan Foodsheds: A Resilient Solution to the Climate Change Challenge? *Journal of Environmental Studies and Sciences* 5 (4): 573–92.

Lerman, Tracy. 2012. *A Review of Scholarly Literature on Values-Based Supply Chains*. Davis, CA: University of California Agricultural Sustainability Institute.

Lev, Larry, and G. W. Stevenson. 2011. "Acting Collectively to Develop Midscale

Food Value Chains." *Journal of Agriculture, Food Systems, and Community Development* 1 (4): 119–28.

Lieb, David A. 2016. "Over 1 Million Face Loss of Food Aid over Work Requirements." Associated Press, January 30, http://onlineathens.com/national-news/2016-01-30/over-1-million-face-loss-food-aid-over-work-requirements.

Liu, Yvonne Yen, and Dominique Apollon. 2011. *The Color of Food.* Applied Research Center, http://arc.org/downloads/food_justice_021611_F.pdf.

Los Angeles Times. 2014. "Mapping L.A. Neighborhoods." http://maps.latimes.com/neighborhoods.

Lovell, S. 2010. "Multifunctional Urban Agriculture for Sustainable Land Use Planning in the United States." *Sustainability* 2 (8): 2499–2522.

Low, Sarah A., Aaron Adalja, Elizabeth Beaulieu, Nigel Key, Steve Martinez, Alex Melton, Agnes Perez, Katherine Ralston, Hayden Stewart, Shellye Suttles, Stephen Vogel, and Becca B. R. Jablonski. 2015. *Trends in U.S. Local and Regional Food Systems.* Washington, DC: US Department of Agriculture Economic Research Service.

Low, Sarah A., and Stephen Vogel. 2011. *Direct and Intermediated Marketing of Local Foods in the United States.* Washington, DC: US Department of Agriculture Economic Research Service.

Lucan, Sean C., Frances K. Barg, and Judith A. Long. 2010. "Promoters and Barriers to Fruit, Vegetable, and Fast-Food Consumption among Urban, Low-Income African Americans—A Qualitative Approach." *American Journal of Public Health* 100 (4): 631–35.

Mancino, Lisa, and Jean Kinsey. 2008. *Is Dietary Knowledge Enough? Hunger, Stress, and Other Roadblocks to Healthy Eating.* Washington, DC: US Department of Agriculture Economic Research Service.

Martin, Katie S., and Ann M. Ferris. 2007. "Food Insecurity and Gender Are Risk Factors for Obesity." *Journal of Nutrition Education and Behavior* 39 (1): 31–36.

Martinez, Steve, Michael Hand, Michelle Da Pra, Susan Pollack, Katherine Ralston, Travis Smith, Stephen Vogel, Shellye Clark, Luanne Lohr, Sarah Low, and Constance Newman. 2010. *Local Food Systems: Concepts, Impacts, and Issues.* Washington, DC: US Department of Agriculture Economic Research Service.

Matsunaga, Michael. 2008. *Concentrated Poverty in Los Angeles.* Los Angeles: Economic Roundtable.

McCabe, Margaret Sova. 2011. "Foodshed Foundations: Law's Role in Shaping Our Food System's Future." *Fordham Environmental Law Review* 22: 563.

McCormack, Lacey Arneson, Melissa Nelson Laska, Nicole I. Larson, and Mary Story. 2010. "Review of the Nutritional Implications of Farmers' Markets and Community Gardens: A Call for Evaluation and Research Efforts." *Journal of American Dietetic Association*, 110 (3): 399–408.

McGowan, Joshua. 2011. "Communities Aren't 'Food Deserts,' but Healthy Eating Eludes Many." Milwaukee Neighborhood News Service, http://milwaukeenns.org/2011/09/06/communities-arent-food-deserts-but-healthy-eating-eludes-many-3/.

McKinnon, Robin, Jill Reedy, Meredith Morrissette, Leslie Lytle, and Amy Yaroch. 2009. "Measures of the Food Environment: A Compilation of the Literature, 1990–2007." *American Journal of Preventive Medicine* 36 (4): 124–33.

McMillan, Tracie. 2014. "Can Whole Foods Change the Way Poor People Eat?" *Slate*, November 19. http://www.slate.com/articles/life/food/2014/11/whole_foods_detroit_can_a_grocery_store_really_fight_elitism_racism_and.html.

Meter, Ken. 2009. "Mapping the Minnesota Food Industry." Minneapolis, MN: Crossroads Resource Center.

Metro Regional Transit Authority. n.d. "Grocery Shopping Bus 91-95." Akron, OH: Akron Metro.

Meyers, R. 2015. *Residential Organics Collection Feasibility Report*. Milwaukee, WI: Department of Public Works.

Millennium Ecosystem Assessment. 2005. *Ecosystems and Human Well-Being: Synthesis*. Washington, DC: Island Press.

Miller, Pepper, and Herb Kemp. 2006. *What's Black About It? Insights to Increase Your Share of a Changing African-American Market*. Ithaca, NY: Paramount Market.

Miller, Richard K., and Kelli Washington, eds. 2014. "Buying Local." In *Consumer Behavior*, 108–11. Loganville, GA: Richard K. Miller & Associates.

Mohan, Vidhya, and Diana Cassady. 2002. *Supermarket Shuttle Programs: A Feasibility Study for Supermarkets Located in Low-Income, Transit-Dependent, Urban Neighborhoods in California*. Davis: University of California Center for Advanced Studies in Nutrition and Social Marketing.

Moore, Latetia, and Frances Thompson. 2013. *Adults Meeting Fruit and Vegetable*

Intake Recommendations—United States, 2013. Atlanta, GA: Centers for Disease Control and Prevention.

Morales, Alfonso. 1993. *Making Money at the Market: The Social and Economic Logic of Informal Markets*. Evanston, IL: Northwestern University Department of Sociology.

———. 2000. "Peddling Policy: Street Vending in Historical and Contemporary Context." *International Journal of Sociology and Social Policy* 20 (3/4): 14.

———. 2002. "Radio Mercado: Station Format and Alternative Models of the Audience in the U.S.-Mexico Border Region." *Journal of Borderlands Studies* 17 (1): 79–102.

———. 2009a. "Public Markets as Community Development Tools." *Journal of Planning Education and Research* 28 (4): 426–40.

———. 2009b. "A Woman's Place Is on the Street: Purposes and Problems of Mexican American Women Entrepreneurs." In *Wealth Creation and Business Formation among Mexican-Americans: History, Circumstances and Prospects*, edited by John S. Butler, Alfonso Morales, and David Torres, 99–125. West Lafayette, IN: Purdue University Press.

———. 2011a. "Growing Food *and* Justice: Dismantling Racism through Sustainable Food Systems." In *Cultivating Food Justice: Race, Class and Sustainability*, edited by Alison Hope Alkon and Julian Agyeman, 149–76. Cambridge, MA: MIT Press.

———. 2011b. "Public Markets: Prospects for Social, Economic, and Political Development." *Journal of Planning Literature* 26 (3): 3–17.

———. 2012. "Understanding and Interpreting Tax Compliance Strategies among Street Vendors." In *The Ethics of Tax Evasion: Perspectives in Theory and Practice*, edited by Robert McGee, 83–106. Dordrecht, Netherlands: Springer.

Morales, Alfonso, Steve Balkin, and Joe Persky. 1995. "Contradictions and Irony in Policy Research on the Informal Economy: A Reply." *Economic Development Quarterly* 9 (4): 327–30.

Morales, Alfonso, and Gregg Kettles. 2009a. "Healthy Food Outside: Farmers' Markets, Taco Trucks, and Sidewalk Fruit Vendors." *Journal of Contemporary Health Law and Policy* 26: 20.

———. 2009b. "Zoning for Markets and Street Merchants." *Zoning Practice* 25 (1): 1–8.

———. 2009c. "Zoning for Public Markets and Street Vendors." *Zoning*

Practice 25 (2): 1–8.

Mukherji, Nina, and Alfonso Morales. 2010. "Zoning for Urban Agriculture." *Zoning Practice* 26 (3): 1–8.

Muller, Mark, Angie Tagtow, Susan L. Roberts, and Erin MacDougall. 2009. "Aligning Food Systems Policies to Advance Public Health." *Journal of Hunger and Environmental Nutrition* 4 (3–4): 225–40.

Natchez, Meryl. 2011. "The Amazing Original Homemade Compost Buster." Dactyls & Drakes, http://www.dactyls-and-drakes.com/?s=compost+buster.

National Grocers Association. 2012. *National Grocers Association 2012 Supermarket Guru Consumer Panel Survey.* Arlington, VA: National Grocers Association.

Neuner, Kailee, Sylvia Kelly, and Samina Raja. 2011. *Planning to Eat? Innovative Local Government Plans and Policies to Build Healthy Food Systems in the United States.* Buffalo: State University of New York.

New State Ice Co. v. Liebmann. 1932. 285 U.S. 262.

New York Restoration Project. n.d. "Target East Harlem Community Garden." https://www.nyrp.org/green-spaces/garden-details/target-east-harlem -community-garden.

North Central Cooperative Extension Association. 2011. *Report of the North Central Cooperative Extension Association Metropolitan Food Systems Symposium: Draft Executive Summary.* http://www.nccea.org.

O'Brien, Jennifer, and Tanya Denckla Cobb. 2012. "The Food Policy Audit: A New Tool for Community Food System Planning." *Journal of Agriculture, Food Systems, and Community Development* 2 (3): 177–91. http://dx.doi .org/10.5304/jafscd.2012.023.002.

Opoien, Jessie. 2014. "Wisconsin One of Three States to Reject Food-Stamp Increase." *Capital Times.* September 18. http://host.madison.com/news /local/writers/jessie-opoien/wisconsin-one-of-three-states-to-reject-food -stamp-increase/article_ac1cdac8-ef38-55cf-bac6-732341209772.html.

Organic Authority. 2012. "Earth Day Profile: Chef Ernest Miller on a Different Kind of Soul Food." April 25. http://www.organicauthority.com/restaurant -buzz/earth-day-ernest-miller-the-farmers-kitchen.html.

Otto, Jayson, ed. 2016. "Municipal Housekeepers and the High Cost of Living: The Establishment of Gardening Programs and Farmers' Markets by Grand Rapids Women's Clubs in the Early Twentieth Century." In *Cities of Farmers: Problems, Possibilities and Processes of Producing Food in Cities*, 21–38. Iowa

City: University of Iowa Press.

Packer, Melina. 2014. "Civil Subversion: Making 'Quiet Revolution' with the Rhode Island Food Policy Council." *Journal of Critical Thought and Praxis* 3 (1): 6. http://lib.dr.iastate.edu/jctp/vol3/iss1/6.

Patel, Raj. 2008. *Stuffed and Starved: The Hidden Battle for the World Food System.* New York: Melville House.

Patton, Michael Quinn. 2011. *Developmental Evaluation: Applying Complexity Concepts to Enhance Innovation and Use.* New York: Guilford Press.

Paxton, A. 1994. *The Food Miles Report: The Dangers of Long-Distance Food Transport.* London: Safe Alliance. http://www.sustainweb.org /publications/?id=191.

PD&R Edge. 2012. "Community Land Trusts in Atlanta, Georgia: A Central Server Model." http://www.huduser.gov/portal/pdredge/pdr_edge _inpractice_112312.html.

Peters, Christian, Nelson Bills, Arthur Lembo, Jennifer Wilkins, and Gary Fick. 2009. "Mapping Potential Foodsheds in New York State: A Spatial Model for Evaluating the Capacity to Localize Food Production." *Renewable Agriculture and Food Systems* 24 (1): 72–84.

———. 2012. "Mapping Potential Foodsheds in New York State by Food Group: An Approach for Prioritizing Which Foods to Grow Locally." *Renewable Agriculture and Food Systems* 27 (2): 125–37.

Phills, James A. Jr., Kriss Deiglmeier, and Dale T. Miller. 2008. "Rediscovering Social Innovation." *Stanford Social Innovation Review* 6 (4): 34–43.

Platt, Brenda, Bobby Bell, and Cameron Harsh. 2013. *Pay Dirt: Composting in Maryland to Reduce Waste, Create Jobs, and Protect the Bay.* Institute for Local Self-Reliance, http://www.ilsr.org/wp-content/uploads/2013/05/ILSR-Pay -Dirt-Report-05-11-13.pdf.

PolicyLink and Local Initiatives Support Corporation. 2008. *Grocery Store Attraction Strategies: A Resource Guide for Community Activists and Local Governments.* http://community-wealth.org/sites/clone.community-wealth .org/files/downloads/tool-policylink-lisc-grocery.pdf.

PolicyLink, Reinvestment Fund, and Food Trust. n.d. "Making the Case: Why Healthy Food Access Matters." Healthy Food Access Portal, http://www .healthyfoodaccess.org/get-started/making-the-case.

Pollan, Michael. 2008. *In Defense of Food: An Eater's Manifesto.* New York: Penguin Press.

——. "'The Silent Artillery of Time': Understanding Social Change in the Rural Midwest." *Great Plains Quarterly* 19 (1999): 245–55.

Lister, Ruth. *Citizenship: Feminist Perspectives*. New York: New York University Press, 1997.

Logan, Mary Simmerson Cunningham, and John A. Logan. *The Part Taken by Women in American History*. Wilmington, DE: Perry-Nalle, 1912.

Luebke, Frederick. *Bonds of Loyalty: German-Americans and World War I*. DeKalb: Northern Illinois University Press, 1974.

——. "Ethnic Group Settlement on the Great Plains." *Western Historical Quarterly* 8 (Oct. 1977): 405–30.

——, ed. *Ethnicity on the Great Plains*. Lincoln: University of Nebraska Press, 1980.

Lumsden, Linda. *Rampant Women: Suffragists and the Right to Assembly*. Knoxville: University of Tennessee Press, 1997.

Major, Judith K. *Mariana Griswold Van Rensselaer: A Landscape Critic in the Gilded Age*. Charlottesville: University of Virginia Press, 2013.

Marshall, Susan. *Splintered Sisterhood: Gender and Class in the Campaign against Woman Suffrage*. Madison: University of Wisconsin Press, 1997.

Marshall, T. H. *Citizenship and Social Class*. Cambridge: Cambridge University Press, 1950.

Marti, Donald. *Women of the Grange: Mutuality and Sisterhood in Rural America, 1866–1920*. New York: Greenwood, 1991.

Masur, Louis, ed. *The Autobiography of Benjamin Franklin with Related Documents*. Boston: Bedford/St. Martin's, 2003.

Matthews, Glenna. *The Rise of Public Woman: Woman's Power and Woman's Place in the United States, 1630–1970*. New York: Oxford University Press, 1992.

McBride, Genevieve. *On Wisconsin Women: Working for Their Rights from Settlement to Suffrage*. Madison: University of Wisconsin Press, 1993.

McConnaughy, Corrine. *The Woman Suffrage Movement in America: A Reassessment*. New York: Cambridge University Press, 2013.

McDonagh, Eileen L., and H. Douglas Price. "Woman Suffrage in the Progressive Era: Patterns of Opposition and Support in Referenda Voting, 1910–1918." *The American Political Science Review* 79 (June 1985): 415–35.

McMurty, William John. *Yankton College: A Historical Sketch*. Yankton, SD: n.p., 1907.

Meyer, Judith. "Ethnicity, Theology, and Immigrant Church Expansion." *Geographical Review* 65 (April 1975): 180–97.

Morrison, Donald, "Aristotle's Definition of Citizenship: A Problem and Some Solutions." *History of Philosophy Quarterly* 16 (April 1999): 143–65.

Neth, Mary. *Preserving the Family Farm: Women, Community, and the Foundations of Agribusiness in the Midwest, 1900–1940.* Baltimore: Johns Hopkins University Press, 1995.

Newman, Louise. *White Women's Rights: The Racial Origins of Feminism in the United States.* New York: Oxford University Press, 1999.

Nicolosi, Ann Marie. "'We Do Not Want Our Girls to Marry Foreigners': Gender, Race, and American Citizenship." *NWSA Journal* 13, no. 3 (Autumn 2001): 1–21.

Noun, Louise R. *Strong-Minded Women: The Emergence of the Woman-Suffrage Movement in Iowa.* Ames: Iowa State University Press, 1969.

Okihiro, Gary. *Common Ground: Reimagining American History.* Princeton, NJ: Princeton University Press, 2001.

Osterud, Nancy Grey. *Bonds of Community: The Lives of Farm Women in Nineteenth-Century New York.* Ithaca, NY: Cornell University Press, 1991.

Parker, Donald Dean. *History of Our County and State: Yankton County.* Brookings, SD: South Dakota State College, 1959.

Parker Historical Society. *The History of Clay County, Iowa.* Dallas: Curtis Media, 1984.

[Peterson Historical Committee]. *Peterson Iowa 1856–1980.* Marceline, MO: Walsmorth, 1980. Clay County Historical Society, Parker Museum, Spencer, Iowa.

Pratt, William C. "Using History to Make History? Progressive Farm Organizing during the Farm Revolt of the 1980s." *Annals of Iowa* 55 (Winter 1996): 24–45.

Prechtel-Kluskens, Claire. "The Location of Naturalization Records." *The Record* 3 (Nov. 1996): 21–22.

Radzilowski, John. *One Community, One Church, Two Towns: The Poles of Southwestern Minnesota, 1882–1905.* Marshall, MN: Southwest State University Press, 1991.

——. *Prairie Town: A History of Marshall, Minnesota.* Marshall, MN: Lyon County Historical Society, 1997.

Raitz, Karl. "Ethnic Maps of North America." *Geographical Review* 68 (July 1978): 335–50.

Raskin, Jamin. "Legal Aliens, Local Citizens: The Historical, Constitutional and Theoretical Meanings of Alien Suffrage." *University of Pennsylvania Law Review* 141 (April 1993): 1391–1470.

Reed, Dorinda Riessen. *The Woman Suffrage Movement in South Dakota.* Vermillion: University of South Dakota Press, 1958.

Richardson, Heather Cox. *Wounded Knee: Party Politics and the Road to an American Massacre.* New York: Basic Books, 2010.

Robinson, Doane. *History of South Dakota.* Volume 1. Indianapolis, IN: B. F. Bowen, 1904.

Rose, Arthur. *An Illustrated History of Lyon County Minnesota*. Marshall, MN: Northern History, 1912.

Ryan, Thomas. "Male Opponents and Supporters of Woman Suffrage: Iowa in 1916." *Annals of Iowa* 45 (Winter 1981): 537–50.

Saldin, Robert P. *War, the American State, and Politics since 1898*. New York: Cambridge University Press, 2011.

Salkever, Stephen G. *Finding the Mean: Theory and Practice in Aristotelian Political Philosophy*. Princeton, NJ: Princeton University Press, 1990.

Scharff, Virginia. "The Case for Domestic Feminism: Woman Suffrage in Wyoming." *Annals of Wyoming: The Wyoming History Journal* (Wyoming State Historical Society) 56 (1984): 29–37.

Schell, Herbert. *History of South Dakota*. Pierre, SD: South Dakota State Historical Society Press, 2004.

Schneider, Allison. *Suffragists in an Imperial Age: U.S. Expansion and the Woman Question, 1870–1929*. New York: Oxford University Press, 2008.

Schneider, Dorothee. "Naturalization and United States Citizenship in Two Periods of Mass Migration: 1894–1930, 1965–2000." *Journal of American Ethnic History* 21 (Fall 2001): 50–82.

Schudson, Michael. *The Good Citizen: A History of American Civic Life*. New York: Free, 1998.

Schwieder, Dorothy. *Iowa: The Middle Land*. Iowa City: University of Iowa Press, 1996.

Scott, Anne Firor. *Natural Allies: Women's Associations in American History*. Urbana: University of Illinois Press, 1991.

Smith, Marian L. "Women and Naturalization, ca. 1802–1940." *Prologue: Quarterly of the National Archives* 30 (Summer 1998): 146–53.

Smith, Rogers. *Civic Ideals: Conflicting Visions of Citizenship in U.S. History*. New Haven, CT: Yale University Press, 1999.

Smith-Rosenberg, Carroll. *This Violent Empire: The Birth of an American National Identity*. Chapel Hill: University of North Carolina Press, 2010.

Stanton, Elizabeth Cady, Susan B. Anthony, Ida Hustad Harper, and Matilda Joslyn Gage. *History of Woman Suffrage*. Vol. 4: *1883–1900*. Indianapolis, IN: Hollenbeck, 1902.

Stuhler, Barbara. *Gentle Warriors: Clara Ueland and the Minnesota Struggle for Woman Suffrage*. St. Paul, MN: Minnesota Historical Society Press, 1995.

———. "Organizing for the Vote: The Minnesota's Woman Suffrage Movement." In *The North Star State: A Minnesota History Reader*, edited by Anne J. Aby. St. Paul, MN: Minnesota Historical Society Press, 2002.

Swaim, Paul. *Webb, Iowa 1976*. N.p.: n.p, 1976. Clay County Historical Society, Spencer, Iowa.

Swanson, Helen. *Logan Township: A Little History, A Lot of Memories*. N.p: Helen Swanson, 2010. Clay County Historical Society, Spencer, Iowa.

Swierenga, Robert. "The Little White Church: Religion in Rural America." *Agricultural History* 71 (Autumn 1997): 415–41.

——. "The Settlement of the Old Northwest: Ethnic Pluralism in a Featureless Plain." *Journal of the Early Republic* 9 (Spring 1989): 73–105.

Thelen, David P. *Robert M. La Follette and the Insurgent Spirit*. Madison: University of Wisconsin Press, 1976.

Theobald, Paul. "Country School Curriculum and Governance: The One-Room School Experience in the Nineteenth-Century Midwest." *American Journal of Education* 101 (Feb. 1993): 116–39.

Turner, Bryan S., ed. *Citizenship and Social Theory*. London: Sage, 1993.

Vandersluis, Charles. *Ninety Years at St. Paul's*. Marshall, MN: Ousman Printing, 1977.

Vargas, Nancy. "Election Patterns of Lyon County: Comparison between Ethnicity and Voting." Senior seminar paper, Southwest Minnesota State University, 1988.

Walby, Sylvia. "Is Citizenship Gendered?" *Sociology* 28 (May 1994): 379–95.

Webb, Walter Prescott. *The Great Plains*. Boston: Ginn, 1931.

Wilkinson, Kenneth P. *The Community in Rural America*. New York: Greenwood, 1991.

Willard, Francis, and Mary Livermore, eds. *A Woman of the Century: Fourteen Hundred-Seventy Biographical Sketches Accompanied by Portraits of Leading American Women in All Walks of Life*. Chicago: Charles Wells Moulton, 1893.

"Yankton College Notes." *South Dakota Educator* 30 (Nov. 1916): 30–31.

Yankton County Historical Society. *History of Yankton County, South Dakota*. Dallas: Curtis Media, 1987.

Yarbrough, Jean M. *American Virtues: Thomas Jefferson on the Character of a Free People*. Lawrence: University of Kansas Press, 1998.

Zieger, Robert. *America's Great War: World War I and the American Experience*. Lanham, MD: Rowman and Littlefield, 2001.

Index

Contributors

Angie Allen, UWEX, Milwaukee County

Erika Allen, Growing Power, Chicago, and Chicago Food Policy Action Council

Martin Bailkey, CRFS project comanager and food systems planner, formerly with Growing Power

Stephanie Calloway, community organizer, CORE/El Centro, Milwaukee

Marcia Caton Campbell, Center for Resilient Cities

Rodger Cooley, Chicago Food Policy Action Council

Lindsey Day-Farnsworth, PhD student in environment and resources, University of Wisconsin–Madison

Nate Ela, PhD student in sociology, University of Wisconsin–Madison

Nicodemus Ford, University of Wisconsin Cooperative Extension

Jason Grimm, food system planner, Iowa Valley Resource Conservation & Development

April Harrington, Growing Home, Chicago

Margaret Krome, policy analyst, Michael Fields Agricultural Institute

Greg Lawless, CRFS project comanager, food system specialist, UWEX

Jeffrey Lewis, UWEX

Oona Mackesey-Green, CRFS communications intern, UW–Madison

Colleen McKinney, Center for Good Food Purchasing

Michelle Miller, Center for Integrated Agricultural Systems, UW–Madison

Alfonso Morales, professor of urban and regional planning, UW–Madison

Anne Pfeiffer, urban farming specialist, University of Minnesota

Samuel Pratsch, University of Wisconsin Cooperative Extension

Harry Rhodes, Growing Home, Chicago

Greg Rosenberg, principal, Rosenberg and Associates, Madison

Neelam Sharma, Community Services Unlimited

Rebekah Silverman, Growing Home, Chicago

Laurell Sims, Growing Power, Chicago, and Chicago Food Policy Action Council

Desiré Smith, former CRFS project intern, PEOPLE's urban agriculture program, UW–Madison

Shelly Strom, Community GroundWorks

Monica Theis, senior lecturer, Department of Food Science, UW–Madison

Steve Ventura, CRFS project codirector, UW–Madison

Malik Yakini, Detroit Black Community Food Security Network

Index